Dreamscapes
of Los Angeles

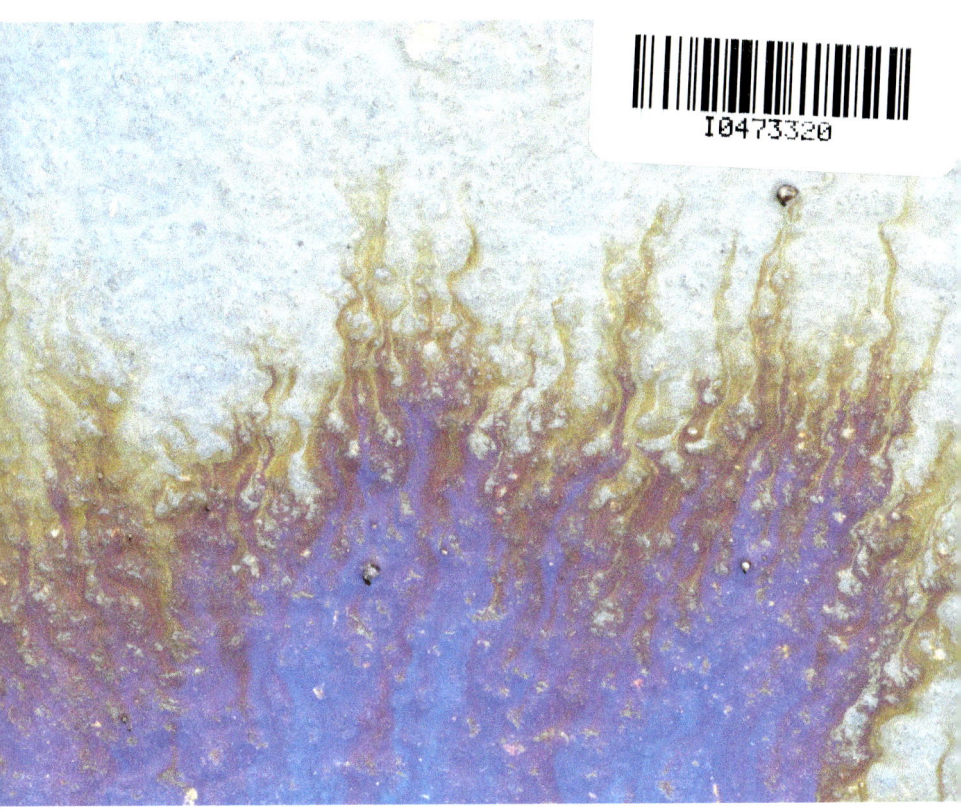

Edited by
Geoff Tuck

Dreamscapes
of Los Angeles

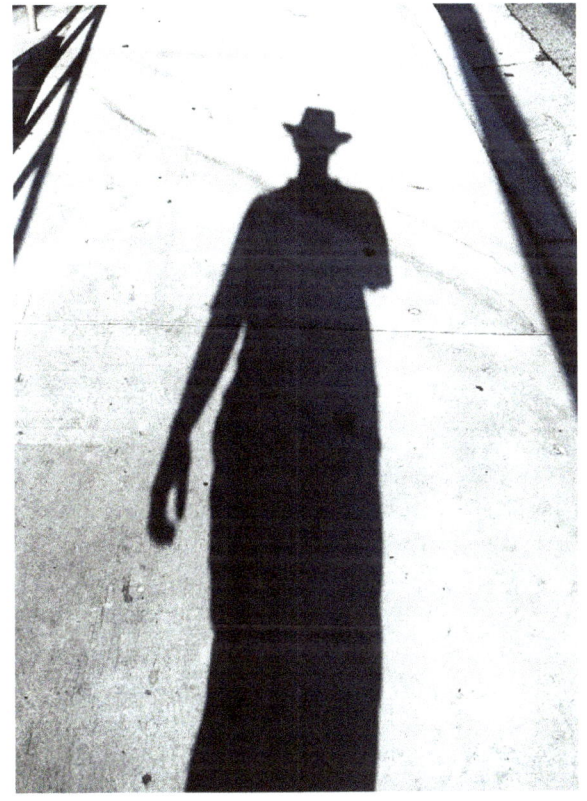

Edited by
Geoff Tuck

Blanc
Press
Los Angeles, California

DREAMSCAPES OF LOS ANGELES
ISBN: 978-0-9911092-9-6
All writing by Geoff Tuck unless otherwise noted
All contents courtesy of the individual authors and Geoff Tuck unless otherwise noted
Insert Blanc Press 2014

This book is published on the occasion of the exhibition *Nowhere to Run, Nowhere to Hide* at the **Infernoesque Set-up 2013** *Die lustige Grube*, on August 9 and 10, 2013, to accompany the piece, *Bingo Bongo Bed*. The artists in the exhibition are David Bell, Anthony Bodlović, EJ Hill, Asher Hartman, Brianne Latthitham, Paul Outlaw and Geoff Tuck.

I would like to thank Sonja Gerdes and the good people at **Infernoesque** for their invitation and for their support. I would like to thank the artists and writers who contributed to this publication.

I am hugely grateful to the people who have made **Notes on Looking** possible over the years by paying attention to, and by offering moral and material support for, my project.

Dreamscapes of Los Angeles is dedicated to my husband and my love, David Richards.

Geoff Tuck

CONTENTS

CONTENTS

CONTENTS

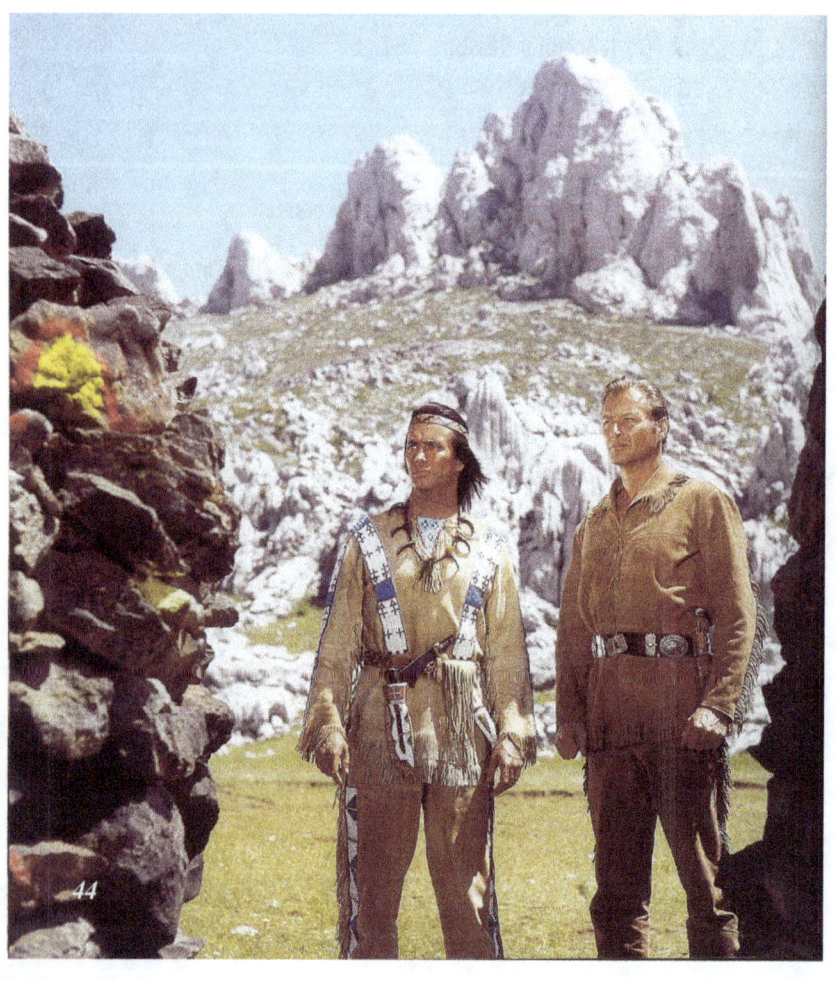

44

OLD SHATTERHAND IN CHINATOWN

Old Shatterhand strides across the American West, a stranger to my cinematic history. He is white but does not speak English; he is a leader of pioneer charges—one who sees beyond questions of competing rights among peoples to the possibility for justice and shared responsibility and opportunity for all. Old Shatterhand is a blood brother to Apache Chief Winnetou, and together, they fight banditry in all its forms, and Shatterhand inspires legions of his contemporaries back home in Germany to become real pioneers in the comparatively free land of the West. He really did these things over the last century, and in a way, he still does. I am a witness!

Karl May's romantic Western-themed novels have been informing German culture since the turn of the last century, and the series of films based on them have been a part of German life since 1962. The Germans' fascination with and belief in these exhilarating stories goes much deeper, I think, than any similar US film does in its home country. I witnessed this devotion last night, when on a roof terrace in Chinatown I watched as a little Swabian boy called Alex appeared in the form of grown-up and married Alexander Wolff and he (both of these characters—the little boy, and the seasoned artist) curled up in blankets with Alexander's wife, Allie, and—along with a brilliant and significant portion of L.A.'s Deutsch contingent—watched Part 1 and later Part 2 from the film series. I have not seen adult faces glow so sweetly in forever. It felt not so much sentimental as essential—but nostalgia was present, too—and each person seemed connected, as though to a source of memory and of identity; and also, they were connected as individuals to each other. In that moment, I was a believer surrounded by souls fearlessly exposed.

The evening was a nice combination of childhood memories, a shared experience that invited strangers to join, an idiosyncratic critique of cultural norms and a beautiful and thrilling movie—a film that is very difficult to find in this country and that our presenter, Alexander Wolff, has wanted to screen here for some time. If this doesn't make art, then I don't know what does.

Alex tacked an impromptu screen low inside the parapet wall (a screen made from one of his large drop-cloth paintings, as yet unpainted), and we sat on scattered milk crates and fluffy blankets and drank red wine and ate popcorn (of the white cheddar variety). "Oh! It's not salty!" Alex observed to Allie. "Yes it is. It's in the cheese," she assured him.

Alexander pointed out to me these movies' use of epic, rather than anecdotal, storytelling, and he's right. Shatterhand and Winnetou are certainly heroes, but rather than having personal struggles and character development, the two exist to serve the needs of larger groups. As Chief, and as a leader among that class, Winnetou cannot pursue his own desires. A hoped-for marriage is put aside when his bride-to-be is wed to a US soldier in an effort to bring unity to the competing peoples. And Shatterhand remains a cypher outside his singular activities of resolving wars and fighting on the behalf of out-gunned Natives who had preceded our law and were denied it as retribution for their precedence.

Visually, the films drive home this communitarian impulse, too. A shot of railroad workers, in near unison, dropping their tools and turning from their shared task to move like an athletic wave of hardened and sweaty men toward the chuck wagon becomes a balletic scene that looked the way reading, in Tolstoy, of troops sweeping across Europe felt. The scene illustrated the power of a community over circumstances: Nowhere was the individual highlighted. Another beautiful moment came at a crisis when tribespeople—women and children—took refuge in a cave and were trapped by bandits. Through a narrow, hidden passage, warriors dressed in beautiful, soft chamois entered single file and, one by one, silently dove into an underground lake, barely breaking the surface with a ripple. They reminded me of pictures I have seen from the caves at Lascaux, where a row of deer appear to fly across the cavern wall to disappear into a defile.

To complete this sequence, the aforementioned evil oil thief Forrester was tricked into an underground box canyon. Panicked, he scanned the crowd of arrows facing him, then glanced up to the cavern's roof at a tempting but out-of-reach escape hole that showed blue sky. Suddenly, a rope ladder descended through the hole, and up this he climbed. Reaching his goal, he crawled through, tossed back the ladder defiantly, and turned and began his climb down the mountain. Warriors appeared, and slowly, shot by shot, Forrester was pierced with many arrows. He was forced to continue to live long enough to squeal with each strike as he slid down the hillside looking for all the world like Saint Sebastian in some Medieval illustration.

No irony, no cynicism, just beauty.

American films do similar things with allegory, but they tend to stress the individual within a group of pioneers or range cowboys. An American hero is brave, silent, driven. Often, he has been betrayed by his fellows or is seeking revenge for some mysterious past wrong. Again, the individual takes priority in American tales. And Natives in most US films were presented as caricatures. I suppose the moral dilemma we felt and feel must be present in the creative act, and either guilt or anger has guided our stories. For the Germans who came here to settle, the "Indians" were no more other than the English-speaking population and, at least in books and films, the division stressed was between good and bad acts. Good acts necessarily benefited a community as well as any single individual.

While charmingly corny and having a wacky sense of historical correctness, the films do present the Natives in their own language. As a sort of grace note, the languages they speak are subtitled with transliterations of the language instead of being in English, which is the case for all the dialogue in German. The given names, too, sound real—or at least they make an attempt to copy the sounds of Native Americans. No one is called Tonto.

Like much of the fictive boosterism that brought people to Los Angeles, these novels by May lured many of the millions of Germans who came here, and the films also seem to have given to all Germans a comfortable place to reserve… suspension of disbelief, I suppose, is the thing. I guess we tell ourselves the stories we want to hear, and they last best when the fictions continue to reassure our myths.

After Part 1, we retired to the gallery for a while and talked about art and stuff, and we finished the wine. People left in ones and twos as the clock moved farther past midnight. Rejoining a small group still outside, now listening to music, Alex (or Alexander) implored us, "Can we watch Part 2? Will you watch it, Geoff?" There was a general flight and declarations of "Good-bye, Alexander, we really must go," as Allie, Alexander and I settled down in the early morning, on a rooftop in Chinatown, to watch.

Published on June 2, 2012 by Geoff Tuck in Miscellaneous, Reviews

DAN FINSEL'S "SELF BOX #1"
a photographic consideration

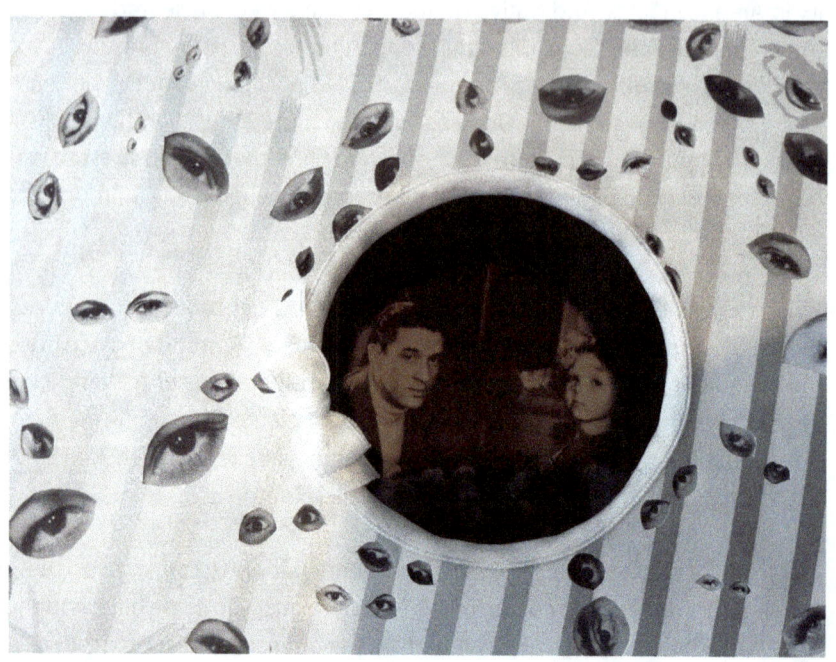

who's the guy? the bow is tender, sweet…

hat box, facepaper__x_covered w/ silver

and white w/ bows

thin paper = eyes cut

out

Shirley Temple glances sort of a flat gaze :: curious b/w outfit

covers reveals protects armoranddesirein 1922

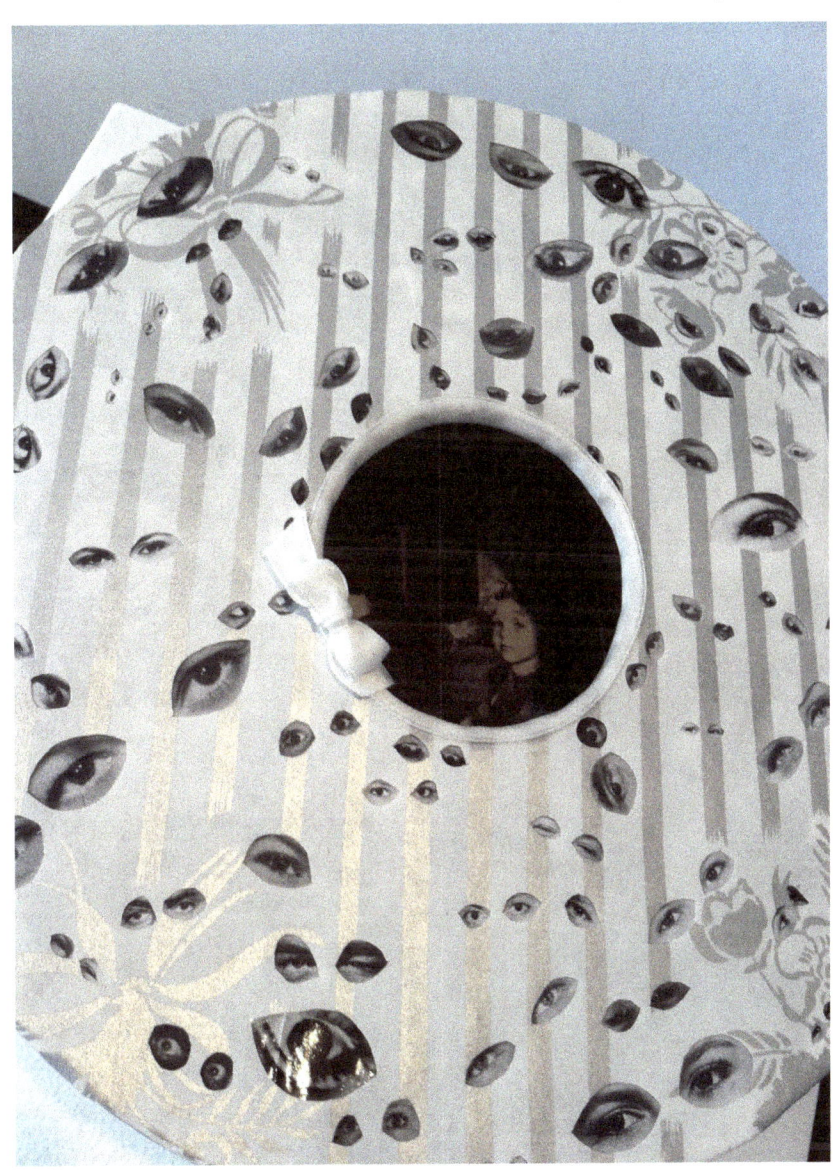

matching wraps @ wrists + right upper arm

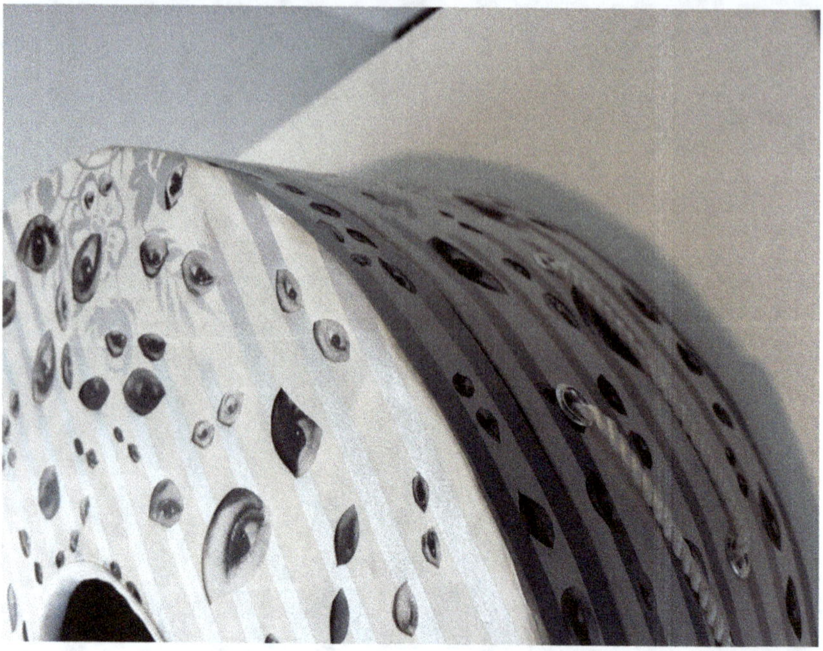

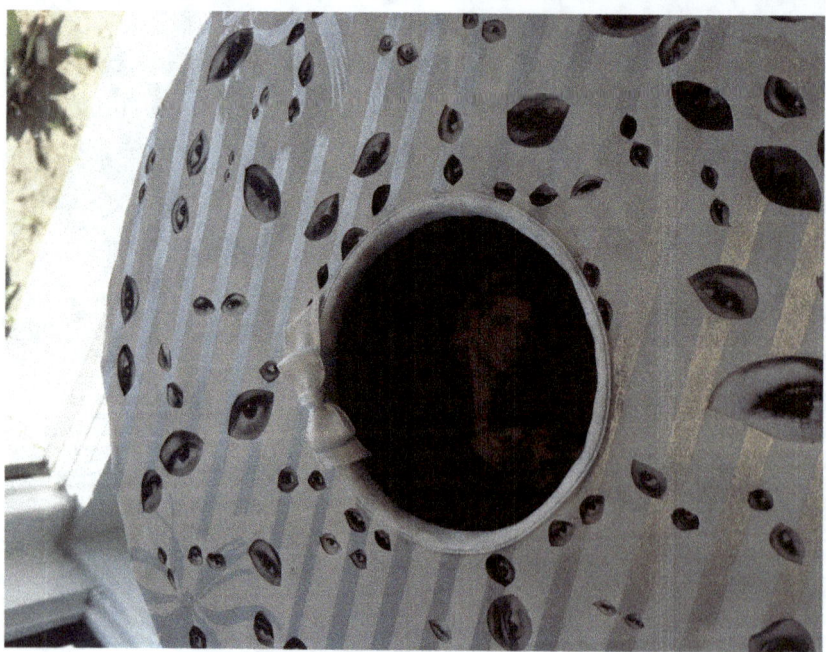

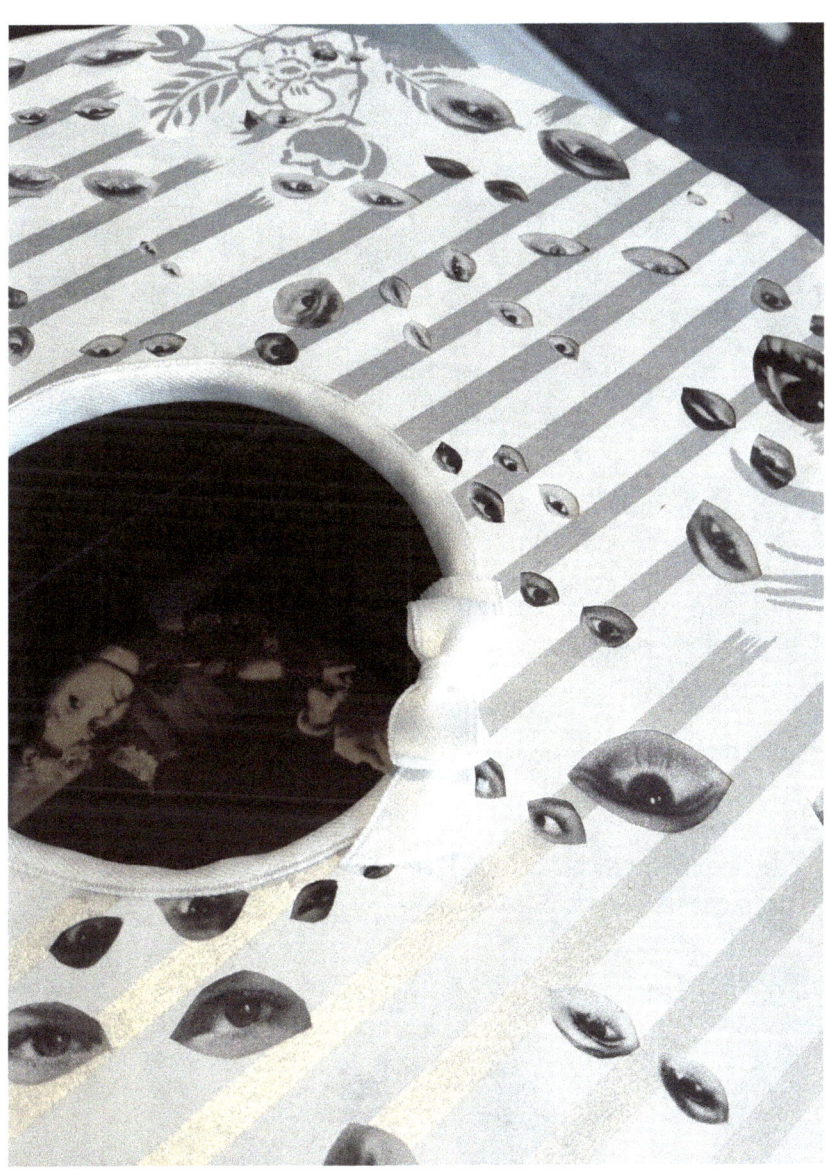

ties twisted but no, that's the next—in a darkened space, windows white with light

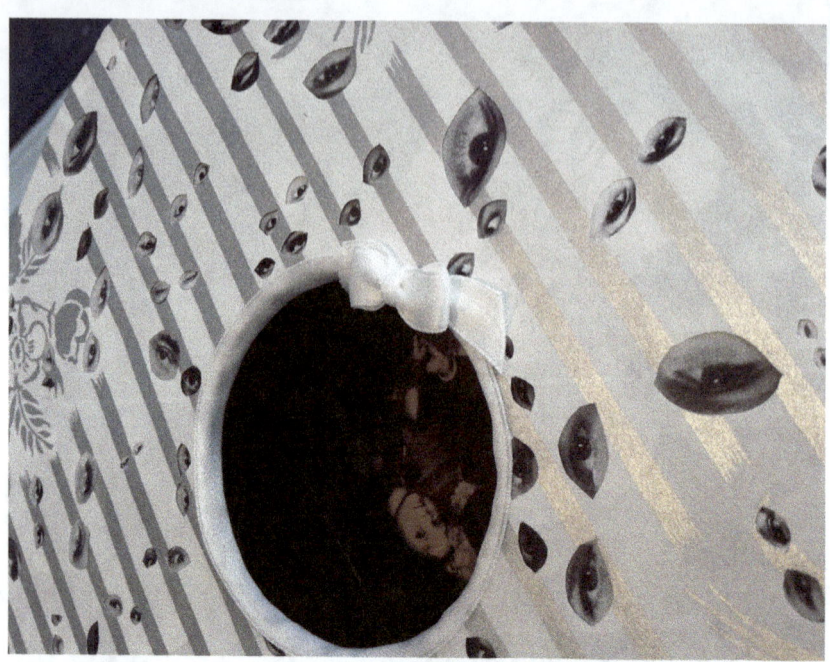

"You know those boxes? There's this way they use art for therapy, you make this box—the outside is what you show the world and inside is... well you get the idea.

I found these hat boxes, from the 1970s or the 1950s. Well, the boxes are still used today.

Shirley Temple sitting on this man's lap...a star, a child, a stand-in for millions of people, in those peoples' own minds.

That was so long ago...

And so like life."

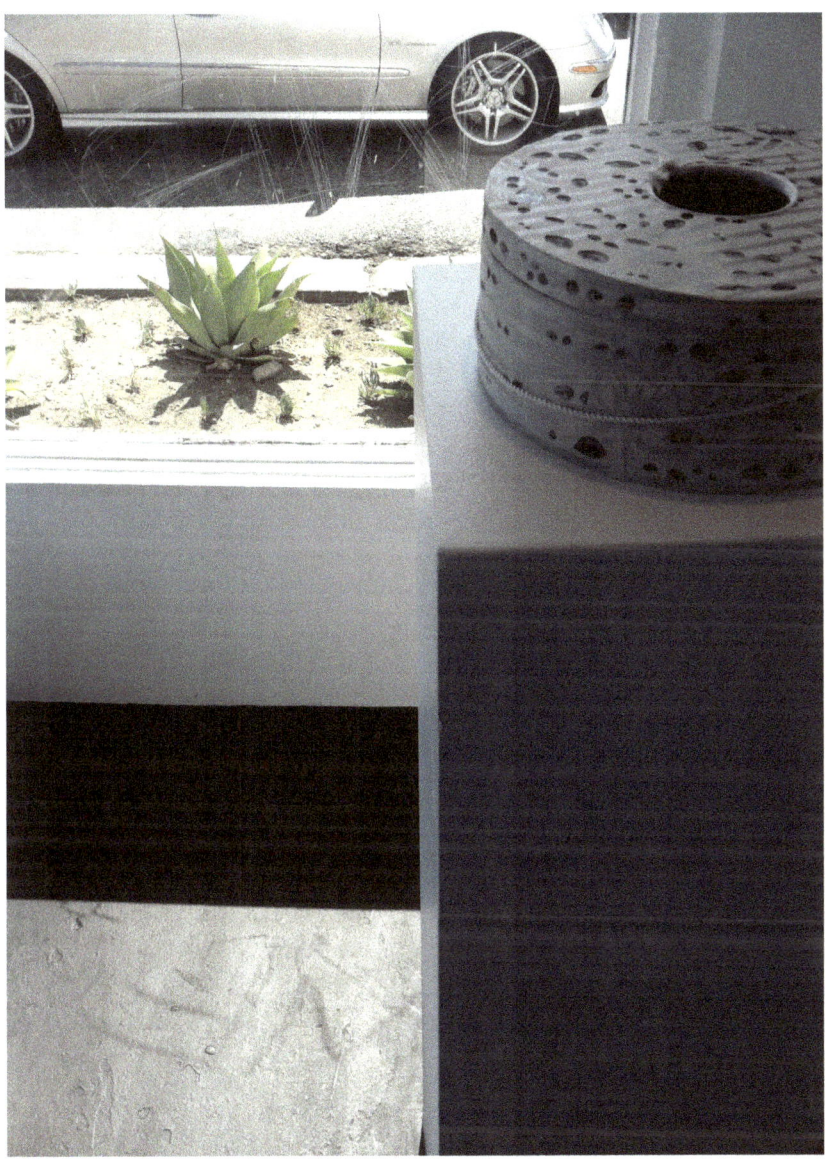

Geoff Tuck, July 23, 11:43 am, 2011

Published on July 23, 2011 by Geoff Tuck in Wanderings

ON MIDDLE AGE AFTER MIDNIGHT
a short poem

The hour is late and the night is dark; the window shows me just myself

when I sit down to write

Sleeping sounds in another room, muffled traffic, Hollywood outside

The city after midnight: I used to know the place

Young people have a wonderful freedom of anonymity that I

lost with age

I stand out too much in the dark

so now I write

Published on August 13, 2011 by Geoff Tuck in Wanderings

SPOKEN WORDS FOR CHARLES GAINES' "SKYBOX"

(Italics indicates extemporaneous performance, regular type indicates quotes read from Gaines' "Skybox")

one hesitates to speak as the darkness gathers

i'm not even aware of it until i see the lights behind the words

…so far 'oppressed' has no stars

'those' and 'rights' have several

(unconscious sounds)

negritude—values—his—the universe—humanism—this point how—contemporary—civilisation—of the universal which is so—before him —slavish fear—inward—to dig—resolution—and further

…and further in the night are the stars

the mind that reads is hushed and shut down

and the mind that wonders takes over.

(more unconscious sounds)

the stars become us—or me anyway

i can't get away from them and i don't want to

i can wonder about the brightness and the quietness and the repetition and the difference

and…to mix my metaphors—my shaking hand cries out for…violence i almost said, when i meant guidance

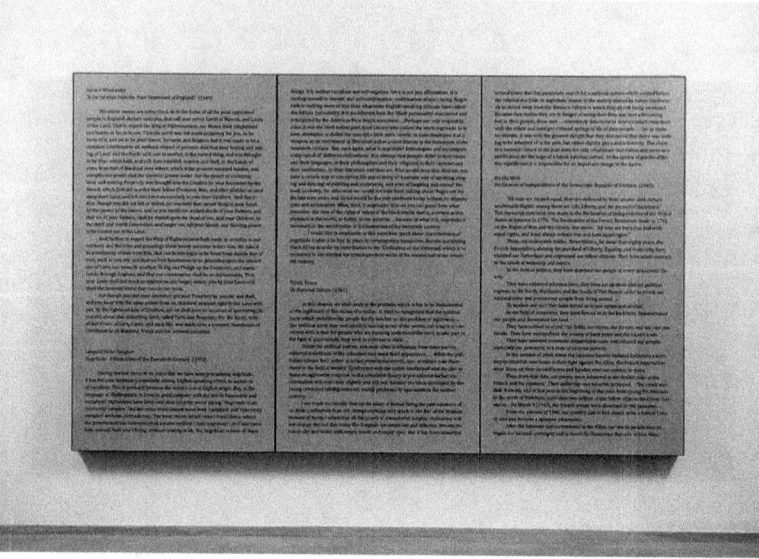

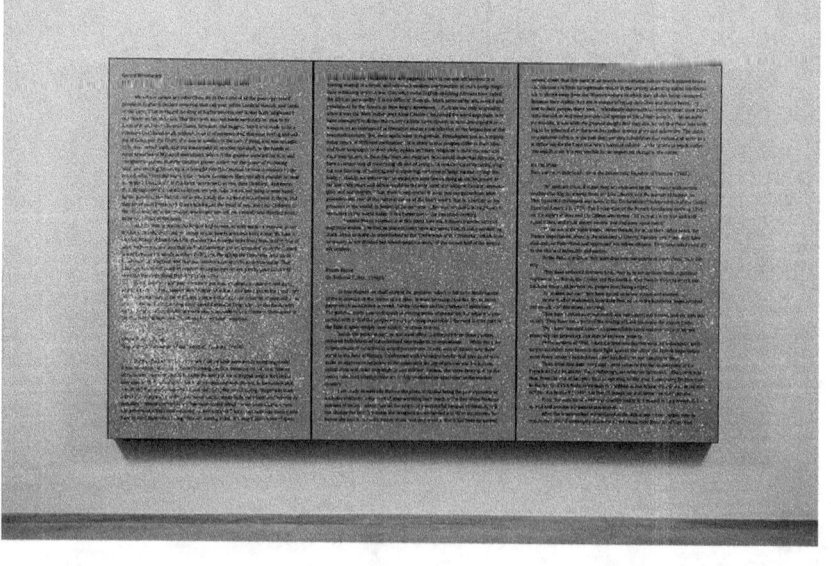

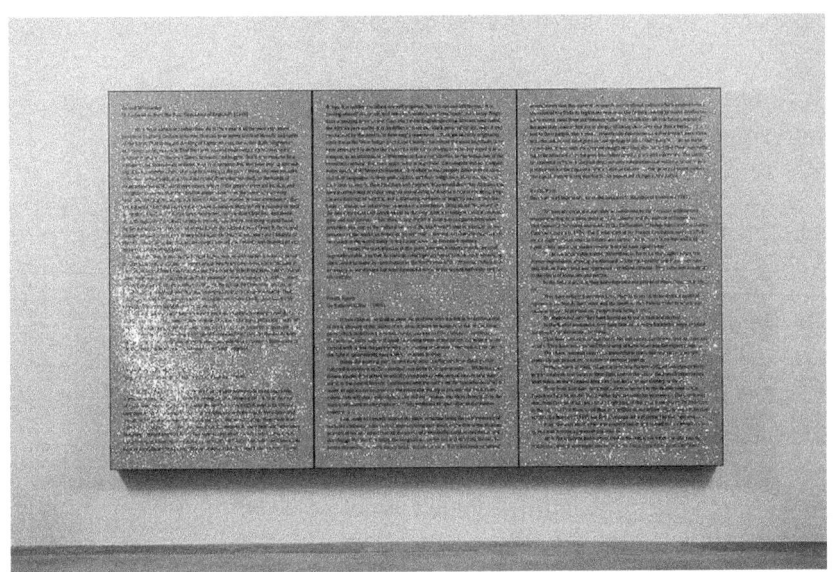

Charles Gaines
"Sky Box I", 2011
Acrylic, digital print, polyester film and LED Lights, changing light system, fix-
tures and tracks
3 Boxes, 84" x 48" x 5" each
Gallery Inventory #GAI213
Courtesy of Susanne Vielmetter Los Angeles Projects; Photo credit: Robert
Wedemeyer

huh.

i wonder if guidance is often violence, or vice versa

all these struggles we have: the rights of man, and the oppressors, those who use, those who take, as against those who share

i wonder, i mean i hate to sound like a Hallmark card—but i wonder what the stars think?

i read a book once, about them—stars, as characters…

…and they did have personalities and they were grandiose and a little bit melancholy

and they lived, and they gave and made life, and their light traveled from one to the other and carried messages

and when they passed, and when they died, that traveled too, and affected everything in the universe

i think the author was talking about people, and using stars as a metaphor

i wonder if charles gaines is, in this piece

talking about people and using stars as a metaphor?

(extended period of darkness, blackness, bare lights, ambient noise)

and the light slowly changes once again.

is it dawn?

hahaha

or is it some sort of rheostat?

and the words appear and almost i forget the night before, and the pure feelings I had, and the thoughts that made me feel whole with everything, and not one but many, and joined.

cultural values—analyze the problem—that the political—legitimacy negritude. proclaiming been have we that years so for thirty last the During—Léopold—livelihood—mankind—corn, cattle—God of Creation—ancestors—to dig, and plough—Kings of Righteousness

charles gaines, susanne vielmetter, closing next week.

bye

Published on October 28, 2011 by Geoff Tuck in Reviews

SHE DIDN'T WANT TO WIN
Brianne Latti

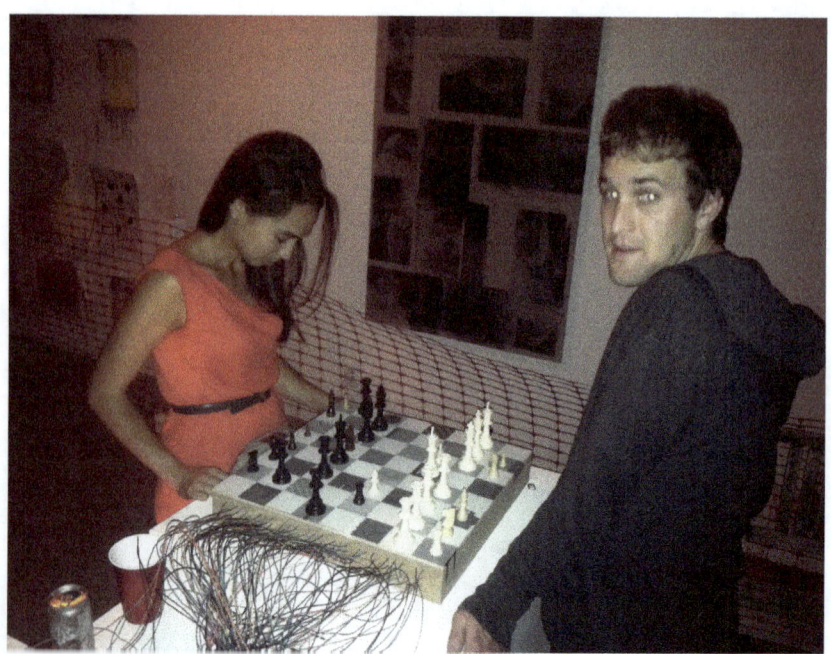

Photo by David Bell

I was totally set up for failure. Not only had every man who had gone up against this chess player earlier in the evening faced miserable defeat, but I was told this young man, a Computer Science Engineering Masters student at UCLA, was literally unbeatable. I didn't even want to play, really I didn't. Yet somehow, last Thursday night, Daniel Lara's chess set seemed more appealing than a game of cornhole (woodwork and hand-knit beanbags courtesy of David Bell…or was it Anthony Bodlović?).

I was still feeling a bit on edge from the performances that happened earlier in the evening at JB Jurve (some of which never seemed to end but rather continue ambiguously in an uncomfortable in-between of performance and reality). Trying to recover from the image of Noah Spindler in pink flared pants and a baby-blue rhinestone hoodie, blasting Top 40 songs over a shitty PA system bought specifically for the occasion; a rigged chili cook-off; and the stress of watching "Chad" deliver a "press conference" after running 30 miles in an overly-ambitious initiative to charm all the gallery owners on the East Side in a mere afternoon, I somehow found myself agreeing to give chess with this young man a try.

The game did not begin well. He had already taken one of my bishops and my knights, and all I had was one of his pawns. As we played, Chess Master X's friends circled me drunkenly, offering prophecies of failure disguised as words of encouragement ("Don't worry, he beats everyone," or, "Dude, he kicked my ass much faster than he's kicking yours!"). One or two of them came up and offered me strategies for winning. I recall someone saying, somewhat condescendingly, "With this guy, all you can do is play defense. He's too good for you to try to win." However, I ignored the advice and maintained my focus. Although I hadn't played a game of chess for years, it was a pleasant distraction from some of the typical artist conversations that I prefer to avoid, such as discussions on the subjects of banality and abjection (I still don't know what that word really means) and simulacral pacifiers and how *obviously* easy it is to die hair in the pattern of a rainbow, or how unsexy sex *really* is, when you start to think about it….

And I suppose the truth is I didn't expect to win. I was just trying to pay attention to what was happening in front of me, and in an instant the power shifted. In what must have been a moment of overconfidence, my competitor left his queen unguarded, and just like that, I took his most powerful piece. For a second I almost felt guilty because he was so upset. Tugging on his hair anxiously, he tried to regain his composure, but from there, it was only three more quick moves until I had him in what I initially thought was just check but, as my poor competitor was forced to point out to me, was actually a full-fledged checkmate. Oops.

My sort-of-accidental victory spread quickly throughout the gallery space and, almost instantly, all of his friends had gathered around to observe their friend's defeat and marvel at "the Asian chick" who seemed like such an unlikely victor. Yet there I was, a winner, and there he was, running off to the bathroom to weep (I kid you not) over his loss. David Bell was so proud he offered to frame the drawing that was produced from my win (hard to explain if you haven't seen Daniel's piece, which is programmed to move a pen on a piece of paper each time a piece moves in any direction across the chess board. And David, who never takes photos unless it is of something completely unsentimental like a bathroom floor or a poster of a missing cat, snapped several pictures that night of the game and told me he would keep them as a reminder of my "perseverance."

To me, I had simply won a game of chess, but David and Noah and the rest of the people who witnessed the game insisted that something truly monumental happened that night—in fact, Daniel Lara himself messaged me just this evening to inquire about this "epic" (his words, not mine) game, and Geoff Tuck apparently was so impressed that he invited me to write this piece about my experience. I find it hilarious that all of these men seem to be so extraordinarily fascinated with the concept of me winning this game. I don't know...I guess I just really like that I made a boy cry.

Yours kindly,

Brianne Latti

Published on June 21, 2012 by Brianne Latti in Additional writing by, Brianne Latti, Fiction

SO NICE TO MEET YOU
Brianne Latti

Sitting in my beat-up car outside the banquet hall, I can see the men standing around. Some talking, some smoking, some peering into the newly-arrived vehicle to try to catch a glimpse of who might be inside. I turn up my music a little louder, savoring my last ten seconds of solitude before I step out into the fluorescent light. The car door opens and I am outside, wearing the black leather dress my boyfriend had zipped me into an hour earlier before I kissed him gently on the mouth and said goodbye for the night. *Have fun*, he said. *I will*, I said.

The tiny, sort of squirrely Turkish man who is my boss greets me with a hug as I walk through the French doors into the small lobby. He is thrilled by my outfit, and suggests the only thing that is missing is a whip. Of course, I giggle and laugh, perhaps gently squeeze his shoulders, and continue toward the table to say my hellos to the guests who are already seated, all of whom I have seen here before. They are regulars. They know me. Well—they know Alexa Grace. That's who I am on these nights.

I wish I could tell you I chose to have a fake name purely for practical measures, as a way to safeguard my own identity from being linked to the game, or the players, or the cash. Certainly, this was part of it. But the reality is I felt my heart swell when the idea of having an alias entered my mind. Mainly, I chose the pseudonym for the thrill of being known to others by a name that was not my own, especially one that sounded so totally absurd and porn star–like.

An iPhone rests inside a plastic red cup, which serves to amplify the sound of rap music coming out of the phone's quiet speakers. It is an undeniably seedy environment, and the room stinks of Chinese takeout. Still, I walk across the tile floor in my knee-high boots with an air of royalty, making the room my stage, because I have one thing in common with these players and that is that I, like them, am addicted to the acquisition of the chips.

The game is close to starting, and my boss seamlessly transforms the players' hundred-dollar bills into stacks of colorful purple and pink chips, engraved with what I've always imagined must be his initials, but I have never bothered to ask—we only go by first names around here. Don't ask, don't tell. Aware of the click-clack of my heels as I strut around the seated men, I take a seat in one of the empty chairs next to Big Eddie and prop my elbows onto the table, resting my chin in the palm of my hand like a child.

Big Eddie is an older Russian gentlemen with a thick accent and a massive frame that is always adorned with beautiful jewelry and designer watches. Big Eddie is also one of the only players who can successfully pull off winking at me from across the room without coming off as leering. "Hello, gorgeous," he says to me in a thick Russian accent, as if he was welcoming home one of his daughters. I like Big Eddie because he almost never arrives without a fresh box of cream puffs for everyone. Tonight, he is wearing a golden Rolex, an onyx David Yurman ring, and a beautiful jade bracelet with a diamond-studded gold clasp. On nights when he has been winning, Big Eddie drinks vodka and cranberry, but he's been on a losing streak lately, so for right now he sticks to Sprite. He always smells of sandalwood oil.

Next to him is Ralphie. Ralphie is a party boy. He is always either coming from Hollywood or going to Hollywood, and he is frequently high. Ralphie drinks Jack and Coke. He's a good tipper, and he's sweet. Waiting for his cards to come, he asks me about my weekend. I tell him I went home to visit family, leaving out the part about bringing my boyfriend home with me. *Never tell them you have a boyfriend.*

The game begins, even though there are still a few empty seats. Throughout the night, more people will arrive. It is early. Big Eddie hands me a five-dollar chip. "For good luck," he says with a wink. "Thank you," I coo sweetly, tucking the chip into my bra.

Superstition runs rampant around here. If I am sitting next to a player and he wins a hand, then he decides that I am good luck and usually asks me to keep sitting with him. They all have their favorite seats, but if a player is continuously losing he may ask to switch seats with somebody else or have the dealer change out the deck of cards.

I watch the game intently. I am picking up the rules, learning the ranking of the hands, and acquiring an entirely new lexicon through this strange sort of cultural immersion: *all in, blind, flop, kicker, side pot, call, check, check raise….* When I first started, Phillip, a handsome but aloof player who rarely speaks or takes his eyes off the game, looked up at me from across the table and asked casually, "You know how to play?" In his eyes I could see he was sizing me up. "Yes," I stated confidently, giving him the answer he seemed to desire. Back then, Alexa Grace knew how to play, but now, so do I.

My eyes dart over to Vijay as he wins the pot. He pulls nearly a thousand dollars' worth of chips toward him and rearranges them neatly in rows of hundreds. Some of the other players compliment him on his hand. I skillfully hide my disdain as he takes a sip of the massive Big Gulp that he keeps underneath the table. The fact that Vijay has the audacity to bring in his own beverage, which he will nurse the whole night long, never asking me for anything and never proffering so much as an acknowledgment of my presence, is maddening. He knows I work only for tips and that, like him, this game is my main source of financial support. Not to mention he plays dirty. *Cheap* bastard.

"A.G., can you get me a Jack and Coke?" Ralphie asks. "Mmmhm," I reply warmly. *Never ask them if they want anything to drink before a player asks first.* This creates the illusion that I am not there to make money, but rather out of the goodness of my heart and an insistent desire to please. "Anyone else want something to drink?" I inquire nonchalantly, making my way toward the door. I take a few more orders before I slip out of sight into the vast, empty banquet hall.

My boots make imprints on the aged synthetic carpet, and then loud clicks as I skip across the freshly polished dance floor. This is only the first of many times that I will walk through this room by myself tonight. In the kitchen, running my fingers along the steel countertops, silently enticing them to remove the dust and crumbs from their surfaces as I make my way to the back walk-in refrigerator. Before I enter, I make sure to flip on the light switch.

I have visions of being raped back here. Raped, or brutally murdered by someone who might slip into the kitchen through the back door, which connects to an alley that leads to the main street. I am so far away from the other men, no one would hear me scream. Or what if it was one of them? Sometimes, my boss follows me back here because he needs to get something too. He's never tried anything with me, yet I remain vigilant at all times, since I know that sexual harassment cases can't exist in workplaces where everything you earn is under the table. My involvement in this game is just as unlawful as his.

I grab a handle of whiskey. Some generic Sam's Club brand, perhaps the biggest bottle of whiskey I've ever seen. As I leave the fridge, I make sure to shut the door behind me and turn off the light—My sense of responsibility to look out for this place, and care for it as if it were my own, is something that has developed against my will over the last few months.

Scoop. Pour. Pour. Mix. I prepare the drinks on the cutting-board counter-top, next to a huge vat of frozen but defrosting chicken breasts. In a way, the griminess excites me. I can't help but imagine the shocked expression on the faces of friends and family if they were to hear that this is how I have been spending my nights. *Sorry, Daddy. I know I'm not in law school, I know I'm not in med school, and I know I'm not preparing to run for office, but this will have to do instead….* I push the thought out of my mind as I run with the tray of drinks through the double doors and back through the dimly lit banquet hall, toward the lobby.

It is a graceful and calculated display: I slide in between them and place the drink gently in the cup holder with my right hand, aware that my breasts meet their eye-line almost perfectly. Then I reach around and rest my left hand on their left shoulder, as if I might decide to stay resting in that position for a while. If they are in the middle of a hand, I wait patiently by their side until they are done. They hand me a chip or two, and I say thank you with a coy smile, closing my hand around the chips without looking to see how much they've given me. Working these games is an art I have now perfected. I have developed my own particular method of seduction, a perfect blend of co-quettishness and confidence and an ability to read in a person's eyes when I am to be silent, and when I am to speak. *Never speak to them when they have a hand.*

I never imagined that it would happen, but I have grown fond of some of the players. Most of the guys who come here are sweet and unsuspecting mid-dle-aged married men with day jobs who come once or twice a week to test out their evening luck. Still, privacy is valued here. In addition to not reveal-ing their last names, few even talk about their professions or their wives or their children, yet I have come to know these men in a very intimate way. I know what they drink, what they eat, and how they take their coffee; I know what they look like when they are upset, when they are happy, or when they are bluffing; and of course, I know how their bodies feel, because in addition to serving drinks, I also am responsible for providing massages to the players who will be sitting here all night, many of whom will be driving home in to-morrow's early morning traffic.

The table is now full, so I stand patiently to the side, waiting for my first client of the evening. If no one bites early, I will stand behind one of the guys and run my fingers gently up and down his spine, putting him in the mood. Then I will bend down and say softly in his ear, "Want a massage?" It's a foolproof technique. But I don't have to do that tonight because Mel, one of the new-comers who staggered in drunk and ready to play, has flipped his chair to the side and beckoned me over. Mel is a massive man, easily 300 pounds, and giving him a proper massage is not only difficult but also exhausting if not approached correctly.

Leaning all of my body weight into him, I roll my elbows in small circles at the nape of his neck. I discovered the elbow technique by accident. One night, I had been giving a massage to one of the more considerably sized players and, because my hands were growing fatigued, I began using my elbows to knead the rolls of fat and lumps of muscle that constituted his back. This produced moans and grunts of pleasure from the seated man, and I knew then that I had discovered a signature maneuver that would set me apart as a favorite amongst the other girls.

I take my massages seriously and make every effort to provide the best qual-ity care that I can. I approach them in a non-sexual manner, yet I am sure that arousal often occurs. Maybe it's only narcissism, but whenever I am giving a massage to a player and he starts speaking to another player in a different language and chuckling, I assume that he is telling his friend all the things he'd like to do to me, if he could. But as long as he tips me generously and keeps his hands on the table and off my body, I tune it out. Still, sometimes, once I've left the game and I am safe at home, a thought creeps up into my head: *How did I come to a place where this sort of exchange seems normal?*

I massage Mel for a long while, losing all sense of time. I have learned that it is the only way I can keep up my energy and make it through these long nights. While massaging, if I rest my chest against his back, it is not in an effort to be sexy, but because it helps me to conserve energy. If I unintentionally stick my ass out, or get down on my knees, it's not because I am inviting objectification, but because it helps me to get the angle right. But…when I take a pause to roll my neck and arch my back, well, in this case I admit that sometimes I make this a more theatrical display than necessary. I don't know why I do this, or why *she* does this.

After an hour or so, Mel hands me a huge stack of chips, enough for me to go out and buy a nice new pair of shoes or treat my boyfriend to a fancy dinner. I thank him by giving him a big hug from behind, and place the chips in my red plastic cup, which is steadily filling with tips.

Hours pass. Empty cups are replaced with full ones. More massages are given. Thousands of dollars' worth of chips slide across the table, taking up residence with a player for a short while before they are lost, and lost, then won again.

It's not until around midnight that Little Eddie rolls in. I haven't seen him in a while. Apparently, he gave up the game because he owed too many people too much money, had alcohol problems, et cetera. I've never fancied Little Eddie. His white wife-beaters, tasteless tattoos, and spiky, gelled hair trigger my vomit reflex. There are some disconcerting characters that come by occasionally, such as Jaleel—a seemingly sweet and gentle man who drops by every so often. His fetish is for feet. "Oh! You have such nice feet, they're so little and beautifully shaped," he'll say, while I giggle nervously, praying that he doesn't plan to go home and masturbate to the thought of my dancer's arch and bubble toes.

Even stranger is Clem, who seems perfectly normal until he starts talking and you can tell that something is amiss inside of his mouth.

"What is that?" I asked when I first met him.

He opened his mouth to reveal that his tongue has been split in two, like a snake. "I did it in prison," he says sort of shyly.

"With what?"

"A piece of floss."

"Oh."

And that was that. But at least Jaleel and Clem have sweet demeanors, unlike Little Eddie, who is loud, abrasive, and overtly misogynistic. Fortunately for me, I was never his favorite girl because I've never entertained his comments by laughing at one of the many jokes he likes to tell that aren't funny.

Still, I am friendly toward him when he arrives, and I greet him with a hug, masking my disgust. He's not playing, but I imagine the urge to play is strong. He paces around the table impatiently, insisting that he won't partake, but I feel that at any moment he might relapse, giving in to the temptation of the cards.

I ask him if he wants anything to drink. He declines, and everyone else seems to be fine, so I walk over to my phone to check my messages. I am standing by the front door entrance, scrolling through my emails, when someone comes up from behind me and unhesitatingly sticks his hand underneath my dress, against the inside of my inner left thigh, and gives it a squeeze. His thumb is only centimeters away from touching my vagina. In an instant, I spin around. It's Little Eddie.

"No." I say sternly, wagging my finger at him as if I am talking to a child. "You can't do that."

He laughs and shrugs his soldiers, then challenges me: "Or what?"

I glare at him, hands on my hips, eyebrows raised, staring at him like the piece of dog shit he is.

"I'm sorry, I thought it was ok," he says.

"No. That is inappropriate. You're being inappropriate."

"Well, when you're wearing a dress like that…."

What enrages me is not that he touched me. What enrages me is this comment. I feel my whole body fill with a cold hatred for this loathsome individual. I have grown comfortable with most of these men. I have even come to enjoy my time here and consider some of them my friends. Yet, in an instant, Little Eddie has taken all of my false senses of security and defecated all over them. I am reminded of my place here, and the role that I willingly subject myself to every day. I am not really safe.

I look around, but the men are engrossed in their game and do not pause to look up at what has just transpired. Did they not hear us? Did they hear but decide it was best not to get involved? Or did they see and hear what happened but somehow come to the conclusion that Little Eddie's actions were permissible?

I am alone. But I am not fearful. I look him dead in the eyes. The words roll off my tongue and shoot out toward him like daggers:

"Just because I'm dressed sexy doesn't mean you can touch me. If you ever touch me again, I'll chop off your dick."

"Ok, I'm sorry," he mutters pathetically.

But I'm already walking away calmly, back to the table to fetch a fresh round of drinks for the thirsty guests, as if it never happened, as if he is no longer in the room. After I've demonstrated to everyone that I am not going to get dramatic or tearful about this, about any of this atrocious display of behavior, I head toward the bathroom to check my lipstick. But when I open up the door, I walk into one of the guys cutting lines of coke on the bathroom cabinet. He looks up at me, unfazed. Without missing a beat, he reaches out his hand to offer me a rolled-up dollar bill. "Do you party?" he asks.

After declining politely, I return to the table. The energy is tense, and I'm not sure if it's because of Little Eddie and me or because a lot of people have been losing money tonight.

Ralphie asks me to come over and rub his shoulders. "Give me some luck, A.G." he pleads. Standing at this angle, I notice that the player next to him, Vijay, has dried-up bird shit on his shoulder. This could present an uncomfortable dilemma if Vijay asks me for a massage later. Of course, I could alert him of the crusty fecal matter, which almost seems to complement the strange, crusty scab on his nose, but I would prefer not to be responsible for making him lose face in front of the other players. It might affect my tip.

Soon, it is four in the morning. Big Eddie is long gone after losing all his chips. Ralphie has gone back to Hollywood to some club that is open after hours, and Little Eddie left hours ago, having slipped out the door while I was in the kitchen making drinks. There are only a few players left. Mel is sticking it out, although every few minutes he falls asleep in his chair, his lumps of fat rolling into each other, billowing onto the table…but then he raises he eyelids for a moment, just in time to place a bet. Nothing can stop him from playing, not even sleep.

When the game finally ends, I wait patiently so the lingering players can cash out their chips in my boss's office. When it is my turn, I go in and shut the door. The chips spill out of my red cup and onto his desk, almost knocking over the portrait of his wife and little boy that he keeps next to his computer. Even after my boss takes a 20% cut, I still have earned enough money to pay my rent for next month.

I say thank you for the money, like a good little underground employee, and I prepare to make my exit. But as I am leaving something stops me. I want to ask him if he saw. I want to see what his reaction would be and what he would say to console me. How would he prevent it from happening again? But then I change my mind. Because I know that if I asked him and he did nothing about it, I would never be able to come back to this place because only *then* would it truly sink in that what I am doing—no, what I am *not* doing—is wrong.

So I get back into my beat-up car and turn on the ignition. Of course, my gas tank is now on empty, before I have even left the parking lot. I face a dilemma: Do I risk running out of gas on the freeway, or do I stop somewhere to get gas at 4:30 in the morning and pray I don't get attacked? This would be a bold and risky move for a young woman to make while wearing a black leather dress and carrying over a month's rent in cash. I can't help but think of the movie *Clueless*, where Cher gets mugged in a gas station parking lot. *But this is an Alaïa!* she pleads. Her father had expressed concern that she was going to be in The Valley, as mine would too, had he known that's where I was. I decide to drive home.

Nearly twenty miles later, I am driving down my street, past the glittery transvestites and the shadowy pimps that frequent my street corner. I have come to think of them as secret comrades, both of us trying to make some quick cash while the rest of Los Angeles sleeps. I breathe a sigh of relief as I pull into the driveway, thankful to have arrived safely to my destination, but there is something blocking my way. A thick telephone wire has fallen across the driveway, and I cannot get into my parking spot without having to pass over it. The wire is frayed and vicious looking, like a black snake on the hunt for living prey. Confronted with yet another obstacle, I measure out my options. Shall I dare crossing this treacherous wire and hope that currents of electricity don't pass through my car and into my skull, engulfing me in flames? Or would there be less risk in parking down the street and walking the long mile past the slow-moving cars, hiding the faces of men who have been searching all night for a petite hooker in a black leather dress? If someone pulled a gun to my head, what would I do?

No. I will not be a cut-up, cold body found the next day. If I am to die, I will go up in flames. Slowly, I ease my foot down on the gas pedal, holding my breath as the wheels turn forward. But then, *victory!* I've crossed the divide.

In moments, I am back in my apartment, the door is locked, and I am tip-toe-ing into the darkness of my room, where I can hear the soft sound of my boy-friend's snores from underneath the sheets. When I eventually lay down to rest, I wrap my body around his body, my legs around his legs, and I lie there, delighting in the feel of his warm back pressed against my chest. I am almost asleep when a memory drifts into my head. Yesterday, I had met someone, somewhere…a friend of a friend who I had been meaning to meet for a long time. But when I reached out my hand to introduce myself, I had stumbled awkwardly over my words—*It's so nice to meet you, I'm*…. And for a split sec-ond, I couldn't remember who I was on that day, during that exchange, and wasn't that so strange? But then the memory escapes me, and I am off some-where far away.

Published on October 30, 2012 by Brianne Latti in Additional writing by, Brianne Latti, Fiction

ACROSS STEVE TURNER
David Bell as Lucas Chaddwick, Jr.

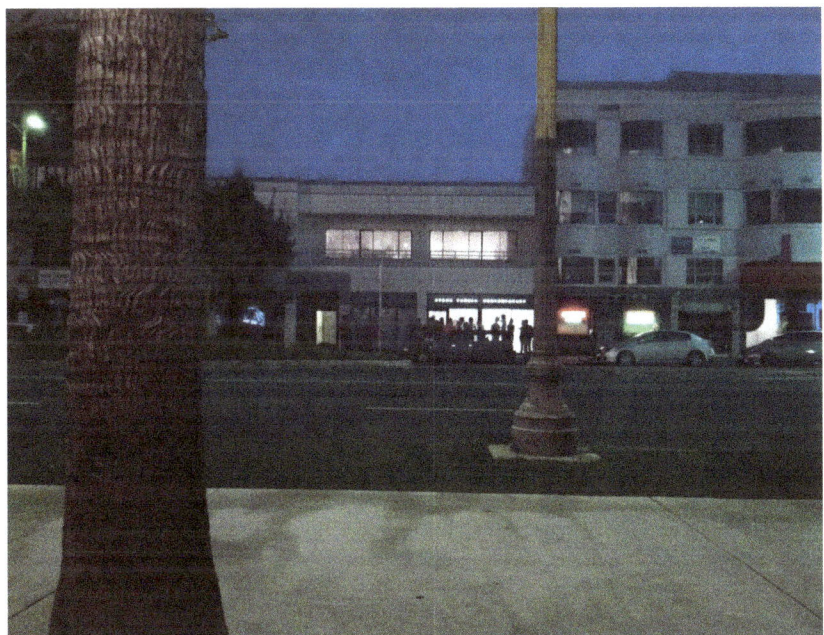

Photo by David Bell

Sitting in the grass across the street on LACMA's front lawn, I squinted but couldn't make out so much as I would have liked at Steve Turner Gallery. Because of the slight slope on the hill I was sitting, I relaxed and didn't feel the need to re-situate myself. I could make out three medium-size paintings through the right window of the gallery, yet their rather dull, pale complexion didn't captivate me to the point where I'd dare to leapfrog through the heavy traffic that still kept the buses moving slow along Wilshire. The cars made it hard to make out faces as well, not to mention the darkness of the street together with the intense light from the gallery left people on their indefinite smoke break back-lit, leaving me to build identities through faded silhouettes.

I could recognize a few familiar faces, being that it was a forever migrating UCLA flock of "art patrons" attending. I may have only been projecting, but I thought I saw William Kaminski walk through the door, yet I never witnessed his exit, and I only know him as someone who spends most his time outside of the gallery with his cigarettes and elevated presence…. I believe I spotted Marcus Perez losing himself conversationally when the traffic stole his attention, although it may have been his older look-alike Jared Pankin, but rarely do we see either of them out at openings. To keep me on edge, there was a very petite man on his phone who paced back and forth obnoxiously in the muddled-up crowd. I found it quite annoying that he would do this in the middle of everyone and not excuse himself from the huddle, as if the sound of his voice in proximity to the others allowed him to remain intrinsically a part of the scene.

Steve Turner himself seemed to be in a constant state of exit, as his face remained always in center view through the doorway, as if he intended to be the first visual a guest would see upon entrance. But he was too late; the show had unarguably been stolen by a tall, maple-skinned woman in a black dress with a contemplated Afro with bleached tips. She demanded attention as she stood near the street with a perspicacious smile that, from afar, acted as sufficient conversation with me for the evening.

After twenty minutes or so, I realized I could not sit there all night alone. The bodies interacting with the lights were too much to resist. I raised myself off the ground and headed to join in on the excitement. After a short walk, I handed over my camera to a stranger and politely asked him to make sure he got all the street lights in the shot as I smiled and said goodnight to the burden across the street.

Published on August 20, 2012 in Additional writing by, Fiction, Lucas Chaddwick, Jr.

METEOR SHOWER
Jonathon Hornedo

I read online somewhere,
without verifying elsewhere,
that many of the stars we see at night
are not individual stars
but clusters of usually two or three or more.
Their starlight travels across space and time,
converging into what to us looks like one thing,
one single point of light.

And John Stuart Mill said
that a man may have been named John
because that was the name of his father.
A town may have been named Dartmouth
because it is situated at the mouth of the Dart.
But if sand should choke up the mouth of the river,

or an earthquake change its course,
and remove it to a distance from the town,
the name of the town would not necessarily be changed.

And because the man of the twenty-first century
is a multi-tasker,
I'm thinking about these things
while another dude and I are groping a nude blond woman
in the entrance hall
at her house in Santa Monica.

I'm sucking on the woman's chest,
her neck,
her nipples,
trying to give her fake boobs a track of hickies
and this guy Todd—who I have never met before in my life—
is nude with only a white t-shirt on his head
and moaning while the blond woman fondles his balls.

The Quaaludes
and the cocaine
and the alcohol
are making me do things I wouldn't ordinarily do,
and I unbutton my pants,
and the blond woman turns to hump me,
and she moans in ecstatic stupor
and I get down on my knees,

positioning myself underneath her bald pussy
so I can lick it
and all of a sudden I'm also underneath Todd's erect cock,
the shaft twitching up to a firm erection,
its shadow cast over my eyes
and he's getting ready to put it in
and I'm uncomfortable in this position
so I stand up again
and begin rubbing my cock across the woman's bare stomach.

Then for some reason Todd stops what he's doing,
and the blond woman stops moaning,
and I look at both of their faces,
and I know instantly that something unanticipated is happening
because they are looking over my shoulder
towards the front door
that I hear open, then close.
My first thought is oh fuck
and I'm thinking that the woman's boyfriend
or husband
is home
and he's probably behind me already,
and I close my eyes,
bracing myself for the fatal punches
that would land on me like a violent meteor shower,

and I'm thinking that this would be a good time to stop the scene
and have my body double finish this off for me
but everything happens too fast for the switch to happen
because the facts all belong only to the task
and not to its performance.

And when two lights converge into one,
and when names change in meaning,
and when the referent of a name is fixed,
it does not matter where,
or on who,
or on which object
the meteor shower lands.

Published on April 27, 2013 by Jonathon Hornedo in Additional writing by

PORTRAIT OF AN AMERICAN FAMILY, OR THIS AMERICAN LIFE
Paul and Damon McCarthy's Rebel Dabble Babble
Aaron Wrinkle

Part One: Written at Home in My Bed

Dean is my middle name. It was handed down to me via my great grandma. Aaron Dean, they'd call me. It's a flirtatious audacity to connect it to James Dean, but nonetheless I have. His looks, his fame, his portrayed reckless behavior and even his death. But we all have, in one way or another, especially James Franco. Dean's is a classic story of an American tragedy, as was *Rebel Without a Cause*. America is tragic today, and lately, so is the L.A. art world. The McCarthys have exceptionally repositioned artistic tragedy by commenting on the former. Specifically Hollywood. One can't help but think of the intentional mirroring that this all places onto the current state of things. When times are bad or weird, make it funny or weirder. But do it right. Do it like the McCarthys.

Rebel Dabble Babble makes me want to Rebel Dabble Babble in my head, out my mouth and nearly out of all ends. I once saw a classic video documentary on Marilyn Manson where Twiggy the guitarist is simultaneously puking, shitting and pissing himself. Luckily, you didn't get the smell through the TV set to create the domino effect, but it's just enough like *Rebel Dabble Babble* to give you an idea. An idea and a glimpse. Ideas and glimpses into what it's all about. New ideas and feelings altogether. Glimpses of what might or might not have led up to the event and what is happening in the present. Enough to know that something is wrong, but being dealt with accordingly or to the best of one's ability. Sometimes one must pull one's pants down to make a point or simply do so to relieve oneself or to get off. Even if faking it. Sometimes one has no other choice and it's a career choice. It's a paycheck. No judging here. Ever. Sometimes we are fortunate enough to experience or come in contact with the people responsible for these acts. To see or hear them tell their stories. Sometimes it's all re-articulated via someone else or through art. Sometimes it's like a re-created reality akin to *Unsolved Mysteries*, with the people and places changed to protect their identities. Sometimes people and their ideas can't be replaced. Just like love. Maybe. Maybe not. Sometimes it's an intervention. I met Marilyn Manson and his band as a teenager after they opened up for the band Clutch. Marilyn drew me snake eyes and 6's on request. I took it back to the household of my American family. It's framed now with all the others. The faces and places have now changed. Or have they? It's beginning to feel like one big scene. A scene you have to learn to live and work with. Something about *Rebel Dabble Babble* reminds me that everything is going to be OK even if the shit has already hit the fan.

Being the first major exhibition I've encountered by McCarthy and his son, *Rebel Dabble Babble* makes me think back to my first interactions with McCarthy senior's work, literal examples from my past, why I was and have become re-interested in his practice, and now his collaborations with his son Damon in relation to my collaboration with my own father. I've always been a late bloomer. It's kind of a flipped example in relation to my own story, but the conversation or link is relevant. My father and I restored a car together…. I'm interested in family collaboration in general. It's like farm work or doing chores. It's very blue collar. Wet sanding the fenders with my dad. Dinner is ready. It's really about teamwork. I'm interested in the American family, my own family and the family of art. Not necessarily pedagogy, but lineage and birthright. There's a certain reality to a kind of reversed adoption as well. A kind of forced idol logic. Some welcome your friendship. You look up to mentors and influences, or you desire to destroy them. Here is more of a token of appreciation for the foreman on the job. Sometimes you don't get along with your peers. Sometimes that's constructed. But, I've never been one to desire the destruction of anybody except myself, and even that was involuntary. For good measure, I'm interested in the artist as self-therapist who also gives their kid Play-Doh or possibly Plato when they're ready. We're getting into the plot now. The thought of a kid not having either is bothersome. But there are always alternative replacements for these things. A family should work together and figure it out, and the McCarthys seem to be doing a great job of this.

I'm quite fascinated by the idea and reality of a family operation. Through Mara McCarthy's gallery (Paul's daughter) The Box and her curated projects existing outside of Los Angeles with artists such as Simone Forti and Barbara T. Smith, she has proven an admirable dedication to issues and influences not just easily tied to her father, but in the greater scheme of things art-related. Specifically through advocating artists connected to feminism and performance. It is a unique reality that gives us glimpses into great relationships and artists sometimes historically under-appreciated. It's hard to imagine the Los Angeles art scene without this reality. With so many others involved, including younger artists and staff, it isn't really fair to call it a family operation altogether, but a collaboration has unfolded currently at The Box that is worthy of noting. Maybe that is a family. Ok, it is. It's also this connection, presumably influenced by her father, that allows one to reconsider just using the common critique of female objectification, shock or machoism attached to McCarthy's work. Meaning there is an understanding of the information the artist is dealing with that goes way deeper than just the immediate or presumed information commonly being viewed or associated with his work. He is aware. Basically, women aren't just objects here, but rather contribute to the overall story very importantly. There is a nod, too, by the artist to his roots and influence from feminism, performance and his relationship to Los Angeles' art history. Sometimes, he even plays dress-up. He has always held up a mirror on his past. He continues to do so. The male position is generally always absurd or pathetic, and there has never been a moment I've seen a denial of this kind of failure, an acknowledgment of possibly needing help. Has this character and portrayal been brought on or triggered by critics? I believe it is more sincere than that, but I can also sympathize with a predicament of being misunderstood. Sometimes, we play out if provoked. Of course Paul has many followers, as I'm sure he has haters. Seems like a no-brainer to me, though, of his importance. There's a certain co-dependency throughout *Rebel Dabble Babble*, which in common relationships is generally looked down on, but here it's one model of making failure a success. Does McCarthy desire to fail or succeed? The question of success is irrelevant in the stature of one's career here. We're talking about the act of making and presenting things. Remove the leg support. Failure is accepted. Here it is a matter of looking at failure and success as possible equals. Either way you look at it, the importance is in the examination of what is being learned and negotiated, whether good or bad. With all of this said it is also important to acknowledge that McCarthy is considerate of all the subjects and individuals at hand. From my understanding, he has always surrounded himself with strong women and challenging artists, which any smart artist should do. He has also supported others, which all artists should do. Not all can do this, but McCarthy is a good example of an artist who supports what he believes in with the support he's been provided. This is still the case with the cast of *Rebel Dabble Babble*. Regardless of rumors on how the collaboration might've gone with Franco, *Rebel Dabble Babble* is a good example of utilizing all roles and actions for their real worth. There is also the relevance of time and place to consider. The '60s and '70s provoked a certain working together that some of us seem to forget. This forgetting is caused in part by a critique placed on indifference instead of a critique of the whole picture that ultimately connects us. I'm not interested in isolating gender and activity in art. You're trying to make me you as much as I'm trying to make you me. I'd never do that to anyone. What do you want—diversity or equality? You're trying to be you just like I'm trying to be me. I'd do that. Identity politics can sometimes create gaps. *Rebel Dabble Babble* fills in the blanks.

Part Two: Opening Scene (Viewing the Exhibition Opening) w/ Extras

The director of the museum is leaving. He's looking for his car. We are arriving. Me, Margaret and Adam. Margaret drove us here. I was annoying her and being a backseat driver. I was expecting we wouldn't get in. We walk in welcomed by Jason and production posters behind the gallery desk. My eyes skim them quickly. No real registration of names, titles etc. They are props really. I'm relieved the place isn't exclusive. Artists should be let in to any art event. The place was already packed. Paul has drawn a map with numbers, and a more common description sheet on the works is also provided. It's nice to have these things to take home as keepsakes. As always, you can go left or right. I go left, get a glimpse of some projected scuffling around a dinner table. I'm jumbled, a little claustrophobic; it's a low ceiling. Mr. Kersels' head is nearly touching it. We say hello. I break from my party and proceed to the spacious main gallery. More scuffling. This time, familiar. Not a family, necessarily, but it's there, it's hinted at. The beds, the inverted household, the stains, the altercations, the recordings and presentations of such abstractions on all of the above and much more. Like a martini party gone bad, but this time it's home cookin'. Like Pollock pulling the dinner cloth off the table. Mark Grotjahn passed out and laying in a median at an AIDS benefit telling women to fuck off. Similar to the unraveling in Hitchcock's *Rope* or Chris Burden being pushed down the stairs. Ask Jean Milant. The stairway to heaven was now the stairway to hell. It's about Hollywood, but not TMZ. It's more involved than that. It's not about James Franco joining the ranks of the art world, either. That time has passed. I'm an artist and I'm in a movie. Everyone is too involved now. It's not a bad thing necessarily. There's no turning back. We're all here, participating and viewing. It all mirrors America and the art world, past and present. It's the best intersection of art and Hollywood that I've ever seen! Inside and out. Domesticated public. Public domesticated. Colonel Sanders. Would you like crispy or original recipe? Extra gravy? There are too many exclusive dinner parties, events and happenings in art today. Who is anyone to hold one? This is all a good critique of that crap.

Everyone is here now, as well as some new ones. Girls on film. Celebrities. Old teachers. Museum personnel. The ones you don't see at yours or your friends' openings. The ones consumed by history and the artists already convenient for their projects. The ones who don't return your emails. Who can blame them? It's psychological, and not in general, but in depth, like an episode of *Hoarders* uncut. The part where you tell your mom to throw out that box of shit and she ends up telling you to shove it up your ass in her own way of saying just that. The father might step in, but will probably keep his mouth shut. He knows when to speak, when to have the family sit down and deliver the sermon. It's critical and not in negativity, but in honest meanderings and excavations of the issues at hand. Gender, consumption, digestion, frustration and a celebration of the tragically absurd. Everyone's shit stinks, you know. You don't necessarily smell your own until that day on the freeway. You usually blame it on someone else. I bet even you have a spanker chief under your pillow. A favorite toy maybe. You ever feel like humping your pillow? Maybe you bite things. There's no such thing as a safe word. It's an involvement worthy of attention and an involvement that requires attention. It's full of surprises. Around every corner and every moment. If you blink, you might miss it, but you'll find the other "it" around the way with that "round the way" girl or boy. Or hear about it now and later. You might even trip and fall. You might fall on purpose. It's memory oriented, it triggers memory. It memorializes and celebrates time. Even Franco is standing there recorded and learning from Paul. He looks somewhat frustrated. He should be. He's playing a character, a role. We are all students and participants here. You signed up for this shit and you love it. We all do. Time to renew your membership. Art is about collaboration, just like the family household, the gallery, the museum, the film set and even KFC. Some people sure know how to pick their collaborators. If only everyone was so lucky. Remember, though, you're always a part of it. Always. Most people love a good conversation or something worth talking about, but even I'm not going to waste my time thinking whether or not you're an artist. It's somewhat irrelevant. Just do what you do and I'll do what I do.

Part Three: Better Description

It is definitely Paul in a disguise. It's a really good disguise. Everyone is in character. They are playing Hollywood. They are good actors. Paul and his stunt double both resemble a mix between Slick Willy (Slick Willy is what my grandpa calls Clinton) and Hank from *King of the Hill* w/ grey hair. Or an aged John from *Garfield*. Maybe even Ed Rooney getting kicked in the face. He did fall down the stairs there. Kind of like a shop teacher mixed with a bible salesman. The principal gets his leg humped and bitten by the Rottweiler. No dogs here. Only metaphorically. There is some harassment occurring from all parties. Both ends. There's a tall male figure wandering around fighting with an unidentified woman. Possibly the mother. It's the "housewife I will beat" type of shit. Pseudo morals. I am the VHS, record me with your fist (these are all Marilyn Manson lyrics). < It's easier citing it this way. On second thought, it's the daughter and her father. Fuck you. Fuck you. Fuck you. More than that. There's a fight occurring in the room on camera that's still felt in the props left behind, now presented to us as art objects. A chair was pulled out from under her ass. She wasn't the same woman on the other screen being fondled/fondling James. She was a stunt double. That one wasn't the same woman either. At the opening she had long dark wavy hair and a skin tight black dress on. Her smile and eyes were there though. She was recognizable out of costume. She said, this is my dad. At least I think that was Elyse, the one playing Judy. Judy's mother is Suzan Averitt. Jim's mother, too. She's a mother, period. Her and Paul's double—the body snatcher—are in a slap session. I didn't see them at the opening. Didn't see them anywhere else, really. The skin has been broken. Blood sticks. Judy is stabbing him with her heels. It's like the victim in a horror film killing the already dead to make sure he's dead. Already dead. There is also an apparent male-to-male ass raping being projected. It is a forced entry. There is grunting. It's like WWF. Sleeper hold. The opposite of the Oedipus complex, fulfilled. Franco is raping Paul. Father yes son. I want to fuck you. Jim Morrison reversed. The table is slightly turned back, though. Don't fuck with a vet. Neck squeeze. The only thing not present is the rectum in the flesh. It's on the screen, though. It's definitely a brown eye. There is a lot of red present, too. I wonder where all of the other clothes went. The men seem to be wearing most of theirs. The women have stripped down a bit in one episode. There's a single bed. There are some linens and garb on it. A family photo, too. Jim's original father in mom's cleaning garb. It's a drag. It's represented on the screen, too. This time it's Paul. Cleaning house. Getting yelled at. The scrapes and the breasts aren't visible anymore, though. The leftover chicken is still hanging out. A splattering of sorts. The inverted dresser/stand with a plant on it mimics its projector counterparts. All recorded actions are projected on the wall in video and in vivid color. There's a lot of movement throughout. Cyclonic. The physical presentation is an altered altar of sorts. The room has been christened. Sanctified. Time has stopped. Things have been broken down and reconfigured. There's a chair with a harp design resembling a W. My namesake. It's enough to know that the situation was mad wrong, whether fabricated or not. But the pieces were being put back together. A possible tape to include into the trial or to put under the couch. As a sick get-me-off. Why are they fighting? Has he had

enough with her games? Her the same? Did she break curfew? He's restrain-
ing himself. She just keeps telling him to fuck off, mother fucker. He's about to
lose it. Who invited the other guy to the party? It was a triangle of sorts, more
than that, actually, and the camera crew had to witness it all. A lot of mirroring. A whole lot of shaking going on. Paul carried a tray of chicken, mashed
potatoes and gravy. It was inevitable. The food would soon become waste. It
would be a waste to waste it, though. Let's put it in the gallery. Serve it to the
customers, anyway.

Part Four: Elyse Poppers as Judy / Natalie Wood and James Franco as Jim / James Dean,
Jay Yi as Sal Mineo / Plato (with Environment and Leftover Altercation, Paul as Nick Ray
/ Father, Suzan Averitt / Jim and Natalie Woods' Mother)

She has beautiful breasts and a pretty smile. Elyse. He has wavy hair like Jim.
It sits weirdly on his head, though. I wonder if he wanted to do it without the
wig on. James. The nighty was a pale copper-ish rose, as were her toenails,
or at least the color was reflecting. Soft and pale. Cream, possibly. It could've
been dirt. It all goes well with that golden brown mid-length wavy hair. All
glistened. On second view, they were clear. The toenails and the fingernails.
The dirt acted as a patina. The residual flowers, dirt, glass and dust were all
left as traces on parts of furniture. Those eyelashes were proper, too. She's an
actress; it's OK to describe how she looked. Her mouth was kissing his lips.
His lips were kissing her mouth. The saliva pulled from both of their mouths
like string. Social lubricant. Franco happily played the role in a somewhat
sedated mood. Blue jeans and all. He looks like someone out of *Happy Days*.
Henry Winkler. She is *I Love Judy*, not *Lucy*. He's telling her about his dreams
of being an artist. Don't be so selfish. She puts his nose in her mouth. Nasal
cavity. His head is teetering back and forth. He already fit the part. At times,
it's hard to do that for both, I imagine. Play a part. Their hands guided each
other. They were both content. It's fortunate, really. An outlet to be intimate.
Lucky guy or lucky girl. If it's not going good at home, go to the set. If you're
not happy with who you are, be someone else. It was all still blurry, though.
As a viewer, you can only imagine what it was like as a re-enactment. It was
still real, though. It was like any desirable presentation of love. They were
embracing each other. Life isn't always like the movies, but the McCarthys
and these actors were definitely proposing that parts of it can be. Art imitates
life and vice versa. A love story, I suppose, but something was still off. Things
were spilled into the crowd. We were behind the scenes, in a way. *Blue Boy*
was on the wall, pervertedly hung. Jay Yi plays Sal at the top of the stairs. It's

kind of like the blue ape w/ his dick between his legs. It's just blurred. He's at the top of the stairs. Lost. Is James dreaming bi-curiously? His penis dangles. It's hallucinatory. Fairytale-like. Identity crisis. Androgynous Male. I barely saw him at all. Supporting actor. Blue tape marks the floor for the furniture placement. There's an area highlighted by light coming through the oscillating air vent in the gallery. It bounces on the floor like a yo-yo. There's a dark brown liquid stain throughout the grayish-brown carpet. A non-working TV set. A relic. You make your way upstairs, possibly smiling. The girl is on the bed. She's pulling you in. Finger in her mouth, on her tongue. You are projecting now. The men are nowhere in sight. Actually, there are only men in the room. She's asking you all to come closer. What are we all thinking? She wants you near her. You're already there. Or maybe you are afraid? Nothing else matters now. Everything matters now. Just give her what she wants or let her beg. Maybe you should comfort her in your mind. But maybe she just wants to be close to you. It doesn't have to always be so perverted. She is innocent. You are guilty from birth.   Maybe there's a chance. You can still hear the fight, though. It's downstairs. It has escalated. If someone wanted to start a fight at the opening, it might go unnoticed. Seriously, someone might call the cops. The neighbors might complain. All of these things go through your head. I go downstairs. There's slapping involved again. Dude, you're way out of line. Punching. I might have to step in. She stepped into a man's place. That doesn't exist. Hair pulling. Kick in the shin. Where am I? Which room? The tone has been set. It's violent. It's sexual. Someone is going to get hurt. We're being confronted by some kind of American demonology. Fuck the police, someone call the exorcist. The second time around, they're in the tub. He's in the tub. It's like the old days. Self-portraiture as woman. Documentation. Like *A Fish Called Wanda*. The demon has spewed a very cold liquid. It's orange cream. *Ghostbusters*. They shiver. Teeth clacking. The real facial of commercial goo. Paul has his blinders on. Fogged-up LensCrafters. A propped-up door to bump into. It'll fuck you up. Weiner on Reinhardt. Lawrence, Ad. A pillow wrapped in plastic. A recycling bin wrapped in plastic. Don't open it. Just put up against the wall.   A tie around his eyes in the other room. Hers too. A baseball bat. Drywall—let me out of here! James and Elyse under the bed. Daddy's home. Get a beer and run for your life.

Part Five: Personal Example 1. The Family Fight, Domestic Scuffle, Family and Academic Merger, McCarthy Era

The spilling of beans was chicken, mashed potatoes and gravy here. We used to have family dinners there. They sold memorabilia glasses with the dwarves on them. KFC. Maybe it was McDonald's. Now they eat together at the nursing home. The food isn't the same there, but the same here. Eat it off the floor. My father as grocery store manager. You know all of the ketchup and shit. Actually, there's a lot of shelving things to that. Even robbery. The kids driving mom crazy. Mom driving the kids home from the theme park. I won't stop singing *So Alive* by Love and Rockets. She's upset now. Broken furniture at home. My brother Brad spilled chocolate milk on the beige carpet. It started to stink the second day. Repressed and then overly presented sex and anger. Here. Things continue to get thrown around, literally and metaphorically. He's older now and listening to Morrissey and drawing on the walls. Dad calls him a fruitcake. It wasn't anyone's fault. Our house was haunted. It didn't help that the babysitter wanted and carried out a threesome with your child. They possibly gave him drugs. His view is skewed. He's experimenting. He's in high school now. Then. He later made it with her sister. Then. Welcome to adulthood. Now. Make a choice. Go to college if you can't handle the real world. Jack off in the paint to make it glossy. Take it to show and tell. Art school might help. Then. It didn't. Now. It's better. Now what?

Wrote a paper in History of Modern Design. Somehow I wanted to adhere ad hoc aesthetics to a critique of modernism. I was naive. I was a kid. It had already happened. This issue. It didn't matter. But I was onto something. I stumbled upon a surrogate depiction of parts of my life at the Kansas City Art Institute in the painting program. To be exact, the library fact sheet/checkout record I had printed out before graduating says so. 9/02/03, to be exact. 3:32 PM, to be exact. Two books exact. One on Paul, the other on Mike. They were the opposite of Takashi. It was too late to do the research on the facts. It's all visual. Might've already happened. I was engulfed by bodies of work more chaotic than my own. It was picture perfect. I wanted them to be my peers. Buszek marked that paper with red several times. Maria. She might do it to this one, too. I made them kids again. I was finding my voice. I was telling a story. Making things up. I forgot their birthdays. Although the parts were mostly plastic and ketchup, there were also saws, drill sets, a sander, a blue extension cord, to be exact. These were mine. Blood, too. I rammed that drill right into my hand the year prior. My future roommate demonstrated the rotation of my flesh to the class on the drill as I laid passed out. He was driving screwdrivers into doll parts. Paul. I used to use dad's grinder to make spears from the broom handles. I shaved the Cabbage Patch doll's head. Doll parts were coming out of his head. Paul. He stuffed those sausages down his throat. Paul. A self-inflicted binge. Paul. There was gauze and mayonnaise. Paul. Dad always puts mayo on the burgers. Bossy Burger. All of these things printed out by my student id #1334 or in my head. Now we're back to my own dad with the air compressor, even the blue extension cord. There's that blue again. It was definitely blue, as was the little chair. Not the broken one that was a rocker. The lava lamp was blue, too. I stuck a knife in it. It blew up. I saw blue and it knocked me out. Coach Hawkins used to call me Smurf. I didn't mind other than the fact that the worst referee in high school history was also called that by my dad and everyone else. This was Nixa, Missouri. The rocker actually rocked one night by itself. The mother had committed suicide there or somewhere else. There's someone in that house. A witch kept me from peeing. Always traces left behind. My brother as my witness. Back to dad. Fuck the grocery store. He just buys things there like everyone else now. He's a little more conscious w/ his budget, though. He was once a manager, after all. Once, his co-workers gave him a fake turd as a gift. The fridge was always full. Grandpa Wrinkle was a milkman. He carried those glass containers like James drinks from in *Rebel Without a Cause*. He harvested beef, though, at home on the farm. He still does. The freezer is always full, too. Slaughter crippled beef. Sailor's Meat. Paul. The grocery store and farm are stand-ins for the prop house, Paul, as was the childhood home, but my dad's real passion is painting and rebuilding cars. Hot rods and classics. '55, '56, '57 Chevys. They used to drag race on the farm roads. Chicken. I was led to here, this place of the McCarthys, by him, and then it was de Kooning, Rauschenberg and Nauman. All teachers, whether they like it or not. Those are all recorded, too. As is *Dennis the Menace* and *The Art of Walt Disney*. This is the reality. I'm speaking the truth. All my connections before have been figured out later or are fakes. I admit it. This connection is real, though. I have the proof. The familial genes don't necessarily matter. Sometimes it helps. Usually that's the case. But it's a hybrid of art and literal family here. I learned it from watching you, Dad. We are all taught to appropriate from birth. Drew an alien at the age of 5. Drew a doll at the age of 7. Took Brad's drawings to show and tell as my own at 8. Don't know what happened at 6.

Part Six: Intermission on the Lawn (actually the Parking Lot), There's a house (recreation of Bungalow #2 at Chateau Marmont), It's time for that beer now. Hollywood Upside Down, Everyone was there, You had to see it, Please let me explain. . .

The sun was setting. Everyone is confronting the crazy neighbor. Paul. There was a house on stilts. It was that sage green, like the Cobain accents in Seattle. It was lit from all angles. The windows were open. Notches were cut out similar to that bathroom door from *The Shining* or the front door of *The Texas Chain Saw Massacre*. There were conventional windows too, though. I looked through one. I saw friends looking through another. Please let me into your house, I need to wash myself (Men's Recovery Project). We exchanged laughter. When does a person get to have an exchange of looking through and into someone's house to see others doing the same? Have a conversation. What does it mean to watch a room? A set? Take a picture, it'll last longer. You could see the props. There was a bath tub covered in a poopy, tar-like substance; a lamp; a couch; a wooden floor. Gel filters. A hot water heater. The walls were lemon yellow. The roof had been pulled away from the second story. Actually, probably never placed on it. It was a fabrication, after all. No tornadoes in California. I could sleep up there, I thought. Hold a solo slumber party. I mentioned that to Karolina and Margaret. Pass out. Presumedly, a retrieved Hollywood Video sign hung upside down on the back side of the structure. That's surely where it's from, Sara said. I move through the crowd and grab another beer. I say hi to Andrew. He kindly says hi, but is in a rush. Where are you going? I have to take pictures for *Artforum*. You can take my picture. Me. He did. Nice blank stare. Him. You gotta act serious w/ these contexts. Me. Not really. Me. Of course it was a promotional stunt. Me. One that I'm sick of. Me. Time to look at the work again. On the second time around, it was like a construction site. One like we used to have balloon and water gun fights in. I looked through the opening to the stairs for the first time. Back to heaven. Daylight helps. The only safe place, perhaps. I could still take a nap up there.

Part Seven: Personal Example 2 / Personal Example and Exhibition Merger 1, Artistic Porn / Adult Entertainment Go Back into the Box, See a metaphorical box get played with by its owner who I'm unaware of until. . . .

When I came upon one of the small back galleries (gallery 10, Adult Entertainment) to find a woman's back side propped up by her knees, her face turned away, with that same hair, I assumed it was the woman (Elyse Poppers) portraying Judy from the scenes before. I was amazed that the scenes had escalated from teasing and common foreplay to the woman now playing with herself. She was doing the v. The butterfly. The shape her fingers made. The gesture. Men do it with their moustaches. Enjoying playing with herself. Acting? Maybe the best kind. Doing it for us, you and them and for herself. Is this the case? I'm sure she enjoyed it. Who doesn't? Masturbation. There is a logic. Who is she? I can't see her face. Maybe she's in the other room. Sometimes I feel dirty afterwards. It made me smile this time. It was flirting with something I was insecure about publicly. Something I wouldn't dare do before going out socializing. I'd still feel that perverted grime. The dirt again. I've reminded myself before just walking down the sidewalk that if others in the art world were weirdos or perverts then I could be too, but it never changed the fact of feeling pathetic when viewing art after I'd surfed porn a half hour before. It's all in will. Is this something to feel bad about? No. You have to clean up and present yourself as educated and professional. Everyone is acting and playing the part. But here I was being confronted with it. It was in my face. It was in all of our faces. This action. This activity of sexual pleasure. From the viewer and the actress. Speak for yourself, you say? But it was calming this time. Almost meditative. Something was definitely changing my views of pornography, art and myself. It was a marriage. It was a good thing. I was unaware of what was happening in the room behind me. She was there all along. In control. It was still about teamwork, though.

Part Eight: Extended Title, Climax, Heather Vahn as Judy / Natalie Wood / Elyse Poppers, James Deen as Jim / James Dean / Franco, Paul as Nick Ray / Director, Jimmy Lifestyles / Director, When I saw her face, I saw her standing there, Now I'm a believer, I'm in love, Just call me Angel in the Morning (I used Angel here before seeing the actual footage of Jimmy Lifestyles calling Heather / Judy Angel—Pop Cultural ESP, more on this later, maybe). . . .

I left the room and decided to take another stroll around, arriving at the front of the gallery. Here, I saw her face. There she was, standing, smiling, dressed wonderfully, and very cute. It was Heather Vahn—a face and body I knew on film, and now she's real, not just a virtual fuck buddy. An all-natural woman, I must add. She was accompanied by women. They were cute and happy as well. They were there together. It was a night out for Heather. She had a glow to her; her hair was pulled up and back, almost in a bun, very proper; she was dressed for an event. She had entered a context of art very happy, ready to participate and excited. I miss that excitement of coming to art. Things were changing again. The art scene was different. Thanks, Paul. Thanks, Heather. If only everyone could be so happy to participate with art this way. There are a select few. Maybe I'm just jaded. Not at the moment, though. She's a natural. Beauty. Her dress was light and a paisley type of pattern in purple, pink and white. Would make for a good portrait or painting. She was wearing wedges, propping up her petite stature. She looked great, like a girl next door dressed for a special occasion. I would happily take her home to Mom and Dad. I took all of this in just in passing. I wasn't objectifying her. I'm sticking to my story. I was appreciating the energy she presented. She lit up the room. Although my memory of her was based in a zone of lust from before, my position was now one outside of her role or my common view of her. She was no longer an actress. I understood the difference. The attraction didn't change, though. Why was she here?

It's all starting to fall in place. The work is peaking. The tent has been pitched. The McCarthys aren't one-pump chumps. The foreplay has turned into something else. So has the imagination. I'm feeling starstruck and weird. I'm still playing the role as artist, though. It's my ego. It's an important club to belong to. Give her the opportunity to stare me down like I have so many times to her? Hardly. What gives me the nerve? Maybe she'll notice me. Notice me for what? Girlfriends have called me handsome. Others have called me a freak. I begin to feel slightly pathetic. I don't follow her or anything. I continue to go through the show again, getting new glimpses and revelations. I go back into gallery 10. It has definitely progressed. I can't believe it, it's Leather Vahn as Judy instead of Elyse as Judy, now flipped around like that girl upstairs, that beautiful smile, almost laughing, and getting kissed downstairs/eaten out by her on-screen companion, James Deen playing Jim. You listened to her. Paul did, too. You took her up on that offer from before. She is glad you're close to her again. She's playing out that fantasy you had before. Or it is that fantasy again? The one from your own bedroom. Which is it? I'm absolutely amazed, but I still haven't connected the overall storyboard. I'm blown away, and all I know is this is something very important happening. My insecurity in perversion meets my life of viewing, making and thinking about art. I get a well-deserved beer. The only thing I now know to do is share this all with Jason, the gallery attendant. "This" meaning my feeling of complete surprise and almost disorientation or embarrassment. What is your art orientation? Not to him. To you the reader. What is your preference? Not to him. You the reader. He laughs at my revelation, knowing who the actress is. I told him she's so pretty/ great and "smart or nice, too," I think he replied. Of course, I didn't go up to her, and to my knowledge I didn't stare her down. I'm not that type of guy. We've all been around celebrities. It's common behavior. You act normal. What are you really thinking, though? I read the paper, and Flea eats his meal at Stella twice a month, usually. I'm actually there every day next door. Good coffee. All I can picture is him playing Woodstock naked. I don't look at him. I read my paper on the steps. It's a form of respect. I had my chance as a kid and got all those autographs. I learned you don't get in Henry Rollins' face and Danzig gets in yours. Maybe that appreciation of bands and pop culture is the same appreciation I have for her. To be fair, I'm not sexually aroused by that stuff, though. I believe me and her had a moment, though. Non-sexual. Or at least, I had a moment with her. She was having her own moment with the show. Had anything changed? I'm not a stalker. If anything, I'm intimidated. This wasn't a gross moment on my part. It was a celebration of her work. Her job. Her acting. As she passed my way, she looked in my general direction, she threw a black coat over her to bundle up. It was getting chilly. I think she was on her way. It could've been a scene itself. Actually, it was. I'd shoot that scene for sure. Her walking slowly by, throwing over that black coat. It was beautiful. She was beautiful. It was Hollywood. I'd shoot the one from before, too. Maybe even participate. I guess it would be considered amateur. By the time I convinced myself to say hello, she had disappeared just as quick as she came to be revealed. I wanted to show Margaret who she was. Margaret wanted to see her, too. Maybe so I'd shut up. What made me want to say hi to her more than other celebrities that I ignore every day? Even the man of the hour, McCarthy, I don't bother. It was an attraction that's not about objectifying her, but rather an experience of normal human desire. She had helped change my views on art and life. I at least owed her a thank you. Maybe we could be friends or get to know each other.

I walked back into gallery 10. This time, Heather and James Deen are engaged in full intercourse. To be crude, it's a plowing. Yeah, fuck me, James Deen. Beat up that pussy. Heather. With a laugh here and there. I've been there. The show me what you got. Tempt me. I don't want to go too far scenario. You're faking. Get it over with. James is somewhat macho. I guess that's his job. Sometimes I disagree with the male counterpart. Take better care of the girl. It's not my gig though. Someone else's clock and cock. I'm not into the mean stuff. I can't watch it. Who am I to claim anything? Judge. I understand it's acting. Paul and Jimmy Lifestyles are surrounding the act. Mumbling and reminding one of a porno genre typically referred to as GONZO. It's a kind of scene where they talk to the actress, ask her questions and ask how she likes it. The mumbling kind of critiques that line of work, as did Heather's blurt-outs. It was actually hilarious. Like she was taunting the dude. Everything else is gibberish. Get to the point. We're here to do one thing. Everyone gets off.

Everyone gets paid. I'm surprised Heather isn't making fun of him. Not in real life. It would fit the plot. I cannot move. I'm kneeling down. I'm frozen. This is unbelievable. It was a moment of throwing myself in and throwing myself out. I couldn't decide what I should do. Good art does this to you. It throws you around like some puppet. Not the girl in the video, but you the viewer. It throws you through a loop. This isn't what one would normally do. You're being mirrored. You can see yourself active but immobile at the same time. Put yourself in her shoes. In the bed. On the couch. In his shoes. In the bed. On the couch. It's an action. A scene. It's all a fantasy. It's a workout. Terrible wig. Hers is nice, though. Pretty feet, too. Nice hands as well. He's doing freestyle. Look mom, no hands. There are things you can think about to make it last longer. She said she was going to cum. I believed her. I wasn't going to, though. Not the time or the place. Pee-wee Herman. Another guy was in the gallery with his head turned as if planted in as some kind of decoy or performer to play the "I'm not looking at this" character. The money shot came. They did it together. We all did it together. You did it! It was important that it wasn't a facial. This was a collaboration. It is also important to bring up that this was greatly choreographed. Maybe improvised. These are professionals. Please don't try this at home. More like please do. Heather jerked Deen's stick till it squirted. It was like champagne. It was like a pillow fight. The feathers flying. The semen was like water. Splashing someone in the swimming pool. Fun and games. We're getting paid good to do this. Everyone gets paid. Grab the soapy sponge. Lather it up or simply just wash your hands. It was theatrical. It was candid. It was fun. It was slap happy. Those are great actors. They make me want to hump. Why was I so amazed to find Heather so pleasant, you might ask? Honestly, I wasn't. It was already something I knew. I was more amazed by the revelation that we are all in this together now.

Part Nine: On the second time around, Gallery 9 (Sorry I'm Sorry) —— (A lot of Mirroring Occurring) Paul McCarthy, Heather Vahn as Judy / Elyse Poppers / Natalie Wood, Jimmy Lifestyles as Director / Paul McCarthy as Nick Ray, and Gallery 10 (Adult Entertainment), Paul McCarthy, Heather Vahn as Judy / Elyse Poppers / Natalie Wood, James Deen as Jim / James Dean / Franco, Jimmy Lifestyles, Cross Examination /, *Superimposed Dan Graham-ian Projection, Performance Audience Mirror, Two-Way Mirror, Oral Reversal, Closer to solving the case, Stories Overlap, She is him, He is her, Back and Forth, Yesterday is Today

I went back to *Rebel Dabble Babble*. Round two. It's a Wednesday. Retrace my steps. I'd never been into Gallery 9 (Sorry I'm Sorry). Throughout all of *Rebel*

Dabble Babble, there is a sense of mirroring. The characters mirror each other. There are body doubles. Art mirrors reality. Even your thoughts are mirrored. Galleries 9 and 10 are split by a window. It is reflective. A mirror that you can see through. Like at a hospital, a bank or an interrogation room. There are videos in each room. Their actions become mirrored. They also meld into one another. If you view one video through the window, you see the other. It's a superimposition. A kind of cross-examination. A delay, as well. Future. Past. Future Past. Present. Present. What you see is what you get and got. What you have. Dan would be proud. There's a conversation occurring in gallery 9. Heather is playing Mommy to James and Jimmy in both rooms. In gallery 10, James sucks on her tits like a baby. In gallery 9, Jimmy begs her like a boy begs his mom to take him to the circus. Please please. Sorry. Paul as his witness. Their witness. I gave you everything. It's too late; she's gone. This seems to be the case. You've messed up too many times. She found someone else. We've all been there. He cheated. She cheated. It's over. She's in control now. Paul as her witness. Their witness. James too. She rides on his back. She's fish-hooking him. Finger pulling his mouth. How's that? You like that? Looking through the window to gallery 10, you see James Deen is doing something similar. He's in control. Paul as his witness. Jimmy too. He's throwing her on the couch or the bed. She's playing along with it. Turning her over. It is all simultaneously merged together. It is all turned over on itself. The manipulation of meaning, if you will. Content. The art. Here, any objectification reading is balanced. It saves his ass. Paul as his own witness. But it's not just that. It is a conscious understanding. A choice in the installation. It's somewhat of a conclusion. The story has come to a head. All of that foreplay before became something. All of the fights. They were settled down a bit. Working on something together. Whether in agreeing or not. They ended up doing it to each other. It became another game. Jimmy is telling Heather she's an angel sent from heaven. Heather spits on him at some point. It was an order. In the reflection, there is more saliva. Oral reversal. She wipes him down. She's sick of hearing the same thing. Do you understand what it means to look at you? She's dressed like the innocence of the '50s. In the rearview, she is getting undressed. That bra looks great on you. My baby does the hanky panky. Him and her. She and him. Them and us. Us and them. You and you. Ed Templeton was there too. The Foundation of Swank had switched industries. Look him up or down. Whichever you prefer. I'm talking about skateboarding, though…. This all seems like good therapy. I'll do it for free. There's a price for everything. The biggest importance in the intercourse scene is in its relationship to the violence in the rest of the scenes. That it resolved some things in the plot. It was a contrast to the slapping, yelling and chaos everywhere else.

It's quite obvious, which line of communication works best. Kiss and make up. If this isn't a conclusion, please put me in the sequel. If this is wrong, I don't wanna be right.

Part Ten: Literal Example 1. My Excuse, Disney-Oriented Porn, Vintage Porn, the Beginning / Penthouse Under the Sink, Aaron what are you doing in there?

Porno nation evaluation. What's this time for segregation. Libido, Libido, fascination. Too much oral defecation. (Marilyn Manson's Cake and Sodomy—A Portrait of an American Family, 1994)

Fuck it. I was influenced by dirty magazines and I'm not going to apologize for being born. Thank you for the advice, Raymond. Present tense. A threesome at 6. I situate it somewhere between my first acid trip and dripping in my pants in English class. The neighbor asked, "What did you do today?" Played sex. What did you do today? Just an experience. A flash. With the other babysitter's daughter it was 69. There were wooded experiences, too. Forts. Like foxholes. Boys will be boys. Girls will be girls. Children will be children. Boner under the hide-a-bed. Babysitters' sisters are freaks. Adults will be adults. There's a pre-pubescent window, you know. A time to figure it all out. You're still shooting blanks. Don't pigeonhole people on experiences. Let them make up their own minds. Admit it to yourself. It really helps. It's all child's play. Some don't experience it at all. Good for them. Very good for them. I mean that. Some experience it a lot worse. You only live once, you know. Don't be a product of society. A book on a shelf. The categorical proportions of identity bother me. Disney is teaching your kids lessons on what? Open your eyes. Disney replaced by Vivid and MTV. Put on your makeup. Stick out your tongue. Just let it sit there. Change the subject. Kind of. From time to time, the adult industry likes to do parodies. This wasn't any different in the '80s and '90s. So as a teenager stumbling upon an old X-rated tape, me and my friends sat around smoking weed and watching a man dressed up like the Beast gruntingly give it to his beauty. I didn't know if I was supposed to get off, laugh, cry or puke. There were times when I puked. It was the weed, though. Everyone's parents had these things. He has a sock around his hand, but what is that thing he's holding? One's uncle had a *Busted* magazine. Funny to put it in your friend's backpack as a joke. What do you know about gays? It was part of liberation. Change your views. Freedom. Respect people. Even the videos had the American flag waving. The saying run it up the flag pole doesn't come from nowhere. It was about Flynt. There are toys, pamphlets and self-help groups for this kind of shit. *Nikki and the Pom-Pom Girls*. A turd on a silver platter for Ron Jeremy. Peter North was in all of them. I now believe adult entertainment to be the ultimate embodiment of art meets life. My brother Brad laughed on the phone the other night, calling it performance art. I realize that might sound naïve to some, but I couldn't agree more. I always took advice from my brother. He painted first and everything else. I followed close behind. Now he has his own family. The kids paint pretty pictures.

Part Eleven: Conclusion / More Traditional Review

Paul and Damon McCarthy's *Rebel Dabble Babble* is exactly what its title says it is. Again, it made me wanna Rebel Dabble Babble. Every single element in this show has some kind of significance to the family situation and relationships in general. That is a hard thing to achieve with anything these days. The fact that an artist can bring his family along to a party, invite guests and tell a story from the wreckage of a completely backward and corrupt society (art included) and make it meaningful is a fact that is well worth celebrating. I also think it's fair to let that celebration be one that gets out of hand as a kind of mirroring. Writing on such acts should be no different.

Paul has been a rebel in the art world all along, and I've only been privileged to witness a small portion of it. He has dabbled and babbled. Again, I've only heard some of it. He continues to do so. I'll continue to listen, as should you. It isn't running in circles in the pedantic way. It's running in circles and retracing those circles to find the blind spots in the dirt. What I mean is Paul McCarthy churns things. He shakes that chicken box to reveal the gizzards. You might not like the taste. You might not even be hungry. But you will eat. You will help with the dishes, even if that means throwing them across the room. Of course, after cleaning your plate. His direction is one any artist or actor should love to participate under and take notes on. I honestly don't have anything bad to say about this work. It's an extremely good exhibition stemming from a genuine practice. It's a masterpiece in failure at the same time. That's the point, I believe. Failure needs to be portrayed and reenacted. So do common acts of love, sex and simulated violence, debauchery and corporate bingeing. An art practice enables one to explore this terrain. I'm not just sugarcoating or kissing ass. It is of no doubt that this work has problems. That's why it is important. It's a kind of problem solving. If people don't see that, they are pessimists. Paul and Damon being approached by Franco to collaborate couldn't have worked out better in terms of what the McCarthys chose to create. I'd like to imagine Paul very happy about interacting with the original content of *Rebel Without a Cause* to inspire not only *Rebel Dabble Babble*, but to serve as further exploration in the issues he's mined throughout his career. To give credit to his son is of importance here also. Who better to know the activities and interests of a father better? This isn't sexist. All the characters play their roles. Remember, it's a family affair. Damon surely helps fuel his father's instincts. He encourages new ways of seeing and participating. A good father will embrace that. If allowed, a good son or daughter will be grateful. The choices that this father and son created along with the whole family, including all of us, give room for improvement on our conversations and interactions on art and humanity. It all proposes we reconsider our judgments on our immediate impulses and viewership. That we take the time to be patient and explore. That we don't just give up on the family down the street because we're the family down the street, too. That your neighbor might like to dress up like a woman, but so does your wife. That James plays with dolls, and so does Judy. A family that works together stays together. There are all kinds of families. There are all kinds of couples. As for the violence, I hope it's something that can be worked out. It's all fun and games until someone gets their eye put out. It's a lot safer to reconsider love. All acts of love. Not just missionary.

Published on **May 18, 2012** *by* **Aaron Wrinkle** *in Aaron Wrinkle, Miscellaneous*

DEATH AS CHADDWICK
David Bell as Lucas Chaddwick, Jr.

I reposition myself on the other side of the booth that I have been sitting at alone, allowing me to finally see the other person sitting across from me. I try to be as hesitant as possible as I take in what I have been deliberately depriving myself of.

Head resting heavily on the tired leather, back bent in, stomach pushed out and free, he sits. From the waist up, he appeared to be sitting alone I self-consciously follow his bare arms down, where I quickly become humiliated, as I am now the intruder, and I immediately hate myself for giving in to my impulse to switch seats.

For an hour or so, in between sips and premonitions, I had nervously watched this man, but only through bunched-up tables and empty chairs, with expected disappointment. He was my unrecognizable friend that I had no plans of meeting.

A figure, reclining on her knees, squats uncomfortably between the man's legs, while the table, as if balancing on her head, shifts rhythmically above her. It is startling to see another figure. As if performing onstage in a mini theater underneath this man's table, she moves her head back and forth, her lips stretched wide, a gaping hole, endless if the eyes allowed it, but they don't, and neither does he. Such constraints are not for him; he yearns for what lies beyond that which she has to offer. My ignominy is what allows my unfettered observation, and as I work my way out of her mouth and into the darkness, his violent tattooed hands steal me away, soaking wet and pulsating red, tighten on the mass between his legs. I struggle to allow the scene its innocence, its communal assurance. My uncertainty prevents me from being aroused; the public disregard, even in a dive like this, keeps me from seeing the passion; and then, the recognition of the tattoo suddenly prevent the man from being a stranger.

I had never actually met Lucas Chaddwick, the writer. In fact, it hurts me to even think of him as such, but I had read his "articles" online and referred to them myself as poor journalism, a contrived and shabby attempt at intellec-

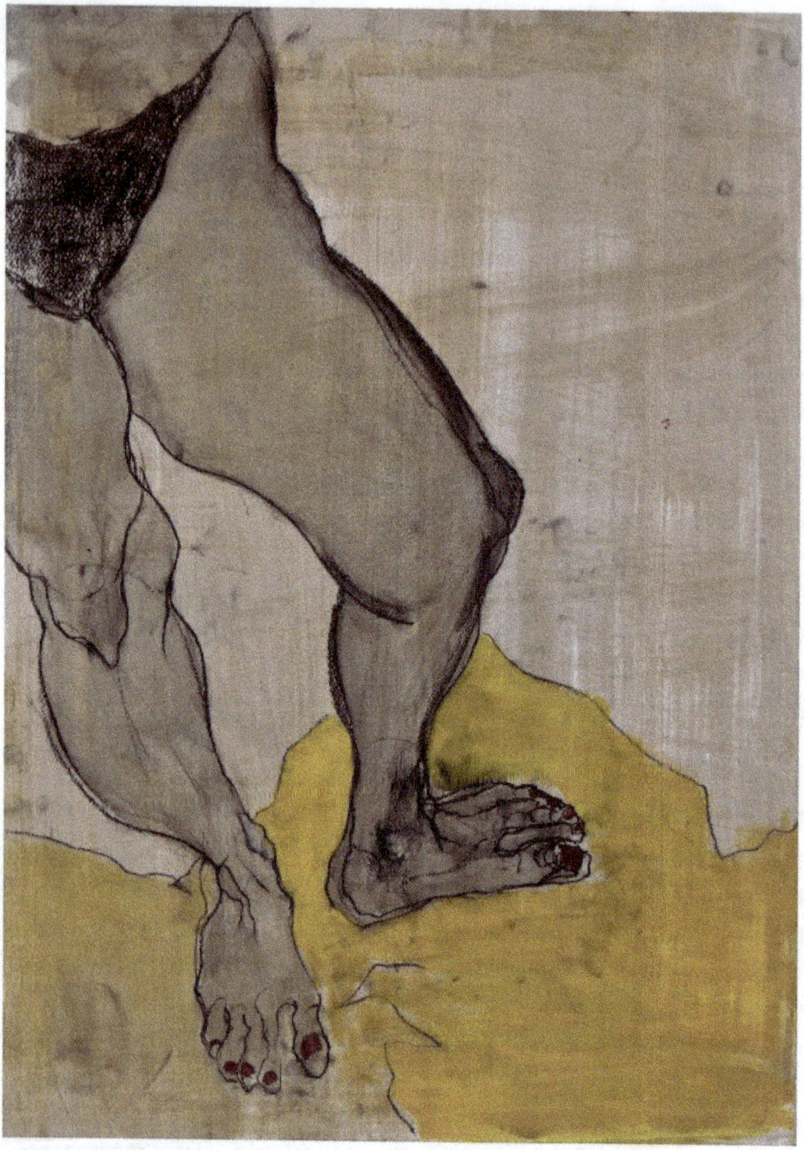

Name: Legs with no Leggings
Technique: Charcoal and Pastel on Paper
Size: 56x76

tual gossip, naming names but never revealing the true hypocrisy and pretentiousness I think he was going for. The few people he managed to upset with his words lacked self-perceptiveness and gave it only the validity he was searching for, and that single thought was as foul as the sight of him in person.

Inward ruminations have now distanced me from the actual scene that is taking place. Trying to refocus, I once again have to fight through my overbearing opponent; I know I can not allow my hatred for his writing to unduly affect the situation. Recognizing the man and boiling over my opinions of his disgusting writing has displaced the moment. I have to start from the beginning.

I do not know this man, and as thoughts occupy a time that massacres the real, I once again feel ashamed with myself, and instead of shifting seats, I now shift focus. My insides begin to shrivel up instantly as I no longer feel the emptiness in my stomach that was put in place to preserve inebriation. Every organ seems to have collapsed inward to form one authoritative mass. I momentarily visualized it inside me, and it parallels the shape between his legs. The inner turmoil that manifests so rapidly inside my gut outwardly takes hold. I thrust multiple blows upon my stomach, smashing the head that had manifested itself. No longer is my own visibility a concern. If they give a shit about me, I'll hear about it in his bullshit article: "Peeping Tom beats himself up alone in bar, donations welcome for massive unpaid tab…."

I'm distraught for being here, and entangled in feeling worse for thinking even for a second of turning a blind eye to what I am witnessing. Although both parties are offensive, I assume only one experiences even the shallowest of pleasures. Randomly, perhaps, I attempt to shove my fist down my throat, a futile endeavor, a hopeful distraction. I gag a little and think of how I'd like to place the blame on my small hands, which are rather large, actually, intimidating even.

The yearning I have for understanding reverts to a brutalizing thought of missing my opportunity to intervene and prevent a crime. Why have I squandered my chance of heroism and replaced it with temperamental, self-diagnosed masochism? I have failed her and myself. I grasp the sides of my face and hold it stiffly in her direction as she looks more and more desperate than just a minute earlier.

I am etched into place. I suddenly realize I am not just looking into her eye, but she is looking into mine. It screams "I am being abused! He is raping me!!!"

Her familiarity is striking. If he cums in her mouth, is it over? If this is abuse and ejaculation is the finality, is it worth intervening? Would I be worth the praise? Am I deserving of the title hero? Clearly, the answer is no.

The distance between them and myself fluctuates within my imagination. *She gets up from under the table and sits lovingly in his arms, allowing me to breathe a sigh of relief; while they sip the last of their drinks and head out the door, together holding hands, laughing about how obnoxious their public display was. She would joke about looking me in the eye right as he was about to explode into her mouth; he would call me an asshole and adjust his pants....* If this doesn't happen, preventing me from sitting alone and running through the entire scenario I created in my head of abuse, I will force myself to take action.

Blood-shot eyes. My sweat has topped the both of them. My heart wants to come out of my mouth as it beats heavily in the center of my throat, literally asphyxiating me. I wonder how she breathes.

"Show me one sign of affection," I plead. "I dare you." No, this man is literally holding this woman's face down onto his cock. With even the slightest motion of escape, he will snap her neck and finish off anyway; he must be murmuring threats down under the table. I feel the need to hear what he is saying. I need to be close to him. I've thought of this moment many times before, falling victim to a victim and arguing for equality.

My face in his crotch, lips wrapped around his unwashed cock, back and forth, every time like a bullet into my brain, carving itself into my memory. His hands on the back of my head remind me of my weakness, my fragility; they feel embedded into my skull. I know if I stop, he will crush me. I start to contemplate, *If I just finish him off...* I could get out of here and forget about it. Yet if it were up to me, I wouldn't be under the table to begin with. Death sounds like a better option altogether. I fully realize, at the same time, that the continuance and the fulfillment of his desire may very well result in that anyway. I'm almost inviting it now.

My hands, without a place to go, have been wedged between the back of my leg and calf; for the first time, I remember them with purpose and pull them gently out. I slide them up my thigh, examining the coarseness of my tattered jeans with the sleekness of my skin where the holes abruptly surprise my senses. My fingers caress up to my hips, and drop down past my waist, and excitedly back down to my ass, and into the pocket of my favorite jeans where I keep my keys.

There are four of them. The smallest one is the key to my front door. It is round at the top and slightly bent due to the lock being constantly jammed. I have always thought how, if trying to escape from someone, this is where I would be caught and meet my demise. The second is to a screen door of the apartment building, about six feet away from mine and my neighbor's doors. If one wanted, they could push through the screen with little effort. We all complain of the nuisance and the uselessness of it, but do nothing about it. I finger my way amongst these small pieces of metal that signify my own little private spaces till I reach the third key. The third one is to my mother's home. She passed away a few years ago, and the house is no longer in the family. When she was alive, I never had to use it; she was always home when I visited. It is longer than any key I have ever seen, a joke amongst my friends. The tip of my finger moves along the teeth, feeling the undulating and unyielding skeletal structure, until the head of it is nestled in my palm and the opposite end juts out through my knuckles.

It all seems to be so simple as I take one last glance up at the one who has forgotten I existed. I put my opposite hand across the space above the navel, and it reminds me of a place we all once belonged. I use it to springboard myself off my knees and onto my feet as I stare into the eyes of my prey, an easy target, weak and pathetic. I raise the key above my head and, to avoid dramatic effect, thrust it down so rapidly I nearly miss my mark…. The key lands in the outer edge of his left eye socket. The noise he interrupts the hollow room with is more than I could have hoped for. I have never received such a standing ovation in my life, but in this gluttonous moment, something tastes even better than applause; without delay, I give them what they want and drive the key down into the opposite eye, then left again, then right, until there is no differentiation, and as I continue, the face of Chaddwick closes in on itself, just a gaping hole in its place. It feels so good that I shove my left hand into the target area and continue stabbing with what now appears to be a glistening saber. My opposed hand sacrifices itself for my need to penetrate and provides a fresh target. After what seems like only seconds of hammering into the pit that now exceeds the skull and reveals the leather from the booth that once provided comfort and support, the bone in my thumb snaps oddly back from one of the blows and extends back in my direction, pointing directly into my eyes.

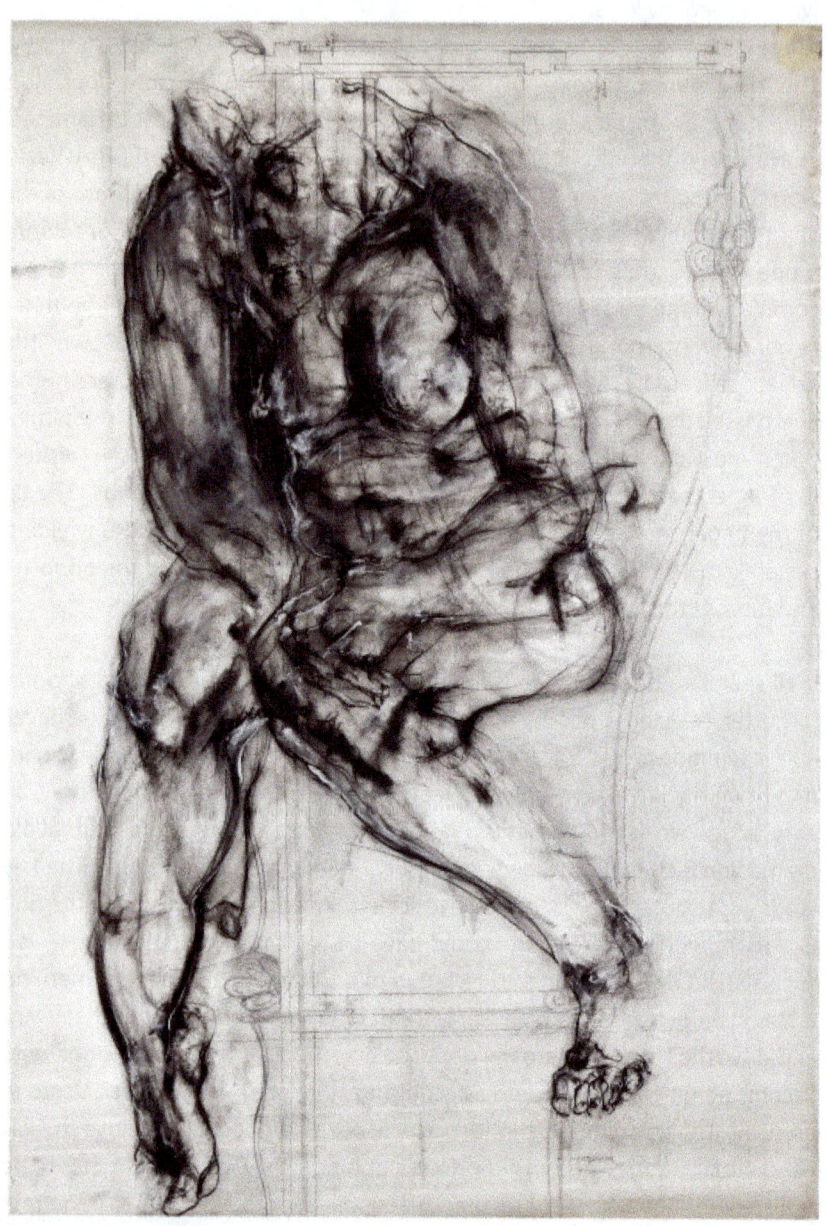

Name: Nausea
Technique: Charcoal and Pastel on Transparent paper
Size: 120x90

I turn away, knowing all too well I have let him down once again. It is time for me to take my keys and go. Shifting my weight over to the left, I reach underneath, into the right pocket of my favorite jeans, and come up empty handed. Shamefully, I look down to face my accuser, who has already found a way to make matters worse, pants unzipped, left hand holding on to a flaccid penis. If I only could have just found a way to get some enjoyment out of this whole thing.

The art in this section is made by, and is courtesy of, Anat Wegier, who lives and works in Tel Aviv, Israel.

Published on October 25, 2012 by Lucas Chaddwick, Jr. in Additional writing by, Fiction, Lucas Chaddwick, Jr.

SELBSTBILDNIS
EJ Hill

"Until the lions have their own historians, tales of the hunt shall always glorify the hunter." African Proverb (Ewe, Mina)

Ever since arriving in Salzburg, Austria, almost two weeks ago, I have tried to find words and images that might effectively describe everything that is happening. Sure, a picture can say a thousand words, but words themselves are rather limited in their capacity to accurately translate, one-to-one, the richness of a direct or authentic experience. Anything that I write or photograph will always fall somewhat short of the actual event. However, it is important that I attempt to transcend the boundaries of language (both written and visual) in an earnest effort to share with you what I have been experiencing here.

Firstly, I have never felt more alive. The air is crisp, and the views are breathtaking. Clouds blend into mountain peaks, which roll into lush hills lined with trees and open fields. Somewhere between all of that, narrow roads bend between humble homes and noble abodes. The entire scene is something out of a movie. Literally. (*The Sound of Music* was filmed here, and tourists from all over the world flock the city to take photographs of locations and landmarks used during filming.) The whole thing is completely beautiful and bizarre at best.

Ironically, along with the elation of being alive comes the heartbreakingly concrete awareness of my own mortality—understanding the fact that someday I, too, will die. Perhaps this realization is simply one that develops with age. Either way, the first of only two absolute truths is this: LIFE is DEATH. Regardless of what one believes of our origins or our destinations, where we begin or where we end up, the fact is: We all live. We all die. Period.

What I find most extraordinary about the promise of death is that throughout the ages, across all borders and cultures, on all ends of the globe, human beings have continually succeeded in achieving immortality. We know their names, we know their stories, and we know them well because, in the words of Medgar Evers, "You can kill a man, but you can't kill an idea." Our bodies may shrink, deteriorate, and eventually disappear, but our thoughts, our actions, and our words harbor the potential to echo indefinitely. We may never fully understand just how far the ripples of our being will travel.

Just a few nights ago, I shared dinner and drinks with people from Turkey, Croatia, Germany, Italy, Austria, Serbia, Brazil, Cameroon, and Czech Republic. And in one astoundingly overwhelming moment, I realized that something very special was happening, something that can only be described as "indescribable." In spite of struggling to understand each other's words, we were still able to collect around the idea of a shared human experience—an experience that goes beyond words, beyond ego—something deep in our core. (See translation: Soul.)

Secondly, I have never felt more American in my life. This realization has been slightly more difficult to come to terms with. Over the course of my life, I have lived in California, Massachusetts, and Illinois. I have traveled to almost 30 other states in the U.S. and have only been to a few countries in Central America and even fewer cities in Canada. Never having left the North American continent, I had always identified as a Californian of Belizean-born parents first before ever identifying as an American. But I come to Austria with a lot of cultural baggage—a lot of socio-political influences and anxieties that are based on a very specific relationship between native peoples of the Americas, early European colonizers, and the Africans they forcibly brought with them. Granted, Austria (and, of course, neighboring Germany) has its own very complicated history that I will not delve into here due to my superficial understanding of it—a lack of knowledge I would need to resolve before making any comparisons between said histories. However, the history that I am most familiar with, most personally affected by, is American history. In America, I know quite well the sense of being the only Black body in a room full of White bodies. I am also accustomed to the way some White bodies will clutch their belongings a little tighter when my body passes by. The fear and discomfort is so thick on some White faces when I walk into an elevator that I can smell it. And it is the most vile and putrid smell. Needless to say, I was nervous about coming to Austria for reasons not unlike these. But the looks that I experience here are not the same. They are not looks that stem from fear, but instead, curiosity—a moment of childlike wonder, as if discovering for the first time that indeed, mermaids do exist. But being that there are so few mermaids here in Austria, I am faced with questions that I haven't had to answer since my own childhood. I am much older these days, and I understand that here, questions such as "Can you sunburn?" are not ill intended, but (dare I say) sincere. However, due to the particular history I have inherited as an American, these questions still sting, perhaps more than a sunburn. Ah, the price of exposure.

In addition to my own complex relationships to the implication of skin pigmentation in an American context, I have also been conditioned to regard my own sexuality with fear, shame, and contempt. At several points in my life, I have used different words to describe my sexual tendencies: curious, bi-curious, bisexual, gay, queer…. This is a perfect example of how language can fail when attempting to accurately represent the fluid and ever-shifting nature of the human experience. We are not fixed beings. I have yet to settle on a proper word to describe my current state of sexual desires, tendencies, and curiosities. But in actuality, I am not so sure I want to settle on a "proper" word because definition and categorization would more likely be for the sake of another than it would be for my own. And there is something rather pleasant about being able to float between spheres, unanchored, untethered. (See translation: Free.)

American. Black. Queer. I am far more dynamic than these three labels may suggest. My existence and my experiences are far more layered than what the rules of language will allow, and the magnificent beings that I shared dinner and drinks with several nights ago are far more multidimensional than the words they employ (and that we ascribe) in order to exalt or relegate their experiences. This brings me back to my point about possessing "something deep in our core." It is important to keep in mind that I am by no means suggesting that our identifications and the myriad of words and terms that we use to describe them are invalid or unnecessary. In fact, I am quite thankful for them, for it is because of these words that we are able to better understand and effectively communicate ideas that, far too often, seem completely insurmountable. But regardless of ethnic origin, class status, race, sexuality, gender, age, ability, political affiliation, religion, belief, background, or any other position on any socially constructed spectrum, all humans are concerned with the latter of only two absolute truths: LOVE. Make no mistake: Every action, every word, everything that we have ever done and will ever do is borne of the insatiable desire to love and the unconquerable fear that we might not be loved back.

To live is to die. And to die is to have loved and lost. This is the human condition. After this, there is nothing else.

Although recounting my experiences exactly as they happen has proven to be difficult time and time again, I am realizing that the attempt to do so is paramount. The frustration and exhaustion as result of continually being misrepresented and misunderstood is trumped by the liberating powers of self-expression, for there is much at stake in recording and sharing individual and collective positions. When we forfeit the task of relaying our own stories, we grant the liberty of writing our personal histories to someone else, someone who may not fully understand, respect, or appreciate our unique positions and tendencies, ultimately risking our very inclusion and presence in history itself, ensuring our absence from the lessons that humans have so courageously fought to learn (and teach) since the utterance of our first words.

*Published on **August 20, 2012** by EJ Hill in EJ Hill*

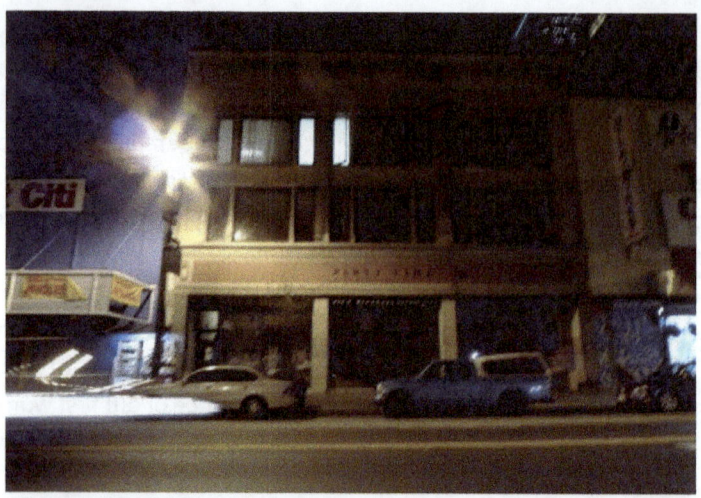

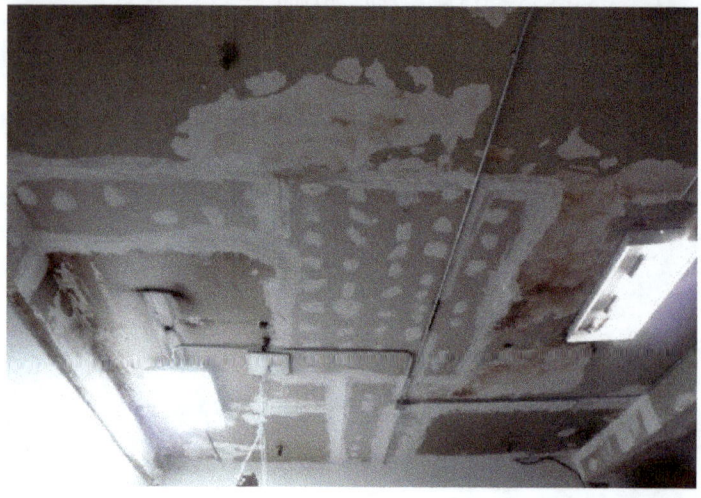

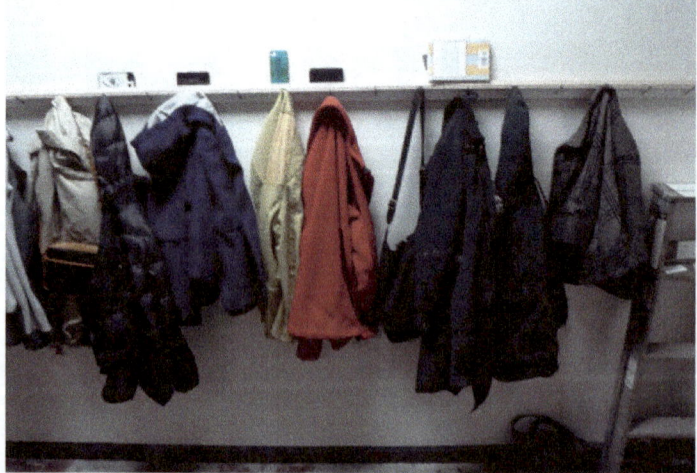

MY LAB RAT SELF DID THINGS THAT SURPRISED ME, AND OTHER OBSERVATIONS OF SILENCE
various authors

Monday, February 18, 2013

David Bell:

I am happy that you have all decided to come to our silent night this Sunday on the 24th of February. Cocktail hour begins at 7:30 PM, followed by a simple dinner around 8:30 and performance and art throughout the evening. Please try to be punctual.

Location: 435 S Broadway, Los Angeles, CA 90013 (between 4th and 5th)

This is not a press release, since you have all already agreed to come, but I thought there was a need to send something out.

I have realized that each individual that I have asked to come may not be on the same page as I am, and that is okay. This Sunday is not a day to put everyone on the same page, but a night where each individual can exist on their own, amongst others without communicating. I have tried to think of a way to not write out a set of rules for the evening because I do not want to put myself in a position where I am acting as ring leader or shssh(er). Yet it is seemingly impossible to invite a specific amount of people to a silent dinner and not explain what I am essentially expecting out of everyone. This is entirely a night where each attendee has chosen to come and be silent.

These are essentially the "rules," for lack of a better word, which each guest has knowingly committed to after reading and upon coming:

No speaking of any kind, meaning no lip synching, noise making or letter writing. Hand gestures, laughter, coughing etc. are inevitably going to happen; try to keep it at a minimum. If somebody speaks to you, please avoid speaking back. You are here because you chose to be silent.

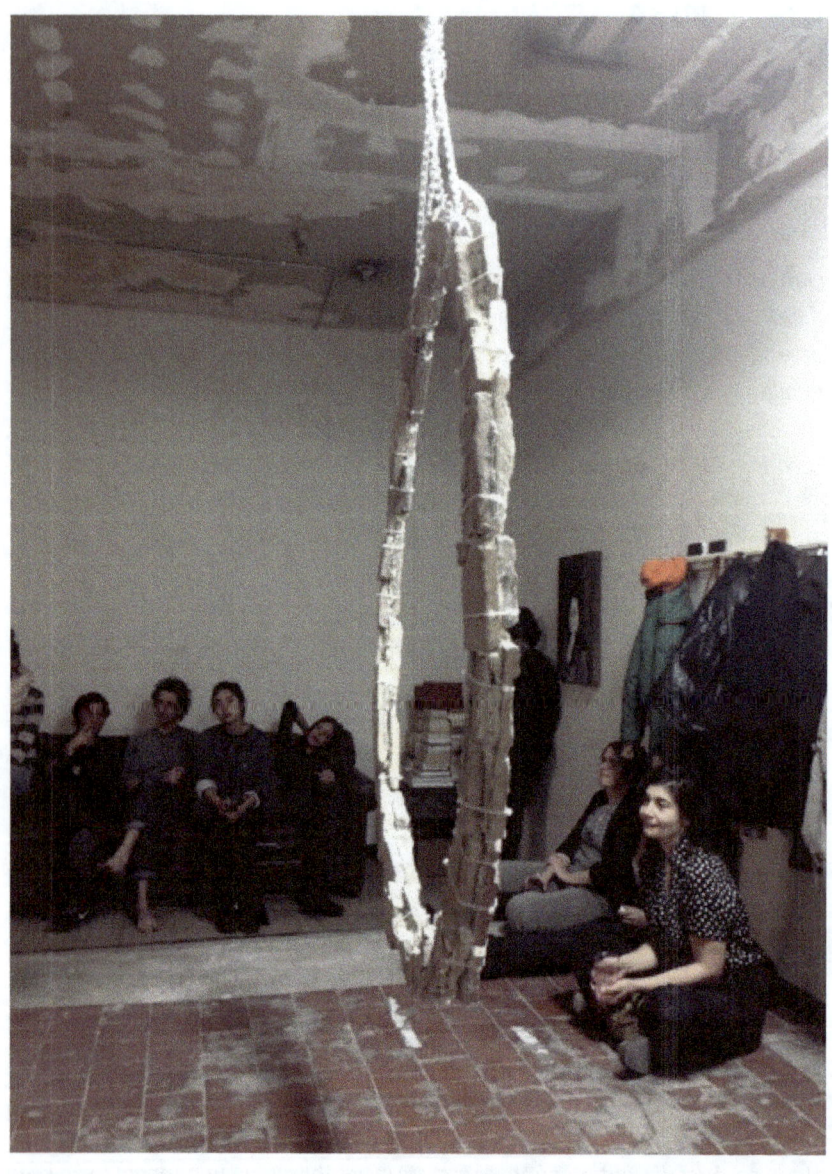

Please do not leave the room unless it is an emergency. Smoking is not an emergency. The event only lasts 2.5 hours or slightly more; there is ample time to smoke before and after. If you have to leave to smoke and be away from the group, then you may as well not have come. (Not to be harsh; I will want a cigarette, too.)

Bathroom breaks are okay in case of emergency, but do so honestly. Do not leave out of nervousness (or to smoke). The bathroom is located outside the door to the left.

This is an invite-only event. The night is based around the individuals who have RSVP'd. Seating, food, space and performances are fit to this certain and particular group. Please be courteous and not bring extra people (if this is a problem, please email or call me personally, in case someone has canceled or it inhibits you wanting to attend).

When you walk in the room, on the left wall, there will be a place where you can place your coat and phone. It is strongly encouraged to leave your phone on this wall; there will be a label with your name. It is also recommended that you leave your phone on whatever setting you usually have it on, whether that be ringer, vibrate or silent.

There will be some sort of cue that the event is over. I ask that everybody leave the room and building at least momentarily before speaking. If you wish to come back in, that is up to you.

Last words:

Since I am a full participant in the event myself, yet understand it is downtown and parking can be an issue, I will keep my phone on me until 7:45 unless everyone has arrived. This is why it is important to be on time. There will be a key to the left of the front door, but I will try to keep it opened. The space is up the stairs; walk straight till you have to turn right, and it is the door across from the stack of dry-wall. I'll make a sign.

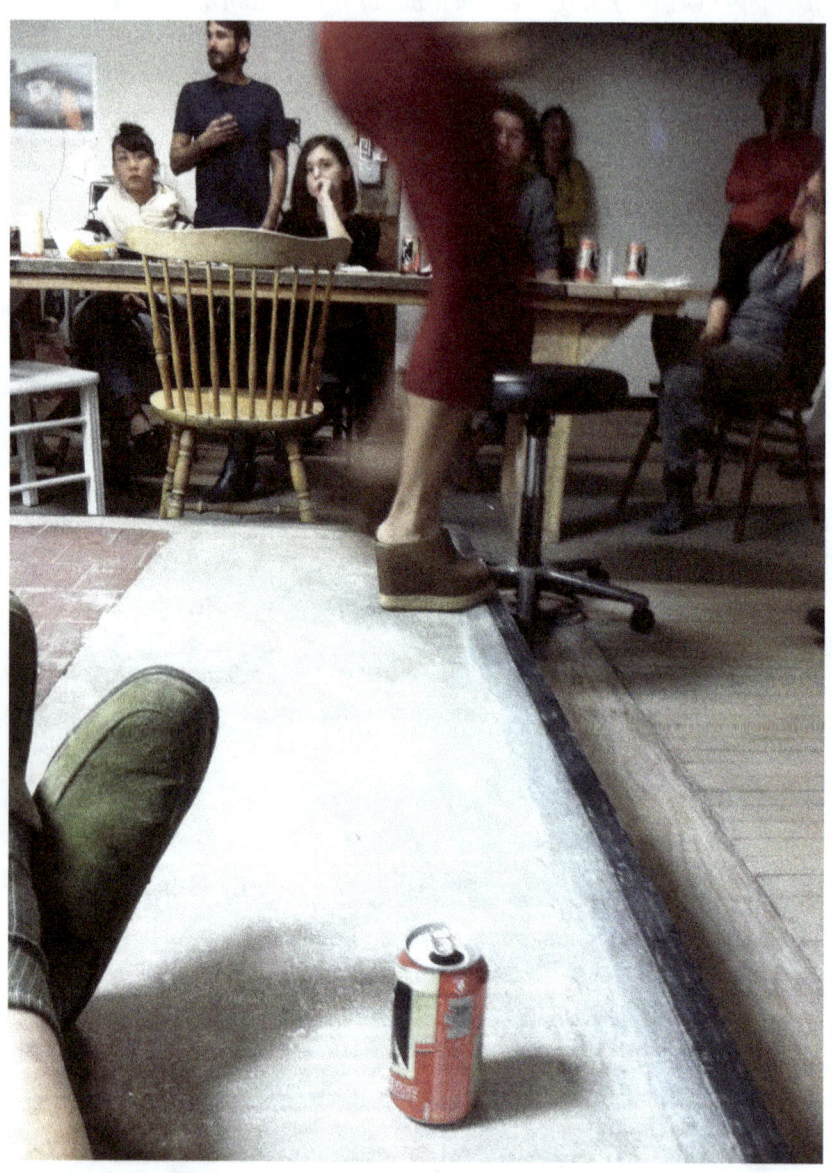

Tuesday, February 26, 2013

Becky Kolsrud:

Here's my take on the silent night:

There was a slow, organic tempo to the entire evening. Everyone moved around the space carefully, stopping at points of interest such as the art and architectural details of the room. The thresholds of the space (the door to enter and the step up to the platform) were the most theatrical spots, where participants drew attention to themselves by entering or rising in to a higher point in the room. Though I was intermittently tense, the tone of the room was thoughtful and composed. During dinner, people interacted playfully, and my most successful interaction of the evening was when a stranger sitting next to me gracefully offered to clear my plate using only eye contact.

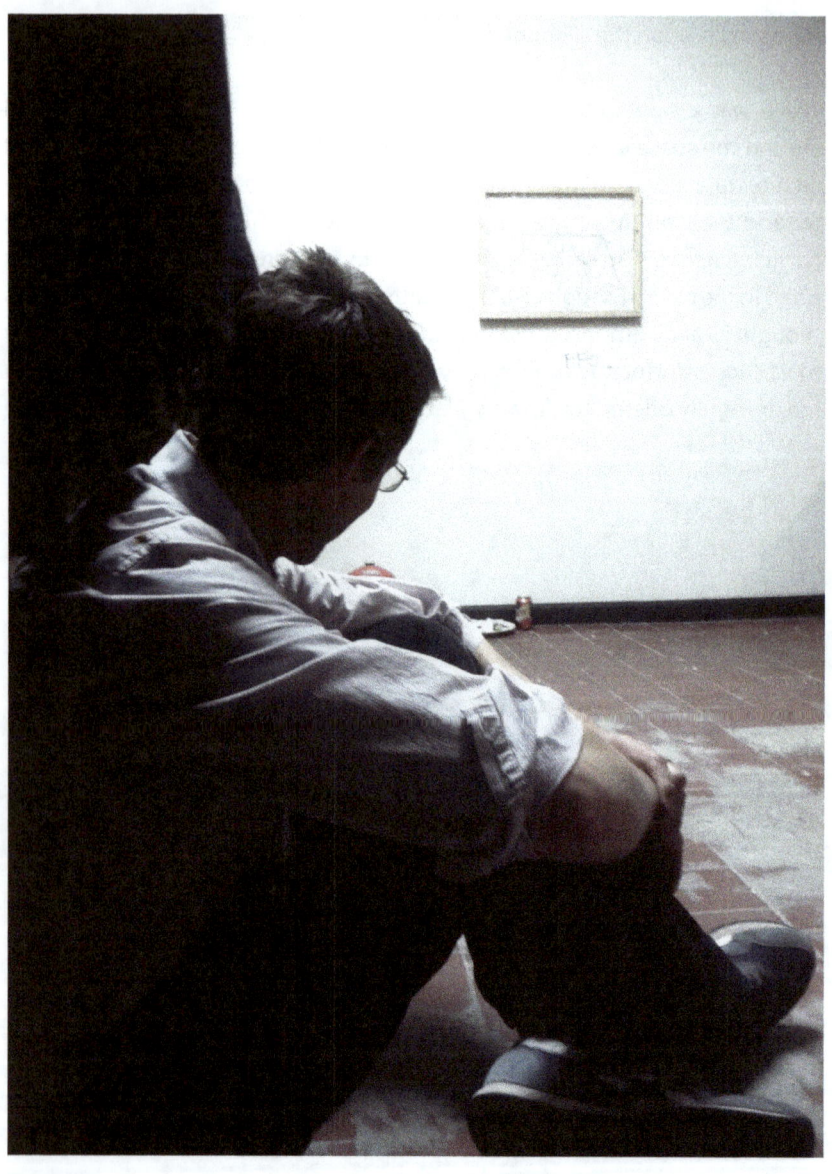

Tuesday, February 26, 2013

Jonathon Hornedo:

"I hope the tone of this email does not sound too authoritative; all you really have to do is be silent and enjoy the art and company. Please feel free to call me with any questions or concerns. No need to contact me unless you are canceling or cannot come; please please email me if you cannot come. I look forward to seeing you all."

I had a complex array of impressions. Throughout the night, I was always curious as to how the night would unfold, what the "tribe" would do or become involved with. With communication restricted by silence, I felt a deep sense of the primitive, and I felt I had deeper access to people's psychologies merely by observing body language. At different moments, I felt more self-conscious, especially after I stepped on the art, destroying the stage where I thought a performance was going to happen. Other moments, I was more relaxed and one with the tribe, especially when moments became very silent, where activity was at a minimum. Then I felt very free. That I could do anything. That no laws apply. That doing something weird or wrong may get a response, but nobody would be able to say anything about it. So do it. I spilled water onto the floor.

John Cage came to mind.

The whole night was fun and interesting. Really enjoyed it. It was one of those rare socially oriented art projects that I didn't want to end.

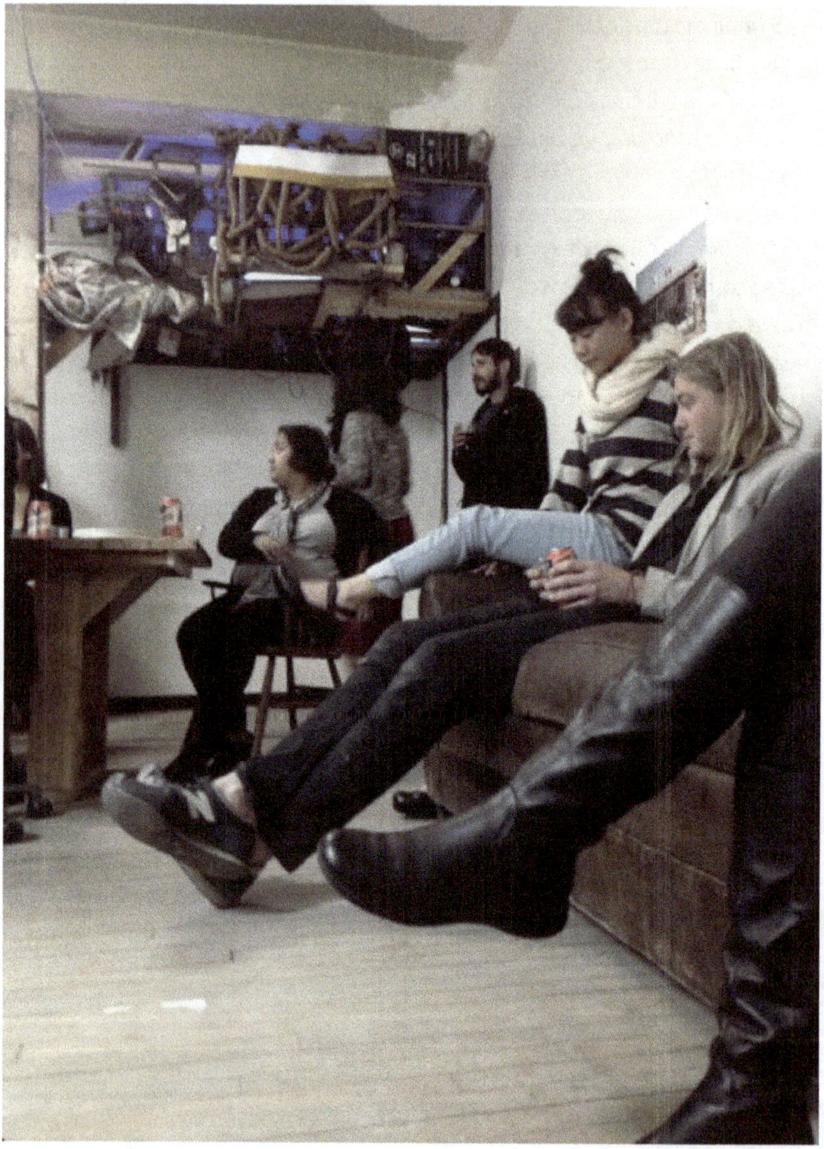

Saturday, March 2, 2013

John Pearson:

There was so much happening and not happening that developed over the evening. I didn't know what to expect, but Pam was a bit nervous, and we made jokes about how this is my type of party because I'm shy and awkward and prefer not to have to talk. Upon entering the room, it very quickly became so cinematic, in part because I was able to just concentrate on looking. People to varying degrees made or avoided eye contact, and that suggested the omniscient, idealized view, the camera and the stage. No language was sort of a gray area, as interactions occurred and were expressive. I immediately thought of *Last Year at Marienbad* for the social party setting, for the silence, for the out of time but in my head space that film conjures. There was sort of a tempo of people shifting location and actions that, in retrospect, felt like scenes. Over the course of the evening, I also thought of *The Exterminating Angel*, which numerous people brought up afterwards up on the roof. But also, with no language, no dialogue or narrative, looking at people suggested the reaction shot in a movie—the silent cut away from the active talker to show the recipient's response. But it was all that shot constantly, continuously! If there was a plot, it rested in you and your friend writing notes or the woman's breasts on the brink of spilling out of her dress. Over one person's shoulder, I began to read his note until I got to the line that read "do not show this to anyone." I read the note addressed to me and realized it as some exquisite corpse, as gender was wrong and it seemed to have an intended provocation, plus it included the line of "don't show this to anyone." I chalked that up to the inherent tense atmosphere of that room and the entry of strangers while you two were writing the notes. As things went along, I decided to commit to the dinner table, as I felt like there was maybe some progression to engaging the sequence of events. Would dinner begin once we all sat down? I also appreciated the décor from the art that didn't seem so strategically present (as a prop) to the long coat rack—that was a favorite! I was curious about the video cameras and wondered if they were recording or just adding stimuli. I appreciated that they were not documenting the entire room. I took photos for a while but didn't want to be so prominent in that way, marking and making moments, so I tried to be a bit discreet (charm). Although I started to feel more comfortable over time, it was not as though I could express that. I think the gesture of smashing the plate came out of feeling more comfortable and that we were all committed to this time.

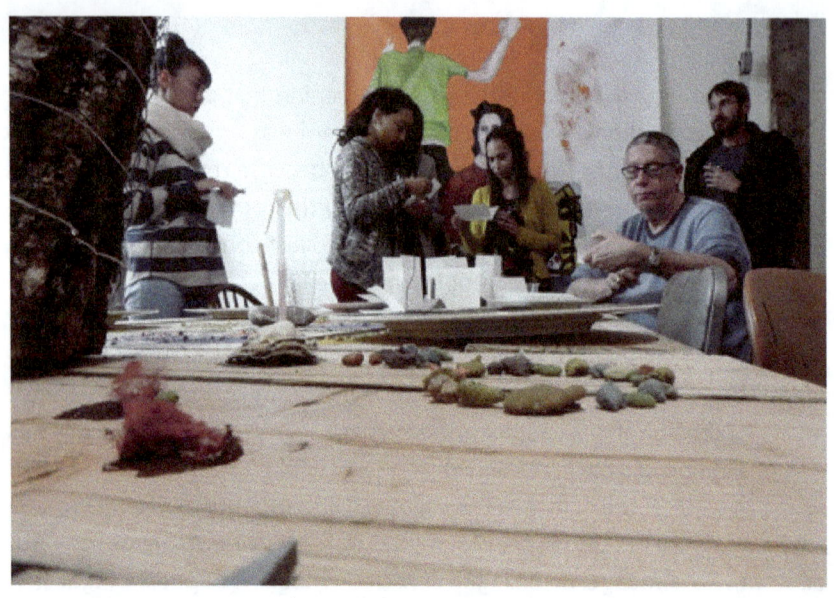

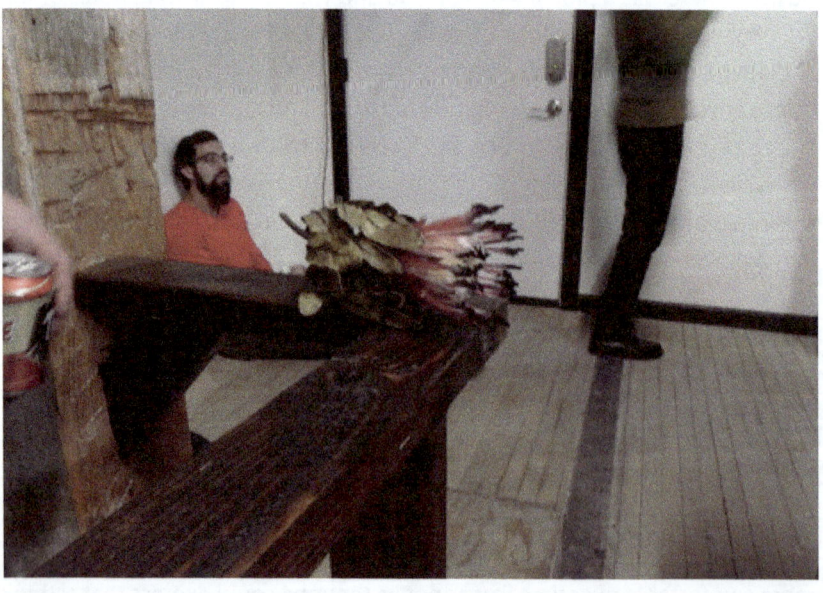

I really enjoyed when you put on the motorcycle helmet and sat there against the wall. There was that component of a lab test as you surveyed the scene and stroked your beard, sans lab coat and pocket protector, but it was also casual and didn't feel that you were separate from our situation. There were so many moments and gestures that took on a heightened significance. To a certain degree, this is how the physical comedy of a Jacques Tati film works. He speaks no words and deals with social situations throughout. *Mon Oncle* is my favorite. I had many cinematic references come to mind. [I guess this also means I had time to think and wander, which isn't so much the case when talking at a party.] I thought of Tarkovsky's *Stalker* for the silence and the mysteriousness of the zone in a landscape that looks very commonplace. The guide leads people into the zone to reach a certain room that can possibly allow you to attain your dreams. But it is not so much the room that came to mind as the trip across the zone when the guide leads people through a typical field of thick grass and requires that they follow his exact steps. It seems absurd, and people don't understand and there is an awkwardness of the group to abide or contest.

And at some point, I decided to smash a plate, as the plates were there, the stage was available, and I could place the helmet on the young guy sitting at the edge of the platform. I had really enjoyed that small windup music box and how sound punctuated and sometimes embellished the situation. I had cranked it at dinner to provide a moment of dinner music. I have to add that in my family, the dinner table was a place of tension and was not so comfortable. So a silent dinner was a bad dinner. But so I thought smashing that plate would be such a great opportunity, such a sound, and we had come to this point where things were controlled and calm. The wildest thing in the room was your long-haired friend who looked substantially hung over. Geoff afterwards said that guy was a "beautiful mess." But so I went through the motions of smashing that plate and, to my surprise, putting on that helmet completely removed me from the space. I could only hear my breathing and wasn't going to get the joy of the smash. But it was also an unexpected privacy, and without my glasses, I was pretty focused on my responsibilities. I didn't want to be aggressive or declarative but just provide this sound. I also felt like we are waiting for what will happen and, well, that would happen. The situation had established itself. I hope that wasn't inconsiderate to use that guy's helmet that way. Also, without my glasses, I couldn't really tell the chips of plate from the white paint splatters, which was a problem when I was picking it all up. The only shortcoming of doing that is if it frustrated the chemistry or dynamic. I'm sorry if that was the case. For me, it screwed up the evening a bit in retro-

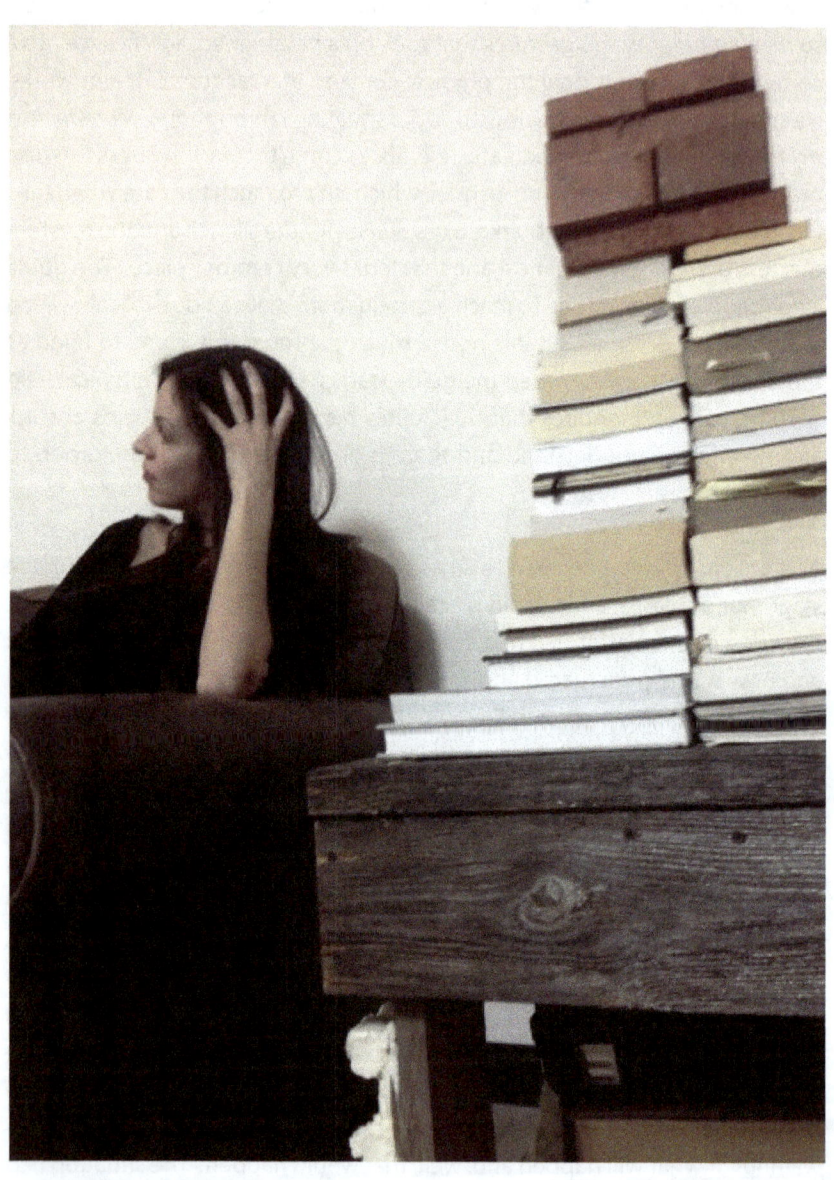

spect because I got so nervous and now today it's like that action is trying to write over so much of the evening.

When it was over, I guess that came around the time the woman started smoking the pipe, or maybe that occurred before the dancing, it seemed so unexpectedly early. I preferred the silence.

Also, before going out that evening a friend had said to Pam that it was going to be like *Eyes Wide Shut*, a Kubrick film that I can find no appreciation for, and it was going to be a sex thing. Ridiculous, of course, but then when the woman spilling out of her dress got up on stage and tucked away her sweater and stood there at the deepest corner of the stage, I thought, oh my god, this might be very unexpected.

The food was good. I enjoyed the company—strangers and friends. Thanks. I can give you some money for the plate. If Geoff and David made any comments about the value, just tell me. So great to garner so much by not talking.

I'll send some photos later on.

(I wrote to you the day after the dinner. Now, a week later, I've had some time to think about the night. John Pearson)

First off, I realized that in retrospect, smashing that plate was so inconsequential and did not warrant retelling to friends. So what? But I think that in the situation with those people, there was an attentiveness and possibility that made it permissible and satisfying. I just don't think that I can convey that experience of the dinner in writing. I also think that talking and language really build a hierarchy. It is how people make themselves comfortable or define the dynamics of a group. It explains (resolves) information (experience). That was what was so nice about the evening, because it developed without talking or clarification. There is so much you take in that doesn't conform to language.

Silence is often the space between words or the time of thinking, so the dinner seemed to create more of that space and that time. It was so generative in that way. It also made me think of this equation: $1/\infty$. One divided by infinity. I came across this while reading about Helen Mirra. It is a Buddhist idea called momentmind that's written about by Seung Sahn. *"This world is impermanent. Everything is always changing, changing, changing, moving, moving,*

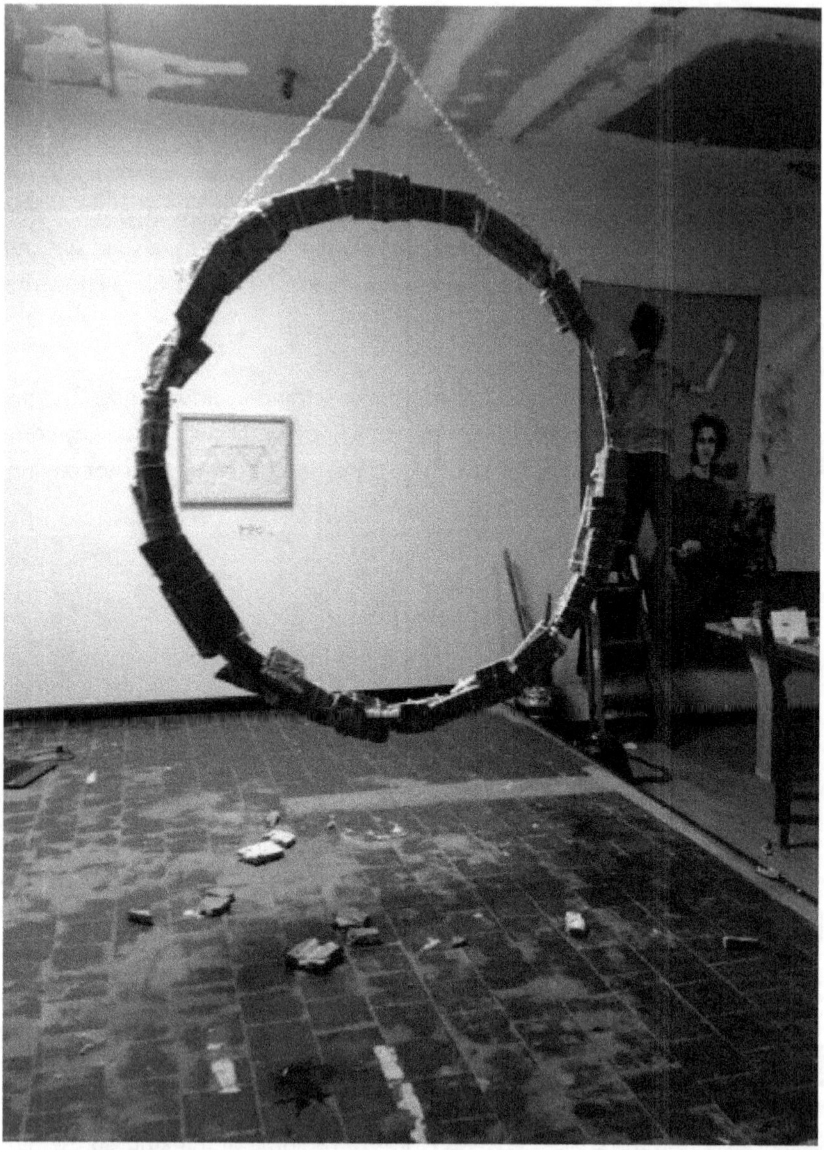

moving, nonstop. *Even one second of our lives seems full of so much movement and change in this world that we see. But your mind—right now—is like a lens whose shutter speed is one divided by infinite time. We call that momentmind. If you attain that mind, then this whole world's movement stops. From moment to moment, you can see this world completely stop.*" I think that's a terrific equation that works in an unexpected way. I also think, although he uses the idea of the lens, that this isn't an idea of stopping time or a problem that you solve with a camera (Muybridge). The moments continue while you attend to the world. It isn't an infinity that pushes an overwhelming vastness, but more a recognition and attention to the moment.

There is an absurdity writing about the value of not speaking and not using language.

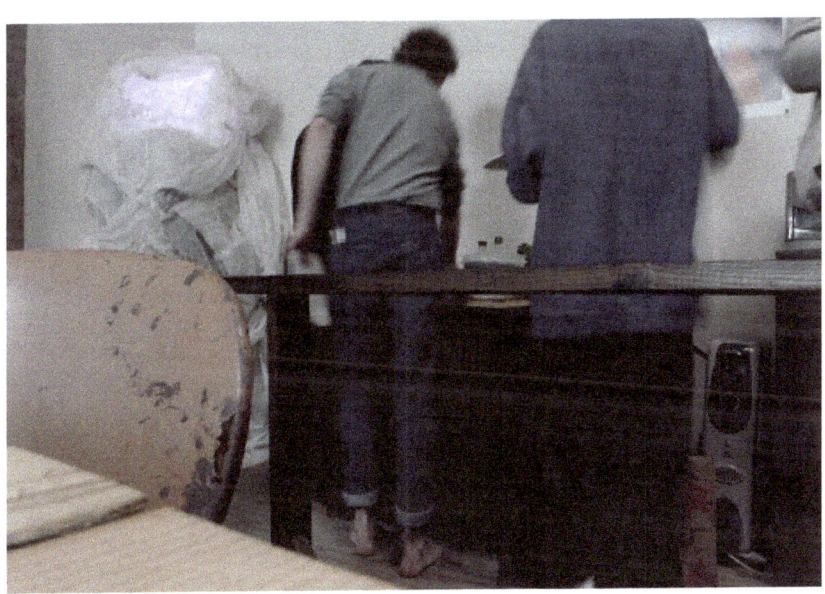

March 4, 2013

Tiffany Smith:

I didn't have anything to say anyway. It reminded me of dinners I've had before where awkward silence couldn't be avoided. I was comfortable in a way because I wasn't trying to think of what to say, and I didn't miss words much. I was so bored. When I describe the event to people, they don't get it. I guess I'm not explaining it well. Fall into your own hole.

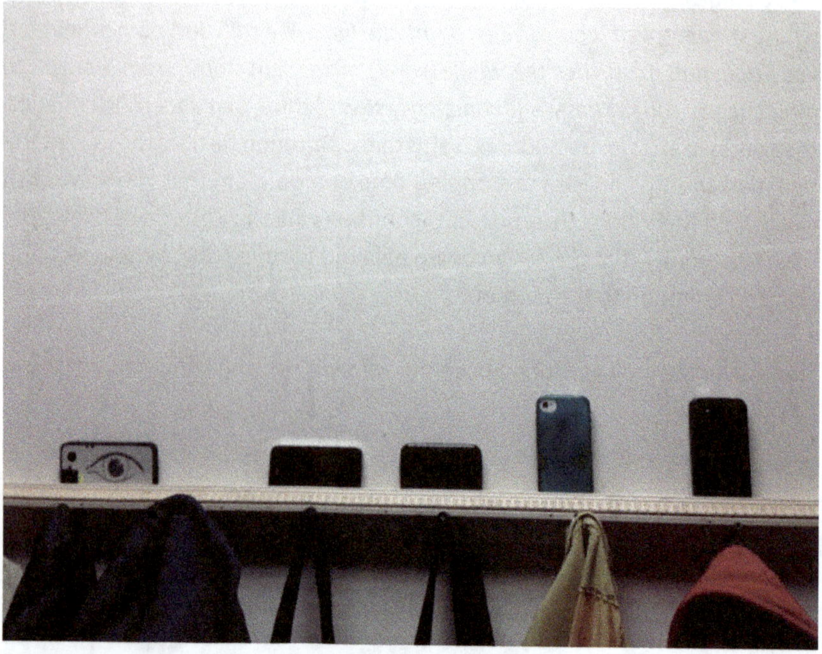

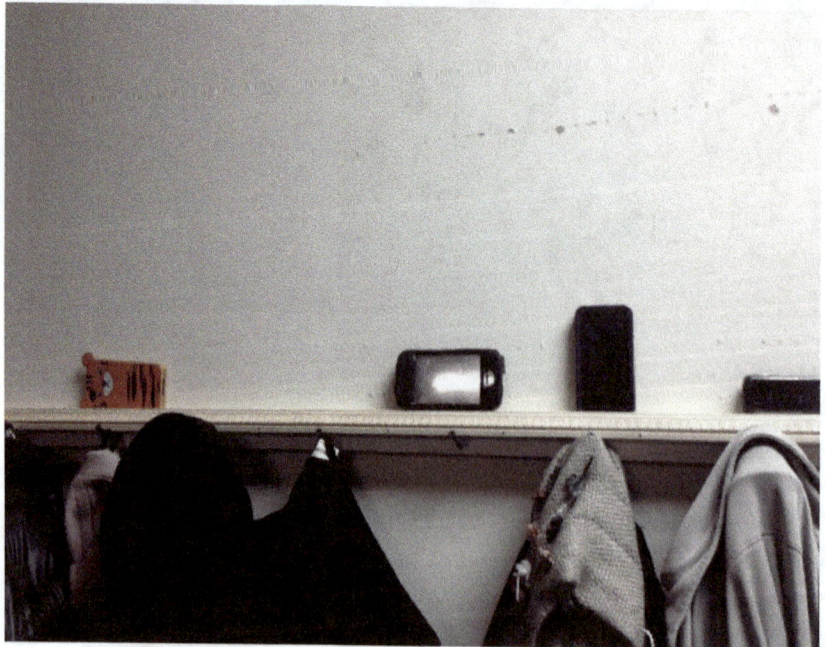

March 4, 2013

Bettina Hubby:

"Be quiet and eat."

If you told me that I'd arrive at a silent dinner party, and that by the end of it I would personally inflict damage on a piece of art without being drunk, I would never have believed you. However, that's exactly what happened, and for the life of me I still can't completely piece together why.

The whole thing had me at hello, though—from the 6-point instruction email up until the last coat was lifted up from its hook and the room of evidence remained left like the used set of an Ubu play. David did something potent by subtracting communication from a social ritual. And thankfully, it was a room of artists, so the results were even more notably strange, uncomfortable, delightful, subtle, and resonant than they would be if it were another demographic.

At first, I focused on watching everyone else, catching people's gaze and turning away due to my inherent laughter rising to surface, but containing myself to witness what a dinner party is without talking. Hearing the clinking of silverware, the small coughs and fabric murmurs of coats being hung, subtle wine-sipping noises, footsteps and chair squeals—these were the only sounds in the room bouncing off the walls between us, and it was strangely exciting. My senses were radically enhanced, and my eyes were wide, not wanting to miss a single bit of the nonverbal evening. This made the ordinary extra so and ended up strangely amping up my adrenaline.

After a delicious dinner, I gravitated towards the large, mysterious ring of zip-tied mortar and bricks on a chain. I began circling it and poking it, noticing it was still wet mortar, and suddenly flicked a bit off and to the floor. There was a palpable energy in the room that gave me an extra pulse of action, or the room's calling may have just existed in my mind. It was as if the congregation silently willed me to make the gesture bigger, to make the intersection of me and that thing more dramatic. But, as I think back on it later, perhaps it was just my nature in the group dynamic to be loud. My laugh is loud, but I couldn't laugh, so perhaps I had to make a big noise or event to replace the laughter somehow to be myself. It was a group dynamic set akimbo so that other behaviors rose to the surface. I noticed people's gestures were bigger, some peo-

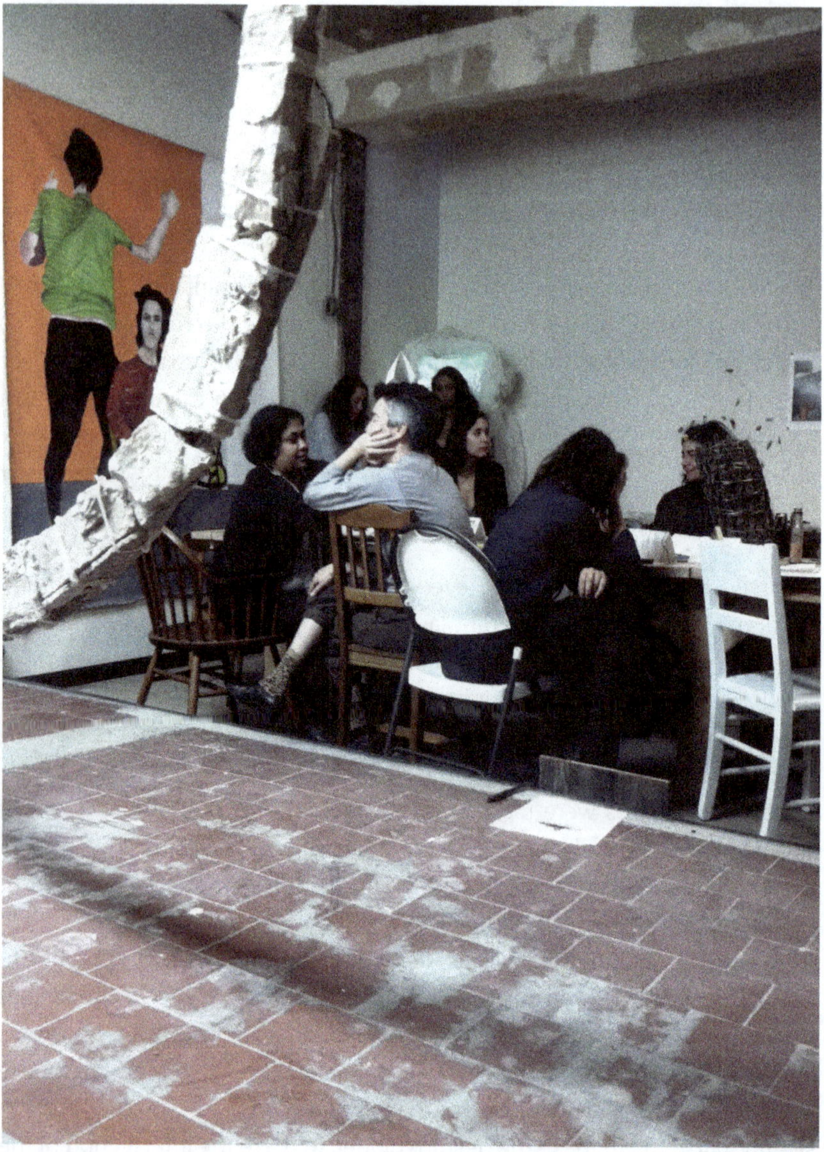

ple's behaviors shifted, and watching was like watching a match near some gasoline—right at the edge of interrupting the order of this skewed order. It was as if we all took clues from those of us who did something first, and then we'd follow and repeat, or do something unexpected for someone else to follow or simply observe—but at the same time wanted to all respect the whole vision that was David's. I was in a social experiment, and my lab rat self did things that surprised me under these directives. I was back home later thinking, did that just happen? Do I need to apologize? I grin to myself now and silently feel thankful to be in this arena of people, thankful to be challenged in these ways to think and to do differently.

March 12, 2013

Carlyn Aguilar:

I participated in this very interesting Silent Dinner, hosted by artist David Lucas Bell at his studio in downtown. As a Speech and Language Pathologist, one who works with non-speaking deaf teenagers, and having worked in a hospital full of stroke victims with aphasia, I was actually quite comfortable being in a situation where no one could talk. I felt like it was just another day at work… but unfortunately (because of the rules given to us prior to the performance), I was unable to bring augmentative and alternative communication devices to assist my fellow diners in expressing themselves. But I also realized that these artists didn't really need words to show the crowd what they wanted, needed and desired. Like I said, just an extension of my typical day….

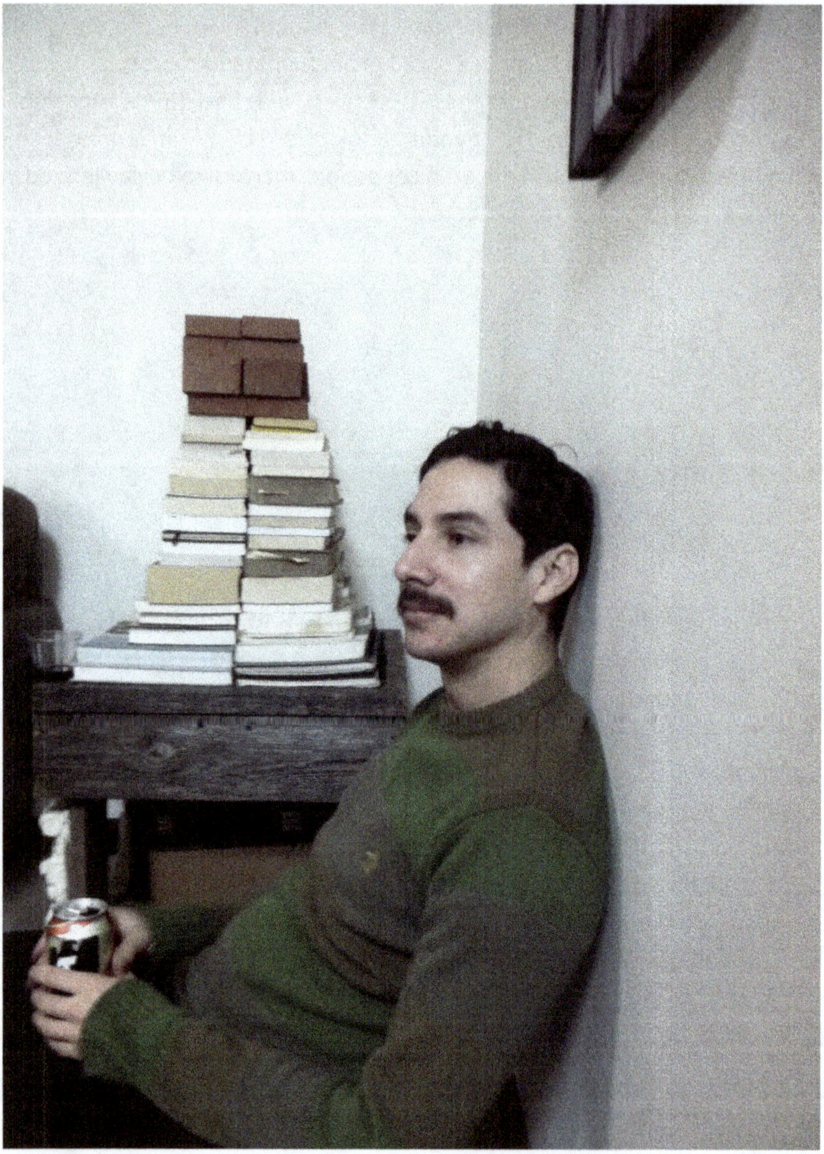

March 11, 2013

Olga Koumoundouros:

The silent dinner that wasn't so silent

This piece was convivial, as dinner parties with food and drink go. I appreciated getting stretched and how it opened up awareness of others movements and postures and time. The overall language of socializing and our unity and ridiculousness in it was most compelling.

I expected myself to generously pursue ways to connect with others beyond vocal, but somehow my own anxiety got the best of me. It began once I was sent the email from David, the artist/host. It was a real game changer. I was initially approaching the event with a "go with the flow" attitude, but the email was serious, and it quickly made me understand that I had made an agreement to participate in something. That all of us had. He laid out the parameters and expectations. They weren't too much to ask, but it was a contract of sorts. I felt stress because I'd never been to the location before and really only knew two other people and had other pressures too. There was no crutch or comfort.

So the fishbowl dynamic happened. I clung to the art, facing the walls, my back towards the group, and looked at the work until I couldn't tolerate myself doing that anymore. Then, I faced the middle, still stuck to the walls, and watched everyone. I was envious of those that could remain still at the table. Just "being" was impossible for me. I felt unable to enter my own mind and escape, nor able to have meaningful connection with others. The sense of spectatorship was intense. Many of us were actively looking in the small room. Every sound and movement was something, a distraction and a welcome tension release. Thank goodness for the crash, got that over with. Someone played a little music box on a chair with wheels, and that was a particularly exquisite moment. The sounds together in memory felt very Dada. Small, sentimental-seeming objects and consciously earnest notes, which stated they were personal, were laid around the long dinner table for everyone to read, exposing our hunger for words but then revealing themselves to be an affectation of intimacy, lumping us all into the human (6 degrees of separation from David) pot together.

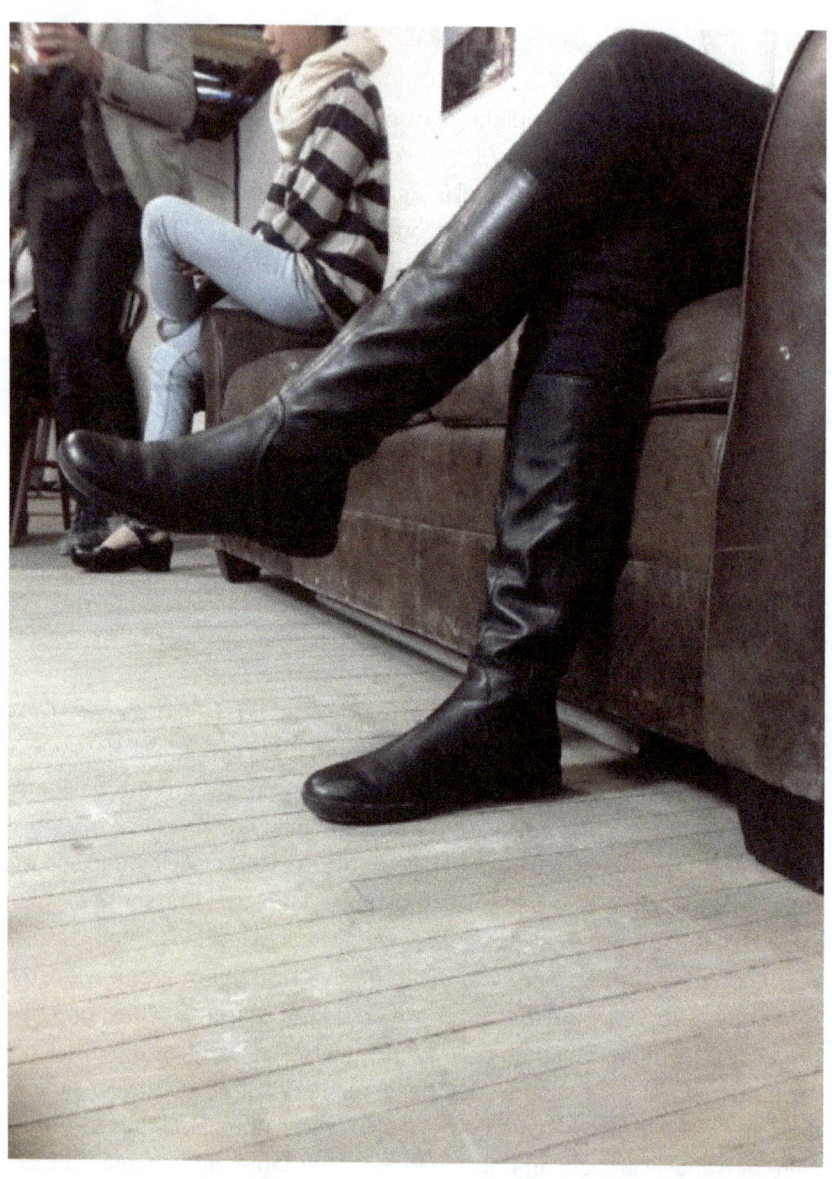

The gathering went in and out of performing performance, tension between everyone waiting for something, entertaining ourselves, resistance, passing time or dealing with the constraint. Then really lovely, unselfconscious and subtle affects, twitches, misunderstanding and coping gestures occurred in between the noted points. Those were the juiciest moments for me.

The evening ended with the artist playing a song on his laptop and dancing awkwardly. The song lyrics were an ode to all our foolish humanity trying to get close to others and then asking "What do you do?" It was a nice summation of our bungling fragility, guardedness and agency in the room. Moving bodies in a shuffly dance was a good way to shake off the tension and finally lose myself and everyone else for a minute.

Photographs are by Bettina Hubby, John Pearson and Geoff Tuck.

Published on March 11, 2013 by Geoff Tuck in Additional writing by, Fiction, Interviews and Conversations, Miscellaneous, Wanderings.

THE DISCREET CHARM OF THE BOURGEOISIE, OR "I ONLY PAID FOR IT!"

considering a performance by EJ Hill—an exchange with Ari Marcantonio

Ari Marcantonio with Geoff Tuck

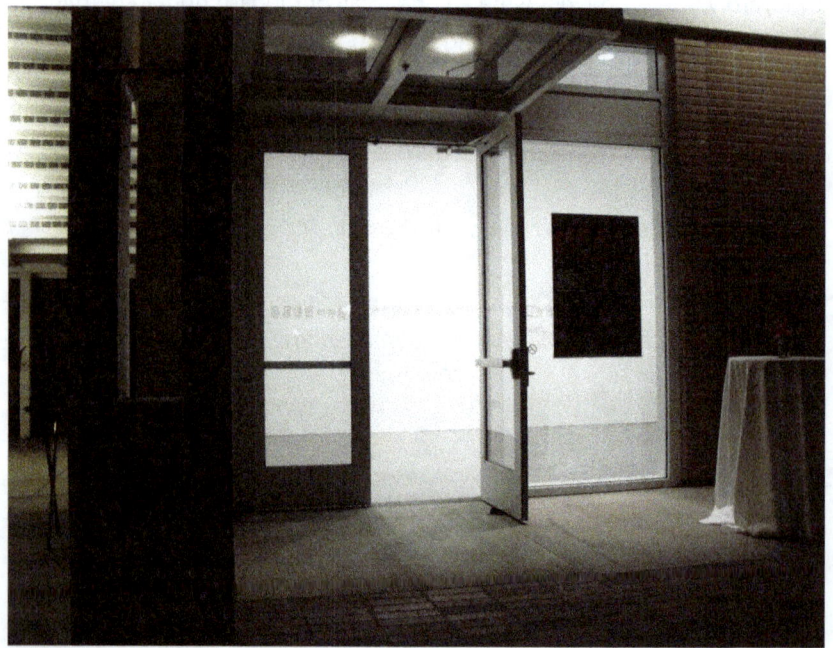

Photo by Ari Marcantonio

Ari Marcantonio:

After the performance ended, I went to get a glass of wine with a friend. As we stood in line, a man, sporting the magnetically attached name tag and real wine glass that signified his position as a member of the donor preview group, stepped in front of us. I politely informed him that we were in line. My friend admonished me for my frankness. "It's OK," the gentleman replied to her. "I only paid for it."

But let's back up. Moments earlier, by occupying the space between the public and the private, an artist had physically manifested a socioeconomic boundary that, as art patrons, we tend to quite readily ignore. Moreover, by denying the formalities of performance art and the exhibition space, the artist had reframed the context of his work and the show at large. He refused to accept the supposed objectivity of the space around him and, recalcitrantly, he insisted on a specific context for the display of his piece.

The piece effectively created two audiences, two contexts, two performances. One was placed on a stage of warmly glowing halogen light for a group of art donors, MFA students, faculty and staff while they enjoyed hors d'oeuvres and speeches; the other was foregrounded by a dimly lit patio occupied primarily by undergraduate students, miscellaneous Los Angeles artists and otherwise interested passersby.

Geoff Tuck:
I came that evening to UCLA with Adam Feldmeth, and as we drove across town, Adam told me of his recent visit to artists' studios at the University of Houston; he had been invited by a colleague currently teaching at the school to bring his curious, expansive practice of conversation to share with them. The visits were quite a success, and Adam was assured that "we want you to come back! If you take some time to meet with collectors here (in Houston) and explain to them your project, you are certain to get funding for a return trip." People in Houston have an almost quaint sense of civic responsibility. It's not exactly selfless (a state probably reserved for saints), but it is effective in supporting the community of artists and museums. We talked for quite a while about patronage that evening, without realizing how our conversation set the scene for our later experience. As it happened, we both misunderstood the time of the opening event to be 5:00 PM. At 6:20 PM, we crossed the lawn to the door; despite each of us having the promptness gene that states "to be early is to be on time," we arrived—as Adam put it—fashionably late.

Surprised to find a pair of tables blocking our entry, we were given to understand that a private function was underway, which would conclude at 7:00 PM. I asked about press access, and I mentioned *Notes on Looking*. The woman behind the table kindly went out of her way to locate the event manager, and this man assured me we could gain access at 6:45 PM—15 minutes before the general public.

As we waited in place, it became awkward when several artist friends came from inside the private party to greet us and express their personal embarrassment at our position. One grad offered to intercede on our behalf, and we asked her not to, as it would make more difficult the jobs of people who ultimately had no say.

Our concern—and Adam and I discussed this—was to not miss EJ Hill's performance. We had each been waiting. We understood that performances were scheduled at 6:30 PM, and that they—or it—would take place inside.

Sometime in this waiting period, EJ came out to say hello. Adam hugged him in greeting and commented on his new shirt.

I think, Ari, that at this point you came, up and we decided to visit a nearby undergrad painting show, where we met more friends and hung out for a while. As it neared 6:30 PM, we returned to our place by the tables and joined a now growing crowd as the private function guests made their way inside the gallery for what we later learned were the usual dedicatory speeches. At the time, all we heard was polite applause from inside the gallery.

At about ten minutes to seven, EJ appeared from inside the gallery to pull the exit doors closed. Through the glazed storefront and swinging glass doors, I saw him set his feet, grasp the push bar panic hardware and lean back, thus engaging the outside lock as well as blocking any exit. I do not recall people inside swarming him or anything; I could see a few guests inside come and speak with him, but I could not hear their words. They looked curious more than upset, although shortly, their exasperation at being separated from the outside bar became apparent. The divide, which previously had been manifested by decorated tables and polite staff, was now enforced and reinforced by a young artist, an artist whose face was set in single-minded focus on his chosen task. EJ's demeanor seemed to say, "…I don't understand much about tonight (it's a show of work by grad students, it's a donor event, it's an opportunity to show the community my work, it's the culmination of two years of work, it's a lot of pressure to succeed, it's my life, no it's not, etc.) and I'm conflicted by some of it, but I do recognize this structure of 'us and them' and I do not know where I fit and I can't think why anyone does, and I am going to focus on it and bring attention to it until I have to stop."

Several things happened quickly in sequence—you, Ari, were taking pictures; Adam and I stayed close enough to observe and moved once to gain better access; I watched as Adam checked his watch, and I saw what he was thinking—what would happen at 7:00, the time for the public to enter? Guests inside began to struggle with EJ to open the doors, and by pushing on the panic hardware, their efforts offered those outside (any of us) the chance to pull one of the doors open. In the struggle, some donor guests were able to come out to get wine, and a few from the public used the opportunity of each exit to

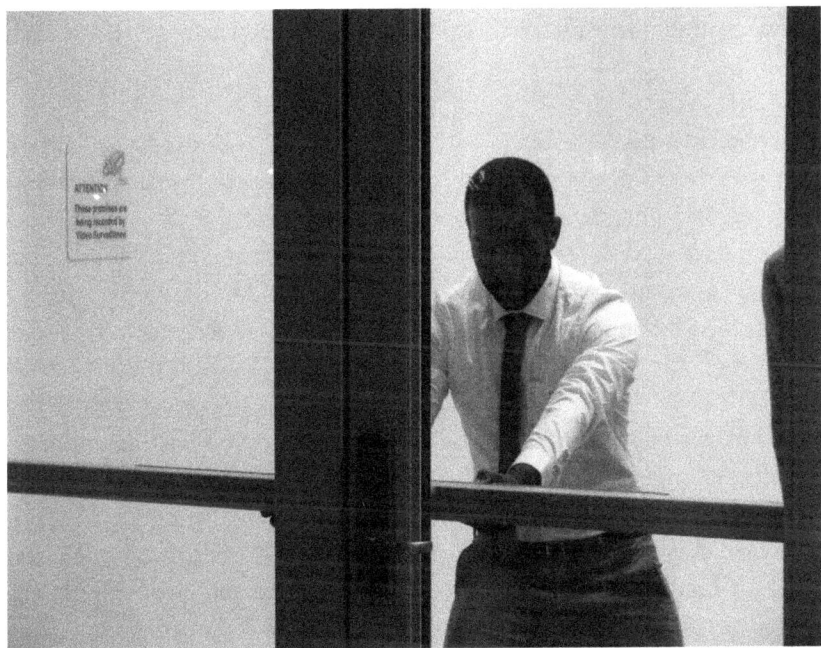

Photo by Ari Marcantonio

enter the gallery; this border was permeable, but to cross had to be uncomfortable and confrontational.

I felt the tension physically and emotionally. After fifteen fraught minutes, a roughly dressed young man carrying a glass of wine and wearing a cast/boot on one foot wedged himself in one side of the doorway just as one of the privileged guests forced their way past EJ; once in place, he used the inertia of his body to brace this door open easily while EJ struggled to regain his hold, leaning at the waist and pulling hard, and all the while attempting to maintain his grip on the other of the two swinging doors. There came a particularly grotesque moment when this human doorstop sipped his white wine over EJ's head and smiled with satisfaction, as though proud of some feat. EJ, with his eyes closed and sweat running down his neck, could not see him, and the scene resembled a tableau vivant of a Daumier cartoon, with some yokel royalist running dog toasting his supremacy over…something. Meanwhile, at several points, faculty had urged us on the outside to wait until the 7:00 public opening, and now, a few minutes after seven, the door that EJ had released in his struggle was held open by a faculty member, and we were invited inside. I think only one person entered, and in my mind we in the public square were unified in not breaking EJ's line. Then, words were exchanged between EJ and the faculty member who held the door, and EJ released his own hold and left the scene.

For fifteen minutes, Adam and I watched the door—out of respect for EJ's performance, out of curiosity, and to converse in place about what we had just seen. We, and others, were still strongly under the spell of recent events. Slowly, the natural waves of the party washed away any remaining intent about the doorway as a barrier; without the college's reinforcement (to keep "commoners" out) and lacking the artist's struggle (to keep the privileged in), it was just a doorway, doing its job.

It was at this point, Ari, or near it, that you returned from gathering photographic documentation and told me of your experience with the entitled man in the wine line. Is it crazy that, as you related this story, I thought of an obituary I read that morning of Letitia Baldrige, a famous etiquette expert? Writer Rebecca Trounson gave a great quote where Baldrige summed up her thinking on social interactions: "More than any hard and fast rules, kindness and consideration are at the heart of good manners. It's thinking about somebody other than yourself. It's being aware of other people and helping them out and not doing anything to offend them and just being nice," she went on, "And it hasn't anything to do with money. It has everything to do with character."[1]

With greater distance from the event, I wonder if your gentleman's experience with EJ's performance was as emotionally charged as ours, but perhaps from the other side? Maybe he felt accused by EJ's underlining of the separation and was on the defensive? I spoke after the performance with a person who was on the inside of the gallery space, inside EJ's performance, and [this person] characterized the artist's performance as hostile, as "a takeover" [of our party]. "It made most of us angry. He didn't do any good for himself." There is a lot present in these comments: that art can make one angry, art can be inconvenient, and that unwilling participants are, well, unwilling. It also seems that the border that EJ was emphasizing, the structure of exclusion, was all but invisible to the privileged side of the party, or was a natural feature of their landscape.

Ari:

The idea of etiquette as the foundation of social interactions is certainly interesting, and I agree that empathy and compassion (kindness and consideration) are cornerstones of civil and respectful human relations, but I disagree that it is necessarily a bad thing, a character flaw, even, to offend someone or make them feel uncomfortable. This idea implies complacency and a lack of accountability from person to person. It suggests that the actions of others are not your business and that it is impolite to take issue with those actions when they strike you as socially insensitive, even destructive.

The fact that EJ's performance "made most of [the people inside the gallery] angry" might be equated in the minds of those people with unsuccessful, distasteful art, but to jump to this conclusion is to deny the potential of art to incite discomfort and disagreement. It is to beg complacency from producers, especially those who are being supported by institutional powers. It is to deny artists the right to critique the systems they operate within, and to deny this right is to deny one of art's most powerful introspective and self-critical tools.

Geoff:
Or not. I agree with the gist of your argument, Ari, but I fear we are putting words in people's mouths so we can argue with them. Indeed, artists must be able to critique the systems in which they operate, and I think it always *is* a struggle. Systems and institutions do not like challenges. I don't find in the quote any suggestion that to cause another person discomfort is a character flaw, merely that to be nice is usually better. In any case, by calling it art, we have moved EJ's interactions out of the social space and into something else, where other rules reign.

I do wonder, though, about his continuing to enforce the structure after the 7 PM public opening. In the moment, I was all with him—I had tears in my eyes and longed for…something, I wasn't sure what. In retrospect, I think the performance became aimless after 7.

Ari:
You mean the exercise began to feel futile? I guess I wonder about the difference or common ground between EJ's performance and political activism. I've spoken to a few '90s anarchists who say that the moment when they chose to stop any given protest was the moment when further participation necessarily precluded a future protest. This way of thinking assumes that people are more useful to the movement on the streets than they are in jail. Do you think that EJ continued his performance to the point that it became directly detrimental to his agency as an artist? Or was your point more of a formal

one—that the work dragged on, to the point that your viewing experience was negatively affected as a result?

What does it mean that EJ's performance lasted exactly as long as the reality of the situation allowed? You wrote (remember, I was in the back when the performance ended) "the door that EJ had released in his struggle was held open" and "EJ released his hold and left the scene." Did EJ begin to realize that his efforts were physically futile? That he could not recover from the bait-and-switch he had stepped into? The performance was not planned beyond a few primary intentions, and the ending was always up in the air. At Parkfield, EJ told me that he would continue the performance until it felt "insincere." I was not sure what this meant when he said it, and now I find it even more ambiguous. Did EJ feel insincere? Did he feel those around him were insincere? The gentleman propping the door open? If there was an impetus for the end of the performance, what could it have been?

Geoff:
Tell me, Ari, what does it mean to *you* that the "performance lasted as long as the reality of the situation allowed"?

Ari:
It is an interesting point to consider, as EJ really did relinquish a sizeable amount of control over his work. There was not a narrative trajectory that the piece intended to follow other than it will last as long as it will last. This comes in stark contrast to more formal performance art, which often defines for itself a start time, an end time, and often an expected duration, all of which are formalities that make it easier for viewers to consume the work and plan ahead. EJ offered none of this pragmatic information. It was not even clear to most people that a performance was going to occur, and thus, when the work began, there was a great deal of confusion. Was this person just being totally socially awkward? Were they having a nervous breakdown in a most formal and inappropriate location? I think that by asking viewers to parse through the potential origins or definitions of what they are witnessing, artists can disrupt conventional ways of understanding art. This work was not prefaced by the rapidly hushing crowd, brief remarks or other common formalities that tend to introduce performance art while simultaneously framing it in the alternate reality of art. Viewers were not primed with the suspended reality of "an art-viewing experience" that often allows us critical distance in decipher-

ing meaning, but rather were thrown head first into an unlikely scenario that is framed not by the supposed objectivity of a gallery but by the insistent subjectivity of our shared present.

Geoff:
But then, was his a fight for "the people"? This, which was my emotional understanding of the performance in the moment of it, seems inaccurate now.

Ari:
It seems to me that the performance was never a fight for anyone in particular but just a call to notice the structure we were/are participating in. It is so easy to take for granted the way things work, the social barriers that have and will forever exist, but EJ did not let anyone off that easy. If he was fighting for anything, it was recognition of a social reality.

Geoff:
Ah, indeed. Yet I still feel a lack to his effort, or to the success of it as art. By not completing his response to the structure, the border, the division between us and them, EJ's action might be relying upon the sensational nature of his act. This moment is where, in conversation with David while editing an earlier version of this document, I talked myself closer and closer to and inexorably smack *into* the recognition that what really bugged me about EJ's performance might be, probably is, that after 7:00 he made me feel like one of the people on the *inside*. My commonality with them was as one inconvenienced. I became crabby about *my* loss of agency. I begin to understand *really* that the focus of EJ's performance was the border itself, and not the people on either side of it; therefore, continuing his performance was necessary. His actions did not judge the border, they drew attention to it. The division might be said to have remained despite the border being made permeable. Nah. Thanks, EJ.

In the days after the performance, as I related my experience to David and we discussed it again and again, he brought up Luis Buñuel's film *The Discreet Charm of the Bourgeoisie*, in which wealthy, entitled characters suffer a series of denials of what they see as their right: pleasure, social ease, food, access, etc., do you know it? It provides a remarkable parable for EJ's enigmatic performance at the Broad Center last weekend.

Ari:

You are right, the film seems to be invested in a very similar critique, and is totally bizarre, funny and great. I guess the difference for me is that EJ is directly implicated in the group he is "denying." He would not be able to perform this piece at all were it not for the event, and this complicates the story for me. This complication raises questions about support in a slightly different regard. The people who come to this preview event are potentially supporting EJ's practice with direct economic funding, but they are also necessitating a specific context for his work (although it is initiative on the part of EJ that realizes it as such). This poses a more tangled web of interdependency. I wonder, then, how the people at this event benefit from their involvement, if at all. Is it possible that other forms of currency are being exchanged from artist to donor? What cultural or social value is gained by participating in such an event?

In *The Discrete Charm*, in the dream sequence nested within another dream sequence that culminates in the Colonel's dinner party, the ambassador to the (fictitious) country of Miranda is questioned by several guests regarding social issues in the country, questions regarding poverty, unrest, homicide, etc…. After each question, the ambassador assures the questioner that the allegation is false and excuses himself, only to be approached by another guest with another question. The ambassador rapidly determines that he does not belong at this dinner party.

Woman: "You have some student unrest."

Ambassador: "Students are young. They need to have some fun."

Woman: "What is your government's policy?

Ambassador: "We're not anti-student, you know. On the contrary. But what do you do if your room is swarming with flies?"

The ambassador's attitude indicates a kind of administrative denial of turbulence. He assures everyone that there are no issues, yet he keeps receiving questions of concern. It is in the ambassador's best interests to pretend that everything is running smoothly, to deny reality and insist that there are no problems for anyone.

We haven't really touched on the greater political and economic climate that this performance occurred in, days before the election in which Proposition

30 would be voted on, the first major move in California to reform taxation since the 1978 Proposition 13 slowly but surely drained the state of property taxes. Proposition 30 is a huge accomplishment for education in this state; had it not passed, the tuition at UCLA (I cannot speak surely of any other UC) would have gone up by 15% this spring with another increase of 10% this coming fall. Does this performance draw attention to the increasing privatization of the supposedly still public education system in CA? I should be clear, I am not taking a jab at the faculty or administration for bringing in private donors; I am pointing to a somewhat frightening impetus for increasing private support of a public institution and to the potentially related shift in value structures of this country as a whole.

Geoff:
Hmm. And so we come to policy, the place where, like love, money and religion, no person seems reasonable to another. You mention specifically Props 30 and 13. Prop 30 is the first time I have voted to directly raise a tax, and given that it passed pretty easily, I think other fiscally conservative Californians joined me. Let's leave Prop 13 aside, as it is history. I mention my vote only to indicate how dire I find the situation of our schools, not to indicate that I am particularly in favor of singling out wealthy people for higher taxes. I also voted for Prop 38. I offer this as my opinion, and I have no interest in debating the subject here, where it bears little on the matter at hand.

I don't expect that passage of 30 will resolve anything much, but it buys breathing room, and this breathing room may allow serious people in the legislature (my fingers are crossed), in neighborhoods and school districts and at dinner tables, to talk and debate and to work, because I do think we all want a relatively inexpensive post–K-12 education that is open to everyone. (Rant alert: And I *do* mean everyone. Every person who wishes, any immigrant, any queer, any religious person—no matter how they dress—sluts, virgins, whatever. Learning is good for everybody.) This access is the standard I think we seek and is the presumed past to which we wish to return.

But there is much to get clear, and I risk straying further outside our conversation. I will be brief, then, and not tarry much longer. Among many subjects to be discussed is one that several writers, in *The New Yorker* and elsewhere, have documented: the exponential rise in administrative costs at private and at public colleges and universities—wtf?; also deserving of discussion is whether high schools should be priming and encouraging *every student* to undertake a college education. There are many alternatives, and I don't know that college is always preferable; it may even frustrate the ambitions of a person who would rather pursue another form of study—apprenticeship and technical training are two alternatives. There is also, in recent history, the practice of guaranteeing loans to college students. It seems that this has simply enslaved, now, two generations of students to increasingly overwhelming debts, and it has probably led to the growth of administrative costs mentioned above, with resulting increases in student and taxpayer costs. Whither the sad students? I suspect educational institutions know that, while people will argue with them about spending money for new classes and teachers, nobody will ever question the need for more bureaucrats.

Returning to our thread: the debate, or struggle, between public and private is the American story, or the story we're engaged in now, and I think what I am hearing from you, Ari, is your expression of a fear—which I share—that private dollars will have a chilling effect on freedom of expression and on freedom of research. EJ's performance certainly pushed buttons with the faculty at the event, I was witness to this; and this is the problem, isn't it? Schools are places where one should be allowed to be wrong, to make mistakes, and to offend— one should even be encouraged to do so! College is a place where the free spirit of a child is matched with the intelligence of growing adulthood. Without open space for expression and in which to learn, one might just as well be out in the "real world," punching the clock and paying the piper. Current trends toward professionalization notwithstanding, education is for learning about the world and growing into it; education is not about a career. Unless you want a really sad life where you only know one thing and you lack critical thinking. Hah. And then you're just fodder.

Geoff:

At UCLA, in the New Wight Gallery, the *MFA 2013 Exhibition* continues through Saturday, November 17. In this exhibition, you will find the work of 17 soon-to-be grads. These include Jonathan Apgar, Leon Benn, Lucas Blalock, A'alia Marilyn Brown, Martin Elder, Brennan Gerard and Ryan Kelly, EJ Hill, Janna Ireland, Michael John Kelly, Devin Kenny, Hans Kuzmich, Dylan Mira, Gerardo Monterrubio, Katie Sinnott, Christine Wang and David Fisk Whitaker. At the back of the gallery and to the left hang, or were hanging, two empty white picture frames; these have glass or plexi in them to protect future photographs that will document EJ Hill's performance at the exhibition's Thursday, November 1 opening reception. I'm guessing that the frames will be filled by the time I visit later this week, and I encourage you also to visit the gallery to see the work of each of these artists, these students. It's a trip worth making.

The gallery is at 1100 Broad Art Center on the UCLA campus, and parking is close by—just south of Sunset on the west side of Hilgard. The New Wight Gallery is open Monday through Friday, 9:00 AM to 4:30 PM, and on Saturday from 10:00 AM to 6:00 PM.

[1]Rebecca Trounson, Los Angeles Times, November 1, 2012

Published on November 12, 2012 by Geoff Tuck and Ari Marcantonio in Reviews

THINKING OF THE NIGHT
a poem for Andrew Berardini, Michael Dopp, Mieke Marple and Davida Nemeroff

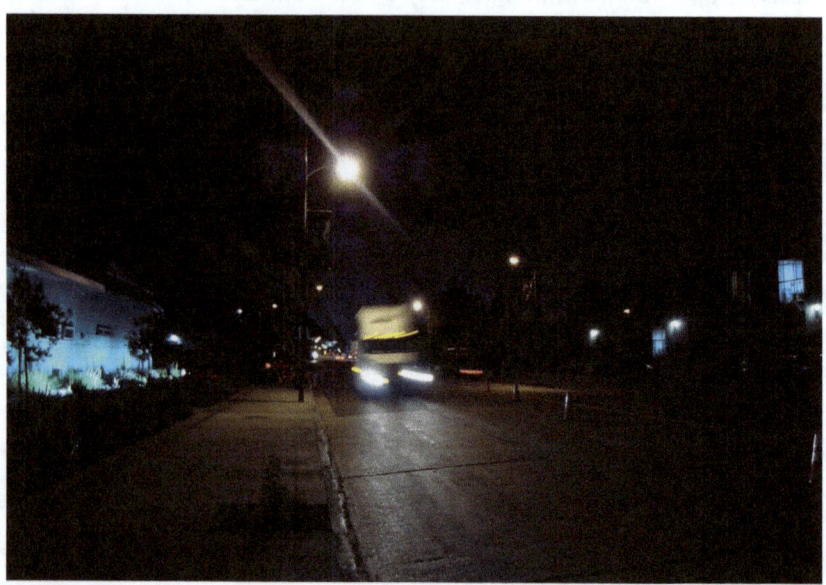

At Night Gallery the air is unsettled

when I leave and the wind

catches my face

in the car. It blows hot and cold (lord, we're not yet into November)

and

"…there may be a come-down" and "the Supreme Court and the recent decision" and "revolution is ugly but it's another man's civil war"

opined our local young sage of political discourse at his polemical best,

earlier, when the night still was not young.

And two gentlemen, one being me, did not discuss beer and pasta and men in grey suits and jazz and Ethiopia in Swahili for twenty minutes,

and the hoodie that he wore in Delhi, and the jagged road and the jolting, pissing ride with goats and the belt that he pounded with a stone, shown to me—he shone—as they all do in my eyes, these people of the Night.

And after 2:00 AM, those who are left have work in the show or work for the show

or have nothing but their need to display and their shiny corded heavy woolen clothes and their loud words and pretentious tiresome phrases and they just won't

leave.

(for Andrew and Davida and Michael and Mieke) Geoff Tuck, 3:40 AM, October 12, 2011

Published on October 12, 2011 by Geoff Tuck in Wanderings

EJ HILL AT UCLA OPEN STUDIOS

Sometimes when I am looking, the space between the work of art and me is too close to get any distance necessary for representation. Photography fails me, or, rather, my impulse to photograph the work disappears in the intensity of my experience.

Saturday at the UCLA Open Studios I watched—rapt, worried, teary eyed, wincing, clenching, and generally in awe—as EJ Hill crawled around the Center Bay gallery space with his tongue pressed against the wall. I think that he probably was caressing the wall in strokes with his tongue, rather than applying constant pressure. I know that at first he left a trail of saliva, which quickly dried and became indistinguishable on the painted drywall. Within a few yards of his start, at the second wall, EJ's trail of saliva was tinged with blood, and over the course of the 200 or so feet of gallery wall, blood became more and more the thing that the artist left behind.

I watched as Hill stopped and gathered himself to continue. I imagined that he was attempting to generate spit. I imagined that these attempts at salivating failed to lubricate his path. I wondered whether he had counted on bleeding, and I thought about marking one's territory with spit and then blood. How quietly animal-like and crude. How confident. How disgusting. How good.

In the context of an art exhibition, where EJ Hill's peers were showing paintings and sculptures, I found it wonderfully aggressive that Hill would abase himself by crawling on the floor, licking and bleeding and underlining his superiority by leaving permanent marks of his own body throughout the exhibition. He certainly stole my gaze from anything else.

In my brief look at Hill's other work, in the studio and on his website, I find that Hill often uses his mouth as a place of communication beyond words. In the performance Saturday night, Hill made his mouth the aggressor and the thing that was acted upon; he used strong language with no words. Hill's performance has left me wondering, "Why?" and, "Was this a self-aggrandizing endurance piece?" and, "Wow, I can't wait to see what else this artist does."

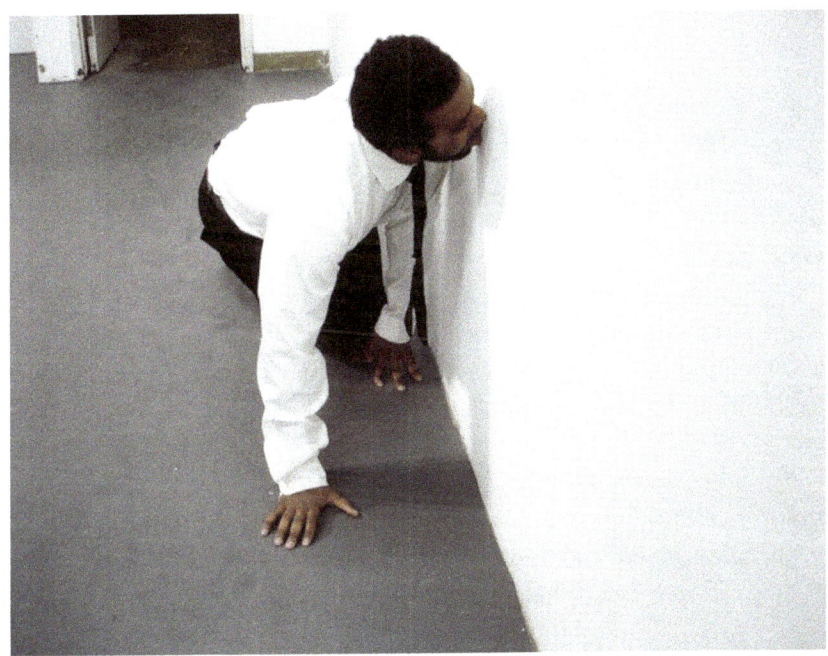

Photo by Matt Austin

Published on December 12, 2011 by Geoff Tuck in Reviews

THE BODY AS A SITE OF POLITICAL STRUGGLE
an exchange with Asher Hartman

Geoff Tuck:

Can you tell me about the importance of gender issues to your work? Looking at the history of your performances, I see that gender, identity, differencing, and the action/reaction of a more gender-normative larger culture have all been concerns since the beginnings of your work as an artist.

I have often observed (and then wondered whether I am really observing, or simply projecting) that the differencing experienced by queers has corollaries in our hetero friends and neighbors. I tell myself that this is a way that straight people can access work that deals with queer issues.

Does this resonate at all with you?

Asher Hartman:

I think gender has always been a concern, although I've never tried to make it one, but given that I am trans, it arises, and will probably always arise as a reflection of whom I am. I experience life as someone who is queer and transgender and different. I see through that lens. Yet, in some way, I'm not particularly interested in narrowly focusing on the avenue of my experience, with some exceptions. Indeed, there are major corollaries away from the specificities of queerness into difference along lines of race, nationality, culture, the trials of prescribed femininity and masculinity, and so on. I think what I'm most interested in are the ways in which Western cultures and ideologies affect the construction of self; how we fashion behavior, movement, speech, even facial gesture and, of course ideals, under the aegis of these systems; how willingly we do this, and not unconsciously. But I have a long, long way to go to really explore this. Still, I imagine that some of the fundamental political quagmires we find ourselves in on the left come from the inability to let go of the basic tenets of capitalism, for example, as they are lodged in the body and lodged at the body. Perhaps because of who I am and who my friends are, I see the body as the site of political struggle, the basic unit of struggle, and I would like to really explore what this is.

Geoff:
In my initial email conversation with Brian about plans for the performance series and publication titled *Native Strategies* and about the program that will be at LACE, *So Funny It Hurts* he used a nice quote:

"Start with something you oppose.

Move towards it."

And he continued with,

"Satire is a ferocious drag in which the artist infiltrates enemy lines by masking him or herself in the skins and uniforms of the enemy. [...] This grand finale is intended as a punishing humiliation delivered to an enemy that mistook parody for sympathy. But what of artists who feel no such objective superiority to their enemy? Artists who work closely with any material inevitably develop an empathetic understanding of that material."

I have an understanding that Brian was speaking from his own background and of this entire project, and not stating his or your wishes for thinking about your own piece in the performance series. That said, how does your piece address the notion of opposition through empathy and understanding? Or, perhaps a more open query—tell me a little about your practice and how it draws on an understanding of what you oppose to then explore "the opposed" with an audience. Also, can you see an opportunity for a member of this "opposition" to find in your work a place of understanding that might make them feel safe enough to go a step further and then question, as you question, their own world view?

Asher:
Well, I wish that my work was evolved enough to really allow in members of the "opposition" through empathy and understanding. That being said, one part of my practice, my intuitive practice, is meant to do exactly that, to teach the use of intuition as a tool of acknowledgment in face-to-face contact with another human being. It's very much geared to helping people see each other energetically, and I would love to use it in situations where people in opposition are in direct contact with one another. In that sense, there are no members of the opposition to play with or against, only the possibility of grasping the essence of a human being beyond the usual flawed means.

But my theatrical practice is a little looser and riskier, I think. It's really meant to let in all comers, all possible reactions, and sometimes the audience itself is the opposition. I think we are almost a little too comfortable as audiences, especially in theatrical settings where we may think of ourselves as "The Customer" who must be entertained and satisfied. Until recently, my work seemed to challenge that inside a kind of homemade spectacle, sometimes by pushing people past their emotional limits. To be honest, I just tried to think of performance theater in a lot of ways, trying to serve the subject matter at hand in the manner that seemed right. Now, I really want to work with the tropes of entertainments, examining their structures, how they succeed, and to take out the substance, the actual entertainment material, like narrative for example, and replace it with layered and complex ideas the audience can further complicate by making meaning, or not.

Geoff:
I want to make sure to ask about your plans for the show. In an earlier conversation, you talked about 1970s comedians/actors/performers like Paul Lynde, Wayland and Madame, Leonard Frey, Rip Taylor and more who are escaping me just now. I love your plan to mine their physical language—the gestures they used—and to marry them with the angry and maybe violent words of your characters. Can you expand on this a little?

Asher:
I'm starting with a base of Paul Lynde, Wayland and Madame, Barclay Shaw, and Charles Nelson Reilly—not them so much as their gestures, as you say, their essence, because I'm interested in them as icons, as those who inspire, whose fierceness and rage is, as you suggest, transmitted in gestures that are repressed, or controlled, or stylized. They are in my view sometimes cultivated as expressions of nonchalance, defensiveness, intellectual strength; in effect, aspects of personality created for consumption.

Geoff:
Do you think that the actions and even the words these performers used do in fact contain and transmit a great deal of fury? I mean fury at their circumstance of being queer in a world that rejected queerness.

Asher:
Absolutely.

Geoff:
The manner of their performance style is really drawn from the queer culture at large back in that day: fierce, demanding, and outrageous sometimes, conservative at others, but always acting with the understanding that their code must protect them as much as reveal them.

Asher:
Yes.

Geoff:
Can you give us an idea of the influence on you these actors who embodied "the other" to a past generation might have had? They must have inspired and influenced you and your own practice, yes?

Asher:
You know, watching Paul Lynde, there was a faint recognition in me as a youth. This guy was somehow different than other men, somehow more accessible, more like me. And of course I watched him on *Bewitched*, where he was magical, and not particularly nice. He had a kind of freedom and power that I didn't have, but since he was "like me" in some then-unfathomable way, by extension, he gave me freedom. He operated as the more powerful, less obedient me. I think it's the same with the other actors. That same faint, inarticulable sense that the person was like me and subversively powerful felt liberating, although of course I wouldn't have used those words.

I was totally infatuated with Leonard Frey, the actor who plays Harold in *Boys in The Band* and, in an opposite pitch, Motel the Tailor in *Fiddler on The Roof*. I'm not sure what it was about him, that he was apparently Jewish, self-described in the *Boys* as ugly, and glorious in his contempt for everyone, especially his best friend. I think I loved his defiance; his existence was defiance. But this was also true of straight male white actors like Peter Falk, for example. I was entranced by him in *Columbo*, as a kid: his raincoat, his guise of idiocy—he made me somehow into the other. I was aware that I was like him and not him. He was accessible and foreign, "in" as a white male and "out" as a working cop, not apparently elite in intellect, and yet in fact superior to the idealized classes. I think that's why he had such a wide appeal as an "everyman."

Geoff:

If gesture and physical expression can be embedded in culture and expressive of capitalist imperatives, and "normal" social behaviors are taught the way body language is mimicked from generation to generation, do you think that the queer gestures and structures of the entertainment world might in fact date to some sort of queer originators whose actions were, over time, embedded in the physical language of theater?

Asher:

Oh, this is a great question I don't have the answer to. Someone must! I wonder if it does come out of theater and some aesthetic, as in Wilde's *Salomé*, or in some bodily codes to identify one another, and of course I'm making gross, gross assumption and casting all queerness in the same light, which I understand is really tenuous. But queer theater, I mean, there may be commonalities of taste, of interest, among some groups who were successful and spread those ideas through that popular or artistic success. To be honest, I don't know, but it's very interesting to think about.

Geoff:

Earlier, you admitted that while gender issues are not the focus of your interest in art making, they do keep coming up. Why do you think this is?

Asher:

Oh, I think you are asking better questions than I have answers. I do think it's interesting that someone who keeps making queer work (a.k.a. me) doesn't really want to make queer work, but can't get away from it. To me, that speaks to some almost innate connection, some ingrained, even bodily coupling with this work that comes right out of simply being queer and growing up seeing queer, lesbian, gay, trans and bi people make art on a regular basis, out or not. I certainly had never heard of queer anything until high school and by that time had already been bathed in this sort of entertainment. *I Dream of Jean-*

nie? Come on. *Gilligan's Island* could not be more queer. And *Bewitched* was like queer kid religious training.

Geoff:
I have one final question, about geography. Can you talk about your practice in relation to this city we all share, Los Angeles?

Asher:
I came to L.A. to go to UCLA, and I've been here a long time. Right now, L.A. is a great place to work. Artists are open to all kinds of work; there's a real interest in each other's work, and a general friendliness among the different communities in which there's a lot of overlap. I think artist spaces like Sea and Space Explorations, founded and directed by Lara Bank; Mark Allen's project Machine Project; Monte Vista Projects; Pieter; Outpost; Telic; the wulf.; Echo Curio; and many others have been responsible for a change in ideology, in possibility. These are imaginative, open-ended, welcoming places that seem to think that artists are the most well positioned to develop the dialogue, so to speak. I see museums and non-profits like LACE taking a cue from the wealth of ideas and momentum of the artists here and in turn behaving as if they are also in dialogue with these communities. When I first started making art, the feeling was that the critics and dealers were in charge of the dialogue and that the artists waited for direction. I might be biased, but that doesn't seem to be so much the case at the present. This kind of freedom means that I can make art here, really. I think it's very difficult for someone who does what I do to exist in a strictly market-driven art world. I don't think I had a need to make art here at all until I met the artists who are my community at present. In fact, I was very much interested in leaving. But now, I think there's so much to do here, and so much flexibility—you can leave and come back, for instance—that it seems the very best place to make art. I think the city is also incredibly welcoming to artists from elsewhere—since almost everyone is from somewhere else.

Performance-based work is hard to maintain, especially work like mine, that's not performance art and not proper theater. It really almost has no place except the place I make for it. I think that what's also nice about L.A. is that there is still space here. There are pockets of places in which a person can work and invite people to see the work. I also have a great, I should say incredible, group of performers I have the privilege to work with, and they're here. I am hoping to establish a company, a regular group who work with one another consistently. I don't know if I could do that anywhere else now. I think we've established a trust, a working method, and a sense of collaboration that's hard to find anywhere.

Lastly, I have to say, L.A. is funny. You really have to have a sense of humor to live here, because the city is made of so many different types of people who get into each other's salads, if you will. And because of that, you find all kinds of odd behavior and circumstances, alongside tragic circumstances, such as any you'd find in a city. Its metropolitan nature, the great diversity of cultures, all of this is terribly important to me. I don't think I could live in a city that wasn't diverse and didn't have a sense of the absurd.

I'm glad you asked these questions, because come to think of it, I think this must be one of the best places in the world to be making art at the moment, and I'm glad I'm here. I have the best friends in the world. We help each other; we get along; we support one another. What more can you ask?

Published on March 20, 2011 by Geoff Tuck in Interviews and Conversations

BLANK CANVASES AND CLAIRE DE LUNE
an exchange with Jonathon Hornedo

(Find Django Reinhardt recordings on whatever file sharing you use, and listen, beginning with Claire de Lune.*)*

I called from the street at 10:05 AM. In my dyslexic way, I mistook 1952 for an odd number, and so I was looking on the wrong side of Clinton for Jonathon Hornedo's gallery/studio. Hornedo answered fairly quickly, and after some confusion, he met me at the grille-covered door. He wore a dress jacket, a polo shirt and a pair of worn corduroy trousers—urbane and gracious, he was ready to discuss the intellectual properties of art objects, his fondness for jazz, the local bar scene, and the current exhibition in his skylit basement rooms.

Using his hands as well as his voice—in fact, moving dramatically as though on stage—Hornedo led me from painting to painting, offering insights into the work, skillfully leading me to ask questions and generally representing his artists with dry wit and passion. When his performance became mannered, as in such situations with professional dealers it sometimes does, it seemed that my guide recognized this, for with a self-deprecating laugh, he waved his hand as though to sweep away dust and turned the conversation to his project of being an artist playing a dealer.

The panels themselves were quite well made. I found none of the bunched layers of canvas at the corners that appear in paintings of lesser quality. The canvas was tight against the panel, and the lines were sharp, not rounded, and not fat. The hand-made canvas *Set For Jazz Trio*—made to accommodate an impromptu concert played at the opening—was also well finished and interesting. It had a pre-Modern, Constructivist feel, and—as with the show—no one part intruded into the whole.

"Seamless, yet full of evidence" is a phrase that comes to mind when I think of the show and the larger project. Perhaps if I share our exchange—the artist's and mine—it will elucidate my statement.

Photo by Jonathon Hornedo

Hi Geoff,
Yeah, I liked our little chat too. I don't know how I managed it, because I had just awoken upon your arrival. A fine example of my professionalism.

Thanks for your analysis and questions about this project! It feels like you have a very clear sense of what this show can suggest beyond my "explain-all" press releases.

Yes, I replicated an aspect of the art world. It's a world I have come to know a bit about after interning professionally at art galleries for the past two years.

The "seriousness" of the project is merely my brand of dry humor laced with parody. Why are comedies so lacking in the art world? Art is hilarious! Humor, I think, even when presented with a straight poker face, is a highly potent and efficient form of communication. What I learned in organizing this project was how to use humor skillfully.

Your analysis regarding the folkways of our community is accurate. At every moment while organizing the show, and throughout its run, I snuck in small, almost subliminal details that would further suggest the stage, the fiction, the theatricality of the entire enterprise. Those details had to make me laugh, at least a little, to justify my use of them. I even hired an assistant! She barely spoke English, and her presence (and her mistakes!) also rounded out the self-reflexive (*Through the Looking Glass*) aura during the opening reception.

Delegating the burden felt great, as cashing checks always does. Does a blank canvas demand respect? Only when it's made with the finest materials and craftsmanship.

The burden I spoke of is a significant point of interest for me. I can't answer it fully here. But if we combine the "burden" with "support"….

Thinking about this show in terms of what my "job" is, or role, feels appropriate because the whole enterprise was predicated on being laid off. So although the show is centered around art world relations, it's also about economics and being unemployed in 2012.

My role in this project shifted with each phase. Although I'm always the "artist," I'm also a method actor who learns his role on set. Like a method actor playing a method actor in a movie. I played the craftsman, the gallerist, the art dealer (I sold John's painting the other day!). My on-the-job training happened live. I'm not really an art dealer, but I had to do it. For the opening in Part 1, my job description consolidated into craftsman-artist-dealer. In Part 2, I'm more of the dealer, which is why I decided to recede into the background a bit, giving the individual artists the attention, being supportive to their needs and schedules to get the show together on time.

And sure, we can combine whatever "gallery support" and "painting support" connote. Sounds juicy.

I don't have a statement. I stopped writing artist statements a year ago, but feel free to use the content of this email however you want.

Let me know if you have further questions.

Can you remind me when our next appointment was? Was it this Wednesday?

Best,
Jonathon

Previously:

Dear Jonathon,

Thanks again for meeting with me—I really enjoyed our conversation! Will you send me images of the work? I do have the checklist and press release(s) already. I am pleased that Karisa Morante's painting has sold—congratulations! I also appreciate that you noted this fact in red ink on the checklist. Everything is like a *Through the Looking Glass* duplicate of the art world. This is part of your thinking, isn't it? To replicate yet make different? Somehow, the seriousness with which your project re-enacts art world commerce and relations makes clear to me how much the folkways of our community (being in this case the mercantile art world) are false, or at the very least are shared presumptions that have no purpose beyond reinforcement of their own existence (and the profit of the elites whom they serve).

In the initial PR for the Blank Canvas show, you talk about "delegating the creative burden onto (your) collectors." How did this feel? Everyone took your burden very seriously, and evidently, they each adopted it for their own. Is there something about a blank canvas that demands respect? Is this the burden of which you spoke? You mentioned to me being pleased that several of the artists chose to leave plain canvas as part of the work; you took this to be acknowledging your joint authorship, I imagine.

Reading now the PR for *Canvas Panels: Part II*, you announce that the show "belongs to them now, not to me." speaking of your collectors. So although you claim the creative authorship of *Blank Canvas Part I* panels, during either the purchase or as your collectors painted, ownership and authorship was transferred to them, hence your listing on the checklist of artists names and not your own. So is your *making* still present but subsumed underneath these other creative agents? Does this make you the support? Or your work, perhaps? Or (your) artistic "genius" (that being the mystical energy that an artist places in the work)? Haha, after all the years of artists making work about the "support" in paintings, I do not know an example such as this.

I am looking forward to talking with you again next week.

Please send those photos if you can, and if you respond to my questions I will be thrilled. In fact, if you have anything you'd like people to know, or would like to issue as a statement, please let me know!

All my best,
Geoff

Published on August 28, 2012 by Geoff Tuck in Interviews and Conversations, Reviews

SO FUNNY IT HURTS: ASHER HARTMAN WITH CURT LEMIEUX

LACE was crowded for this event. We arrived just as Brian Getnick was introducing the artists. It seemed like an interestingly varied crowd—art people I recognized, some people whom I imagined to be fans of Hartman; I know that LouAnne Greenwald and her class of USC undergrads from the Cultural Studies program were in attendance—so it was a good mix for a performance. Some were believers, some were people open to an experience, and all of us spent our time trying to grapple with the odd experience that performance presents.

Getnick warned us to "stay three or four feet away from the performers—for your protection as much as theirs," but that we were to "Get up, don't sit. Move around the performance, see it from all sides!" Many people did just this, as the costumed actors performed in a circular space amidst the audience. They were dressed kind of burlesque-ey, maybe, old-style "Hollywood Entertainer" suits. These suits were wearable sculpture by collaborator Curt LeMieux, some with feathers and some with wooden placards on their backs. At first, I eased into a "watching the acting" mode—this is kind of defense for me, I think. It makes it easy when I can tag something in my head—this way I feel able to—oh dear, this is a horrible admission to make—control the experience. Carol Stakenas put it well, after the show in conversation with me and front gallery muralist (and coincidentally, also a grad student at UCR) Nick Lowe (hugely paraphrasing here): *"I was tempted into watching the performance and felt like I could choose my understanding of what the actors were doing. But then it picked me up like a kitten, by the back of my neck, and then it dropped me into another reality. This is the thing about performance—sometimes you recognize what's going on and expect it to continue but, being human and active, performance surprises you in real time. In its time, I guess I mean, not in mine or yours."*

Hmm. So can you describe this performance for us, Geoff? Ouch. I am trying now. I'm vaguely recalling individual lines: "Straights are the marksmen of (our) perversity" and "Did you hear the one about the fag magician who disappeared in a poof of smoke?" "Where's the rage? Where's the anger? What's the point?!" "You're the most famous fairy in the world, Paul (Lynde). How do you describe yourself?" To which Lynde replied, in his most queer, affected and drawn-out vocal manner, "Huuummm-b-lllle."

Have I mentioned bitterness? Have I mentioned being alone, in a bar, in a bus station, on the street—before the days of free outness, prior to "Gay Pride," when one would stare longingly at men, never sure—always a little afraid and ashamed because you knew that when you approached one, sure they might let you blow them but as one character stated, "They'll make you pay for it." Each of these fruited dramas were played last night, for laughs and for moments of startled recognition.

It was funny to be taken back there. I sort of thought that was all gone from my life. Sometimes during the action, I laughed so hard I peed my pants, and pretty often I also cried.

(This peeing part is not simply a Julia Roberts quote—it's an effect of a prostatectomy. No big deal, life happens and we move on. But if you want a takeaway—and who wouldn't after this opening?—any of you gentlemen out there who are frustrated with that other rather famously commercialized post-operative dysfunction: don't use the pills and shots. You know, the drugs that begin with "V" and "C." Use a pump. I swear on a stack of now useless condoms. The pump is fun. Everybody involved gets to…take a hand, so to speak. And who wants to put another expensive and creepy drug in one's body? Ask a doctor. If you're shy, hell—I'm obviously not! Ask me where to get one. Cheers.)

Seeing the crowd around me reacting, becoming engaged and enlivened, I was also forced to think to myself, "Well, Geoff. All these people are getting this. We in this room are all invested in the public action, this purgative dance. Did you think it was just you? Do you really believe this *difference* crap? Can you imagine that because *you lived in a different time* and because you are queer that your life is inherently, essentially *other* than these other people who are watching? Good lord, most of them are younger and many are straight. Or even trans, or simply decline to state.

"Difference is *us*, Geoff. All of us. " (This I learned tonight, this I needed to hear. Thanks, Asher.)

Tonight's "So Funny It Hurts" was a magnificent performance. The structure of the event was anecdotal, yes—but I think perhaps that was true to the experiences being enacted: queer men living from trick to trick and seeking fame instead of…whatever else life may have withheld. These lives *were* anecdotal; these men were *performers* on stage and off. They never went home. And at the end, a later generation—several later generations, in fact—have tagged them as "liars" and "embarrassments" and cried out with exasperation (and shame) "Don't call me Mary, you old fag!"

What's the point?

Published on April 7, 2011 by Geoff Tuck in Miscellaneous

DEAR ADAM. ON THE FIRST DAY OF TO THE LIGHTHOUSE

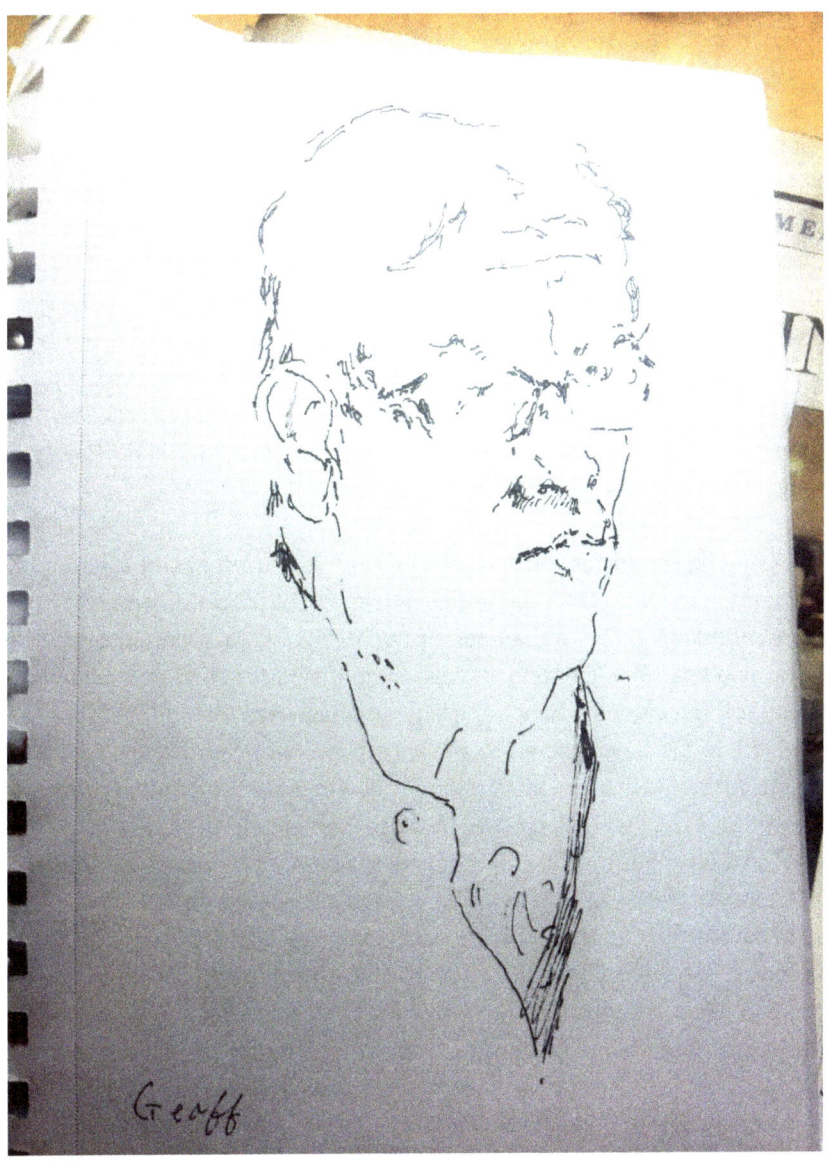

Geoff Tuck by Andy Robert

Dear Adam,

I'm happy that you are in Germany pursuing your engagements within and outside pedagogies, but it really sucks that you were not at the opening! I and we missed you. Visitors were very curious about "What did Adam put in the show? Where is his work?!" I would sort of chuckle and reply, "Well, it's in his CV, with the others." When I returned to the space this week with Andy Robert (about which, more later) I noticed that alone among the printed CVs, yours was lifted. Some eager fan, not understanding that the art of your practice is in the experience rather than the object, must now imagine they hold a precious artwork. I'm laughing because we both know that a studio visit would be more the work of art than a printed paper representing your practice.

Ah, but about that sparkle in your eye that we all missed at the opening on Saturday—despite my best attempts to mythologize you, Adam, as pure intellect walking, when we finally met and talked, you laughed and made jokes and, well, I recognize once again my foolish need to find ease of relating and safety in myth. If I can tag a person I can contain them in my mind. (Have you ever read Madeleine L'Engle's *A Wrinkle in Time?*)

The painting I made for you and gave you before you left has an eye, roughly painted on the verso of a paper towel that droops from the top and hangs over and hangs down. A marriage of two paintings via an intuitive gesture of ripping apart one painting and attaching the parts in other ways to other paintings. The eye was chance, the labyrinth below it also, but together it felt like you. In the days before the show, that eye became a fixation to me (It stands for so much in my life!), as did a need to make more Adam paintings. My thoughts of you boiled down in those moments to the eye as observer. Hmm, observing is a subtle form of action, Adam, and I believe the subjects of your percipience would do well to understand observation as active. There is, of course, the notion of awareness of being observed and how it may alter behavior, see Schrödinger and more, but beyond or in addition to that, looking also directs attention. The conversations that accompany your looking investigate these points of attention, sometimes exhaustively—you are noted for your supply of energy when it comes to looking, talking and asking—and because these are conversations, studio visits, etc., your observation becomes a shared experience. But even understanding you as I do, you remain enigmatic, Adam.

I made two more paintings with rough eye shapes and titled them with reference to you. They act as surrogates for your presence in my work for the show.

I met yesterday with Andy Robert, who I understand you know. Andy and I became acquainted at Human Resources when I visited Helga Fassonaki's exhibition. Andy and I chattered about his projects, about Helga's show in the gallery, and then I scraped myself and bled a bit everywhere. It was unnerving, but Andy handled it like a trooper and grabbed paper towels to clean up. There's nothing like spilled blood to make fast friends!

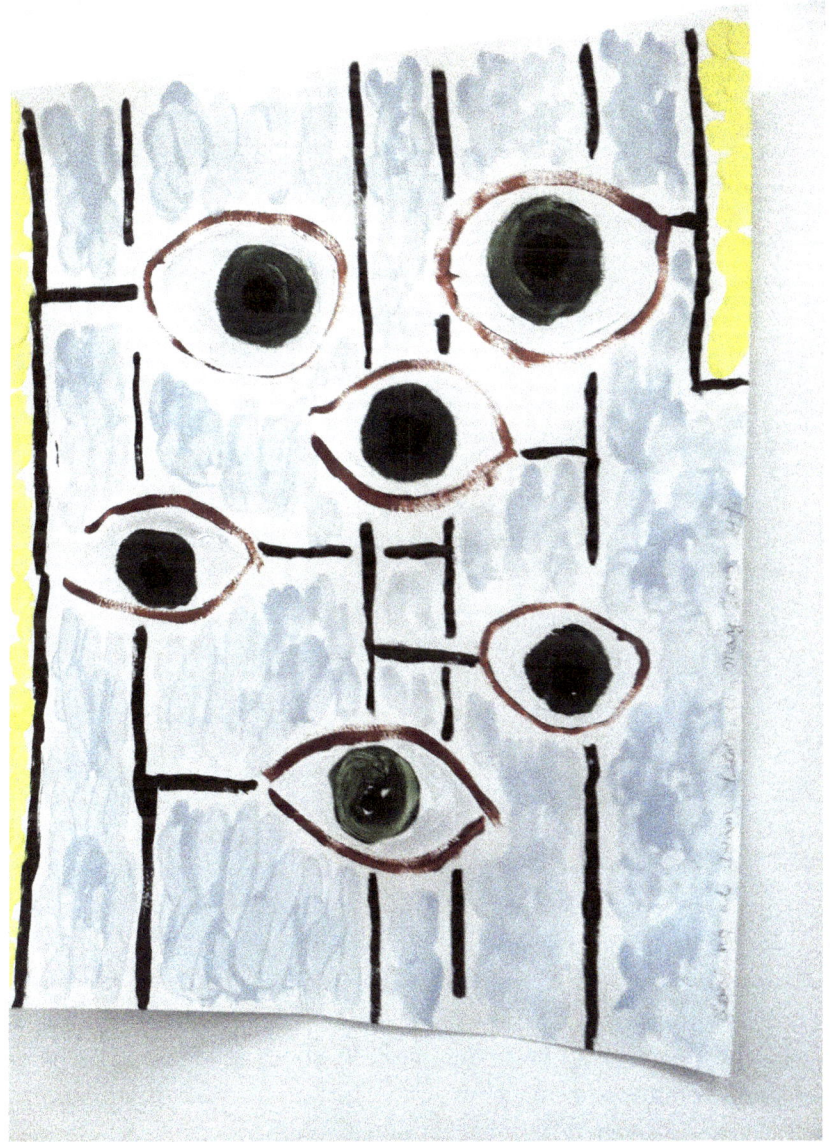

Looking at Adam Feldmeth by Geoff Tuck

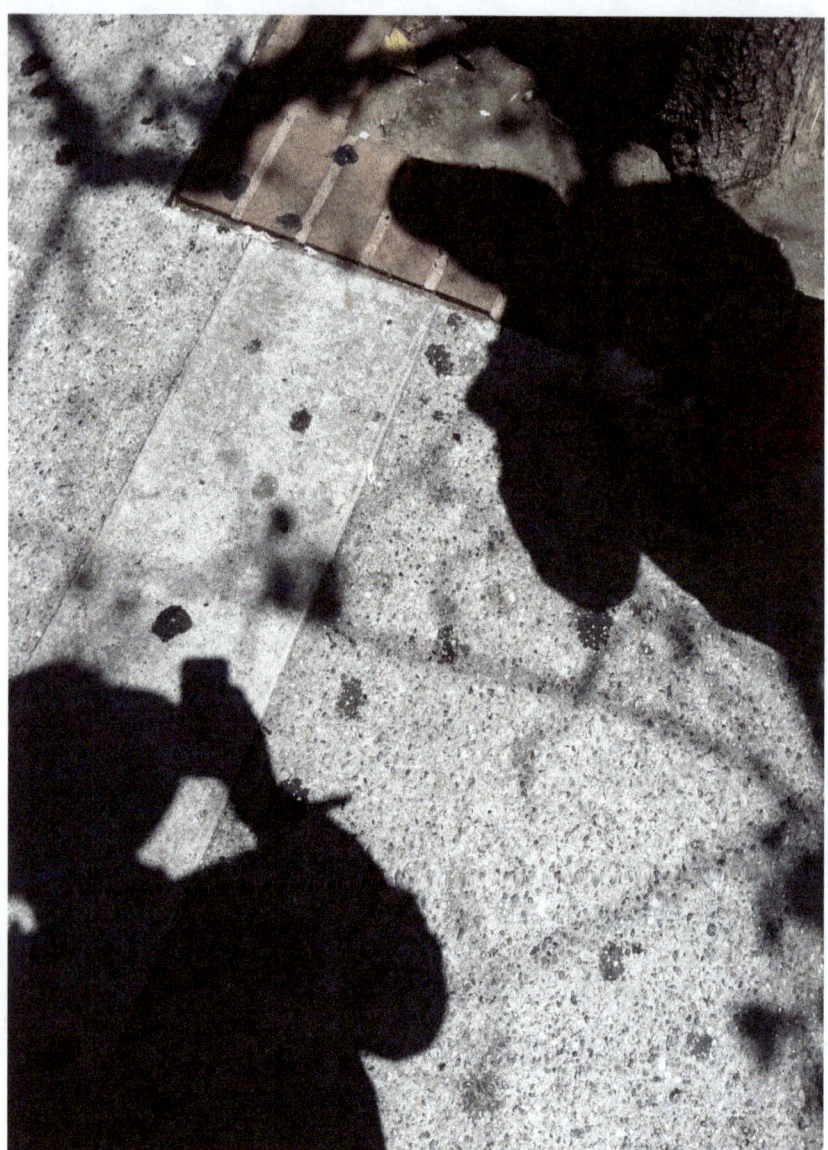

Shadows of Geoff Tuck and Andy Robert

While talking with him at our recent meeting, I learned that Andy is among the CalArts students whose studio you visited this year. What a delightful co-incidence! When we got to JB Jurve, Andy kindly asked about my paintings and was interested to learn that each is a gift to, and is dedicated to, an artist in the show. Such a gift is vulnerable, I think, yet these paintings, with their sweet natures, function as building blocks for relations—or as pictures of my dreams of community.

Andy asked if any were available for a trade, and of the several I indicated, he chose the one pictured above—not knowing it was dedicated to you. His trade was to be a drawing of me, made later after lunch. In our further conversation while he sketched, I learned that young Andy has possession of a certain portrait of Adam Feldmeth—one which, to his disappointment, you chose to refuse on the grounds that "Why would I need a picture of me?" You rock, Adam, and more tables are turning: The above *Portrait by Andy Robert of Geoff* is now hanging at the Jurve, next to Andy's painting by Geoff that is dedicated to Adam. Andy will give me you, and—when the exhibition is done—I shall mail you me. Life has never been better.

(Imagine that Minor Threat's *Salad Days* is playing, and bounce around. I am.)
Smiling fondly and from JB Jurve—I am yours,
Geoff

Published on May 24, 2012 by Geoff Tuck in Miscellaneous, Reviews

YOU'RE NOT A HIERARCHY, ARE YOU?
Radicalizing Pick-Up Soccer with Daniel Lara

"I appreciate now that you let the drawing by Andy Robert in the show. I mean, I noticed it at the time as an act that speaks, but I'm thinking more and more of this show as a process, as fluid rather than fixed. I like it."

Daniel Lara came into JB Jurve early today to talk about his Non Talk event. When we're lucky, conversations stray.

"Oh. This is not what we expect from Daniel. Where are his paintings?" This from a mutual friend who arrived before the opening to beat the crowd, and then this friend inquired of me, "How did you know what he would do?" There was a bit of chiding in the tone of these words, and my friend's face betrayed her consternation as she looked at the unfamiliar, mechanical chess set.

"Well, we talked about ideas. Daniel does videos that show people in exaggerated dependence on mobile gadgets and apps. I am interested in them, and so we began there, with systems of support and with the invisible language of code that underlies every one of our encounters.

"Soon, Daniel was telling me about a soccer ball project that grew from his love of pick-up games. He and his wife travel a lot, and when they do, Daniel inevitably seeks out a soccer game on the street and in parks."

Daniel collects these balls. He exchanges them for newer balls with the promise to re-exchange in the case of failure. A loose network, a community even, is created.

The balls used in these games are well worn, lovely really, and show the history of playing and give evidence of the intuitive collaboration of experience for individuals who, as members of a larger group, emerge from that group as teams, momentary mates who, after one match, rejoin the mass—be it based on neighborhood or employment or chance—to rise once more, altered by the circumstance of adjacency, to play again. The competition that is present is, at its best, as much about keeping the games going as it is about winning. Winning is necessary, and so is playing. (Speaking briefly of competition, there is a loose way of organizing people that allows the more skilled to exhibit their flair while offering to the clumsy but dogged players a rousing and heartfelt cheer on the occasion of a good hit or pass. Although excellence might be judged absolutely, respect is measured on a curve of integrity.)

As it happens, Daniel Lara made an anti-hierarchical chess set for *To the Lighthouse*, a set that makes a drawing as one plays the game. A nervous and repetitive pen skates across buff paper, and where it rests, it makes dots. A final piece in this puzzle is Jorge Luis Borges' story "The Writing of the God," which is coded into the processor that connects one's movement of the chess pieces to the act of drawing. A process, indeed.

"For me, the making is paramount, and putting something out as an experiment, to see how it works, how people react and work with its idea. Then I can learn. These artworks are part of a language of inquiry—I make a proposal, an artwork, and the intellectual critique, as well as what I'll call the physical critique (how it functions as an object, how bodies move around and play in its space), informs the ongoing process of making, creating (dependence, support)."

To the Lighthouse and the Artist Non Talks behave similarly—as open proposals, investigations in which there is an implied invitation to the dance.

"You didn't know what I would bring to the exhibition, yet you trusted my ideas and me. My Non Talk may be a surprise, too; it will certainly involve a pick-up soccer game and will be activated by a piñata, at least metaphorically. Somehow, on Thursday, June 7, the people who come will…collaborate in play. They will give up a little individual control and gain the insight that comes of interaction."

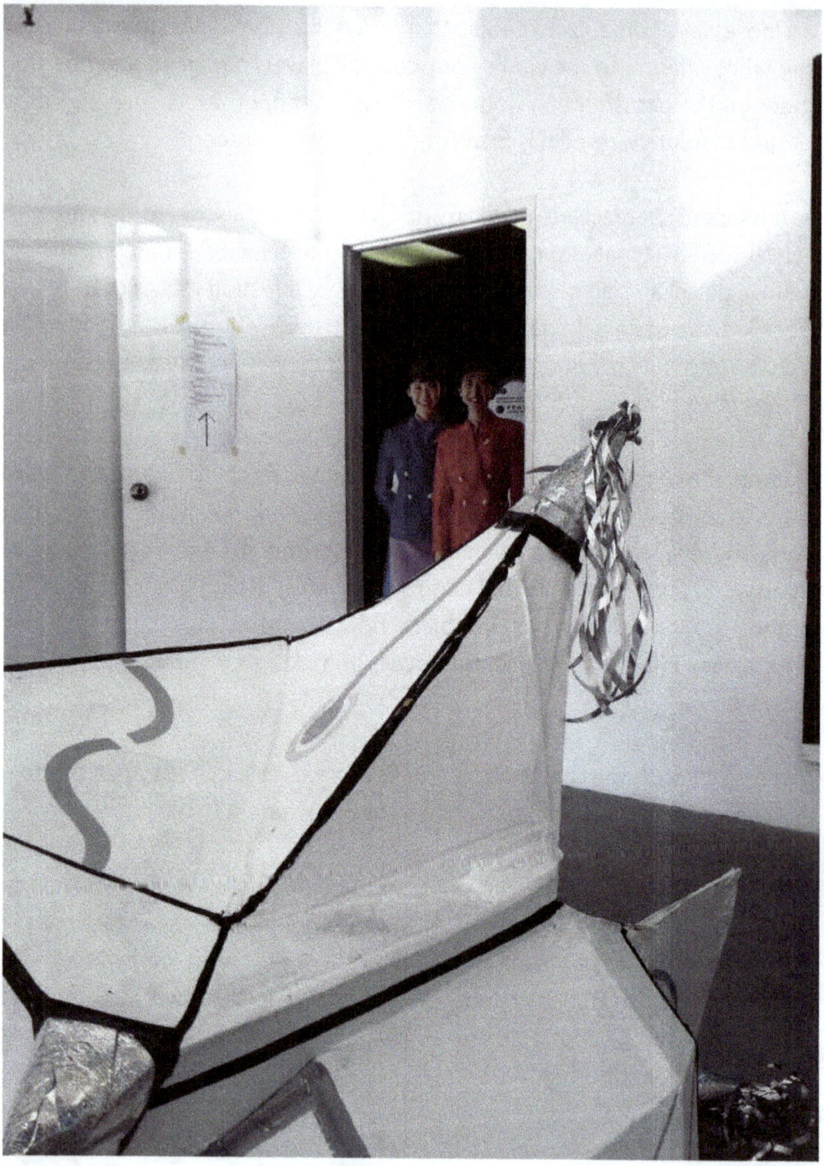

Daniel's fútbol, with cardboard ladies in the doorway.

Published on May 31, 2012 by Geoff Tuck in Miscellaneous, Reviews

"GROUP SHOWER" AT NIGHT GALLERY

It was like a dream, my friends. That night shimmers in my memory as the barest reflection of light off the desert floor will create in one's eye a mirage of water; that I can locate no images from this exhibition enforces my hallucinatory vision.

In *Group Shower*, at Night Gallery, Chris Hanke, Claire Kohne, Ari Marcantonio and Max Schwartz (along with a Jungle-Juice–filled bathtub, which sat at the back of the Lounge like a throne for some darker entity) gave to an excited crowd a wonderful, dreamy party that lasted until three and ended—for me—parked near the storied Buena Vista Viaduct, eating an early-morning burger, trying to become sober. (I want to thank the four artists. In that cold moment on the bridge, I felt timeless, and there was clarity in my mind that was connected to nothing and yet touched on everything I know.)

Less fantasy and more show in a moment, but first: Isn't this what an art exhibition should be? An experience—one that begins (for the audience) at the reception, with friends and strangers mingling in a libidinous, free-spirited festival, and continues for the duration of the installation as, one by one and in groups, people visit and revisit the show and slowly become aware of the magic in an intellectual way. If one was also at the opening party, then all the better, for to have a body memory of an experience and to then approach the experience again using the tools of one's mind has to be the point of art, or one point, anyway.

Ari Marcantonio's large, metal-clad box has its own gravity, and as I passed, I leaned in to brush lightly against the silvery surface. This was hard, but not like steel, and felt less cold than metal sometimes does. The density and mass that I sensed proved to be deceptive, as the cube was hollow, and so—even while heavy—the gravity was weight that I imputed to the sculpture.

The interior space was fitted out with wooden planks, not unlike a sauna (which it proved to be). A plank bench seat, a single-bulb light fixture and a chunky satin-finish brass two-point surface mount deadbolt completed the tiny chamber. Sitting, I noticed a plaque carved with words. I perched on the seat and considered shooting the bolt. (Would this seal my fate?) I lingered, paying attention, looking and listening and touching and smelling. My space became only wood, was filled with wood and bright light and with me. Although I heard voices outside—the universal chatter of all celebration, meaningless in its specificity yet comforting and engaging—outside was another world. Inside was just me, myself, alone. It grew hotter and somehow denser. The feeling of gravity had returned. My sweat made my clothes cling, my eyes hurt from the glare, and I recalled how I used to feel (and still do!) at parties— bigger than I should be, clumsy, surrounded by voices I cannot reach and afraid of judgment.

"Your words, thoughts and actions are not autonomous / Your self is produced and evaluated by all other selves / The tendency to construct physical and psychic barriers between yourself and others is common but self deceiving / Will you feel purpose, validation, legitimacy when your only audience is you? / Will your needs, desires and appearance still be of significance when those that constructed them no longer exist?" Ari Marcantonio, text for *We Want To Live*, 2012

Paper—aqua (?) paper, curling and torn, hung on the Lounge walls. These were lovely and simple sheets of paper doing what paper does: adopt a form, show gravity by drooping, and respond to moisture and other applied and atmospheric materials. The checklist I have calls the materials "seamless paper and mica powder." I know of mica; I have seen mica lamp shades that give a mysterious glow, but I am not sure what might be seamless paper, nor am I sure now that the color was aqua or if color was a trick of the light. Chris Hanke, *Curls*, 2012

Moving again into the larger room, and darting between conversationalists and flirters, I met first Phil Chang, and next Calvin Lee, and both photographers were interested (at the moment I saw them) in Max Schwartz's photos. "Luscious" was the apt term that Lee came up with for Max's compositions of color and the human form. The figures seemed derived from commercial photography: the human parts were as near perfect as an ad agency can imagine humans to be; there were a toned arm and an equally buff torso, a man's chest that had just enough hair visible to suggest musk and eros, and superimposed over these figures were vibrant, abstracting colors. Hmm. Do you know how sexy women are associated in ads with cars? Somehow, these men make me think of the kind of ads Lamborghini might do: use a totally objectified, nonspecific male figure coated in thirty coats of hand-buffed polish to represent a machine. Max Schwartz, *Arm, Kimota, Leg, Shazam*, all 2012

I feel like Chris Hanke had the widest range of work in this show: seamless paper and mica dust in the Lounge; a film was projected over the top of Marcantonio's sauna; Hanke's color photographs of spills were interspersed with Max Schwartz's photos; in one corner of the large room, Hanke had placed a small glass box filled with dust and stuff from his studio. Mounted in a corner, I found photos or xeroxes of brambles, running vertically on both walls. The Fall (April), 2012

Do these xeroxes (for this is what they are) represent the experience of a fall, as in down a hill or into chaparral? Or is it barbed wire? Does the studio dust make me think of the artist's time in the studio, possibly at loose ends with himself and paying attention to the floor? I don't know. The spill photos are beautiful the way many vague abstractions have beauty in them. I think for a moment of Brendan Threadgill's buried photographs. Chris Hanke, Spill (#o1), Spill (#p1), Spill (#g2), An attempt to touch the sun b&w video, Contained space #1 (studio floor), all 2012.

The shower room, the site of so much adolescent angst, the end and the beginning of our covered selves, a place to get clean. "I made the tiles myself," I heard Claire Kohne tell her family, and from Mieke Marple I learned, of Kohne's shower installation, that "they all had each other's back. When Claire first installed the patinated shower heads, they would not adhere, so Max and Ari dropped what they were doing and ran to Home Depot while Claire continued with her installation." This observation of Mieke's interested me because, in an earlier conversation with Ry Rocklen, he contrasted the generation of "the thousands, who came out when the market was flush and were maybe a bit complacent" with "these kids, these undergrads who are coming out of school full bore and ready to take it on." I would put forth that while they may be, and in my opinion are, ready to take on the world, these undergrads and others I have visited and whose work I have seen and written about, they seem to be steeped in a notion of mutual support, of an idea that "for one of us to succeed, we all must succeed." I contrast this with the fixed-size pie theory of success, which holds that for each person who gets a slice, another must lose one. There is indeed more than enough to go around, my friends, and in fact, the more people who are contributing, the bigger will be the universe on which we draw. Claire Kohne, Heaven (Don't hope to drive a stake into empty space), 2012

Published on *May 21, 2012* by *Geoff Tuck* in *Reviews*

OVERHEARD AND SEEN
encounters with Carol Cheh, Peter Harkawik, Dawn Kasper, Karen Adelman
and Samara Golden

1.

"Some time ago, the people at Art21 invited me to be a guest blogger on their site. The requirement for guest bloggers is to produce six posts during a two-week period. I thought to myself, 'Well, should I blather on for two weeks? How valuable could it be for people to only read my ideas? I wonder what else I can do.'" My friend continued her story as she waited to be seated at Public Fiction's *Secret Dinner* event on Friday night. "It happened that the Occupy movement was just getting underway when the invitation came my way—I had spent several days down at City Hall, talking with friends and listening to people. I asked ten people who have a deep involvement to each do a post. I think it worked out pretty well."

Carol Cheh, chatting while at Public Fiction: dinner by Peter Harkawik, performance by Karen Adelman and Dawn Kasper. Enormous is my respect for Cheh's gesture.

Carol's guest bloggers were: Robby Herbst, Elana Mann and Juliana Snapper, Mathew Timmons, Teresa Carmody, Mikal Czech, Anna Mayer, Christy Roberts, Dorit Cypis and Matias Viegener.

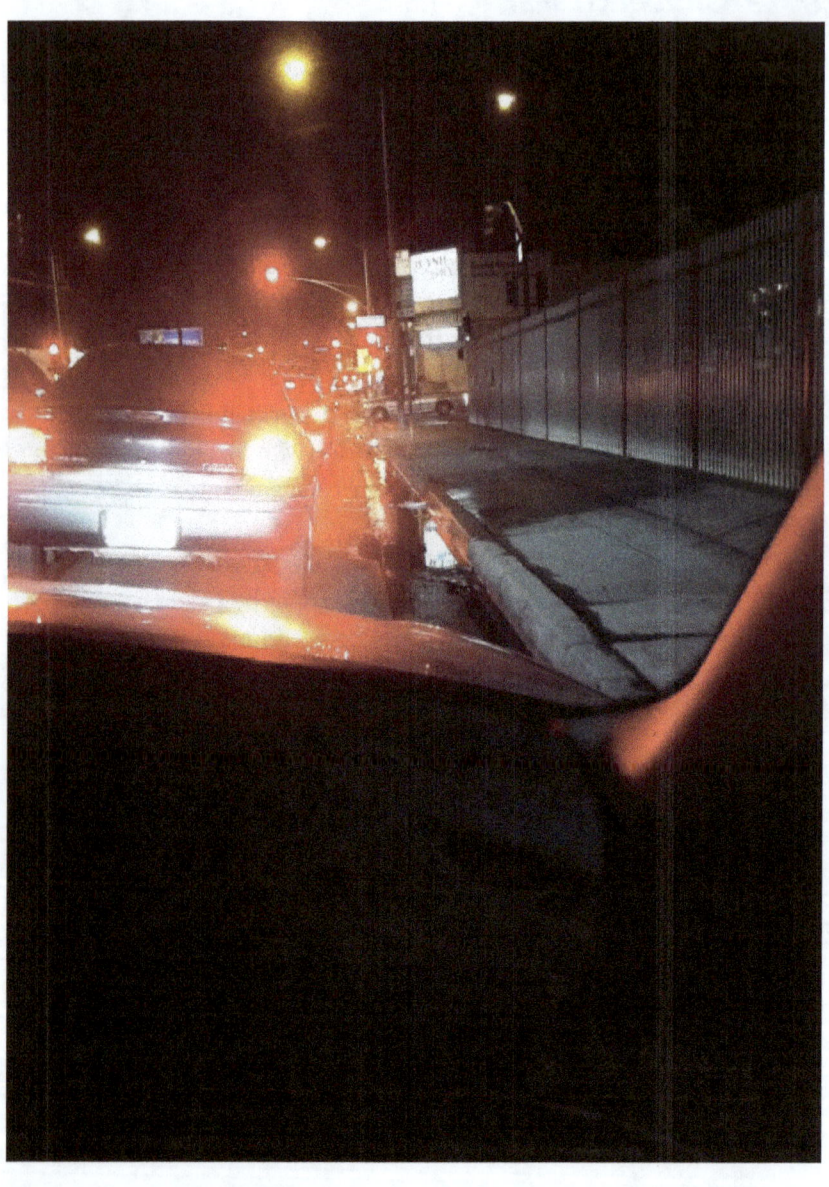

2.

"Does anyone need more meat?"

Chef Peter Harkawik at the above-mentioned *Secret Dinner* at Public Fiction. This was a stellar event. Josh Callaghan interviewed each guest (briefly) to determine the proper series of courses to delight and offer spiritual resolution to a crowd of fast-living, smartphone-burdened, urbane sophisti-cats.

We broke bread together, and the crumbs scattered across the long, bench-style table. Later, freshly boiled eggs were served, and we also broke these, and soon mounds of still-warm shells piled up cheerfully. We were a group of strangers at first, but sharing bread and eggs and tasting the pear butter with rough-ground pepper and Tibetan salt made us, if not friends, then a company of like souls, gathered and joined only momentarily, but still well and with shared good feeling.

A battalion of lovely and patient wait staff transported to each guest a selected variety of delicacies. When interviewed, I confided to Callaghan that while I had my usual and terrific day, if pressed I would admit that I have been stressed and frustrated and the afternoon prior to this dinner had been particularly technologically challenging. I wanted comforting, my dining therapist/coach decided, and indeed, I was served a plate full of fork-tender pot roast, quinoa, sautéed artichoke hearts and incredible green potatoes. Nice.

Interestingly, and I do not know whether this was Harkawik's plan or not, at the first, some among us were served plates piled high with food, and others only got a small bowl of buckwheat noodles with peanut sauce. With my generous and meat-based serving, I felt suddenly like one of the 1% sitting next to and among many who were obviously far less well taken care of than me. I felt guilty and uncomfortable… and so very full. The servings continued, and portions grew and diminished, were eaten and replenished with each round in an elegant dance of plates and fork and mouths.

Food as political art, cooking as conceptual practice—I think that Harkawik's gregarious and human gesture to invite us to share his table reminded us all of our shared place in life.

Dawn Kasper and Karen Adelman were scheduled to perform at 9:00 PM, and they did, and it was raucous and wily and mixed up. "We thought there would be tables." "We thought there would be tables with chairs." This from Dawn Kasper,

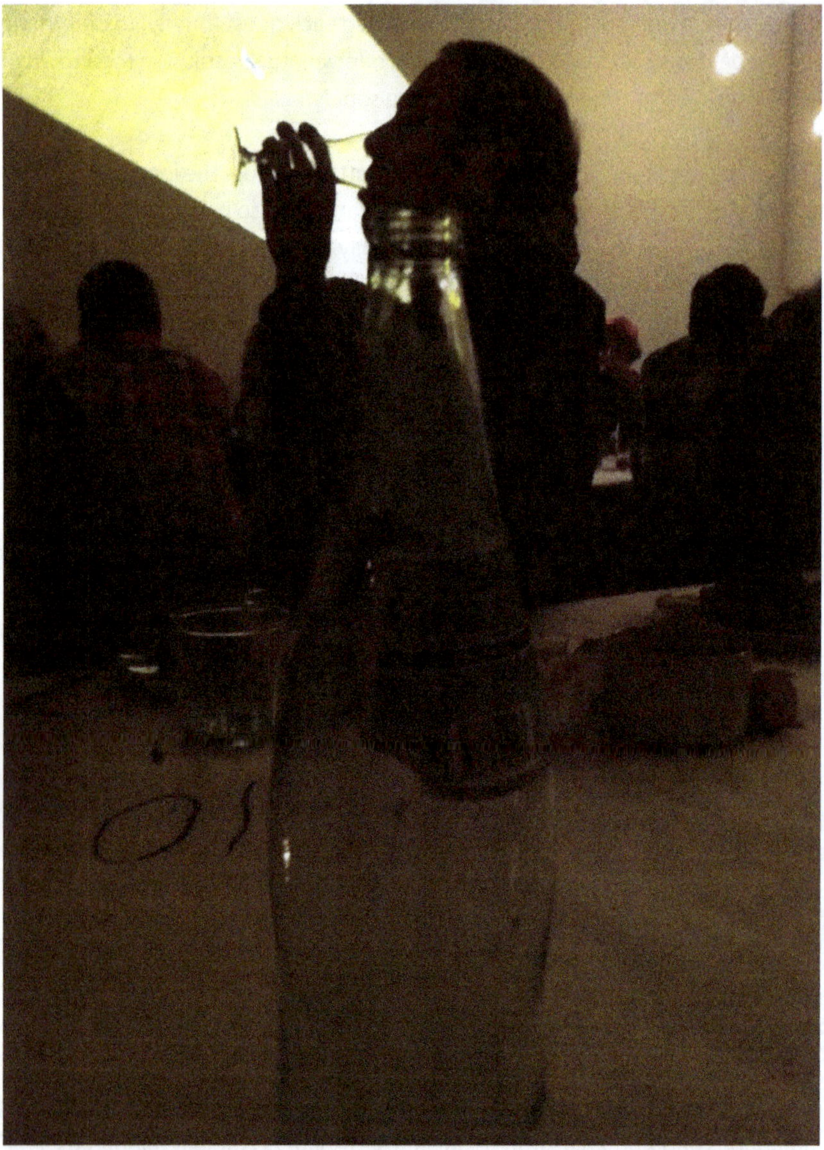

as she strode down the center of our long table, clomping her feet and in great voice. "The tables would be round and the chairs square, or the chairs round and the…."

Karen Adelman chimed in and expanded on the original thought, "We talked about sitting in the center; we talked about maintaining eye contact. We thought there would be tables!"

A gentleman sitting near me put forth that Gertrude Stein was being channeled, and if not *The Making of Americans*, this was certainly the making of a performance, which may and may not be the same thing.

It seems their thought was to exhibit difficulty in connecting and in continuing to be connected. They achieved this expression. A loudspeaker played a cut-up pop song; with each performer's movement, the table swayed and the two lost eye contact. Kasper dismantled one end of our table, and a photo-taking guest with great elan did not trip over the CMU blocks that stood as reminder of the table's former outline.

As things progressed, each performer followed her own pursuits—Adelman led a guided meditation, which she read from her iPhone, while Kasper moved to another table to wreak havoc and to then re-organize her havoc into something approaching ordered chaos. For a second time—no, make that for the fourth time, experiencing Kasper at her work had me thinking that at heart, she is a musical composer: she made so many sounds, and each was so well placed. Clinks of plates on plates, plates on glasses, feet on table, her own focused speaking—to all this, she brings a rhythm that, I notice, is chaotic and is also life-like.

The two actors wound down and began again to converse—they discussed what type of song Adelman would sing, and Adelman told the story of a friend's funeral, which she attended alone and at which she sang, also alone. She ended the performance by singing, as she had at the friend's memorial, excerpts from *Amazing Grace* and *Bye and Bye*.

This last movement was awkward. Spirituals such as these bring a lot into a room, and death is big, much bigger than the performance that I had seen, which had ranged from lighthearted to confounding and was all-over fun, and the parts that were forced went down easily because the whole was good-natured. If seriousness was intended, more work needed to be done to prepare its way.

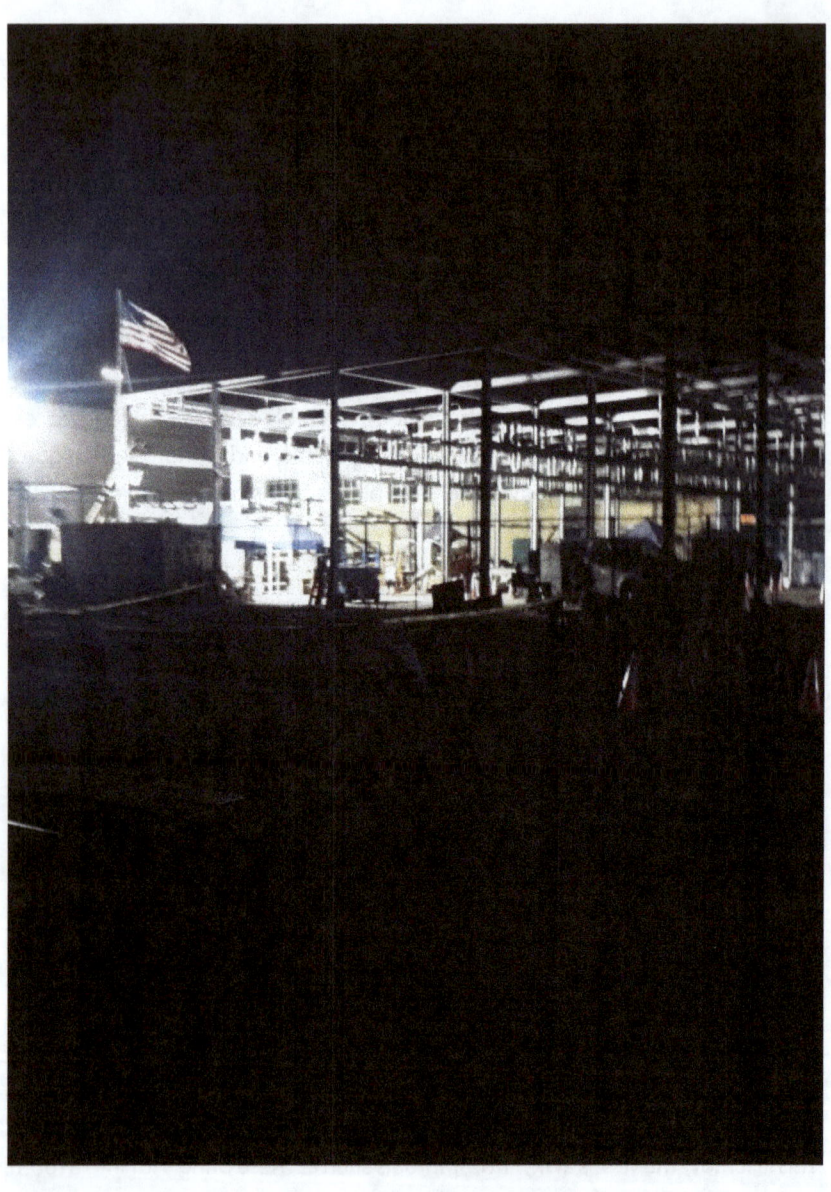

3.
"Would you excuse me for a moment?" Samara Golden asked me politely, as she drew her phone from her purse. "Somebody has been trying to reach me for ten minutes. It's just driving me crazy.

"Hahahahahaha, omigod it's you! You texted me your number, that's right! Look at us—two people talking face to face and we can't connect because at the same time, we are trying to hook up electronically."

Feeling a bit foolish, we continued our conversation uninterrupted. The crowd at Cirrus Gallery was thinning out, and as I looked around, I noted that people were in fact speaking to each other. And were not becoming distracted. Maybe next time, I'll leave my phone at home. Or, well, maybe in the car, just in case.

Published on January 15, 2012 by Geoff Tuck in Reviews, Wanderings

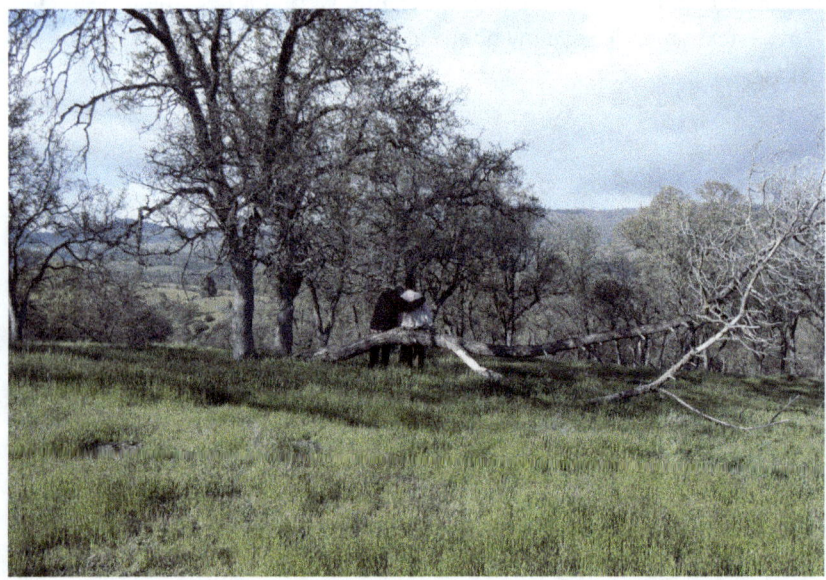

Photo by James Anderson

SOMETHING PERSONAL AND VERY DEAR
queer marriage, Occupy and revolution

I had occasion to revisit my status on Facebook this morning. No earth-shattering news, only updating my employment and other personal facts. While I scrolled around the various opportunities for sharing information, I noticed that sometime back in the whenever I first signed onto Facebook, I had marked my family status as "In a relationship." Hmm, I thought this morning, is there a "Married" selection? Did I miss it the first time? What was my thinking then? I hovered over the dropdown menu and selected Married. I was not able to put David's name in because my angel eschews social media. He prefers face-to-face contacts.

I reflected for a while on the conversations regarding marriage that David and I have had over the years. At times, we have both stated and felt that "we don't believe in queer marriage—we remember our past outlaw status (as queers and fags) and believe that 'outlaw' is a valuable place to be. Personally and for society." I also recall thinking to myself and later discussing with David a desire to stand with our friends and be counted as queer AND members of society—so maybe marriage was OK. There have been straight friends I have talked with, most memorably Karl Erickson, who was kind enough to tell me of his and Gretchen Larsen's decision to forgo marriage "until our queer brothers and sisters can be wed." In addition to being kind with that gesture, Karl also challenged my thinking on "not needing marriage" as being a potential cop-out, and he made me think hard and talk fast before he would acknowledge the sense David and I made.

This dilemma of definition is challenging and, I think, good. David and I must always question our status—which to our brothers and sisters may sometimes feel like an unnecessary burden placed upon them by a conservative culture. I am certain that all couples, whatever their make-up, must work through such questions. No marriage is a gift—such unions are work and pleasure and take time and effort and sacrifice.

Perhaps you discern my own struggle in this conversation. Nothing comes naturally. I am easily persuaded by emotional as well as intellectual arguments. I am happy, and this is enough.

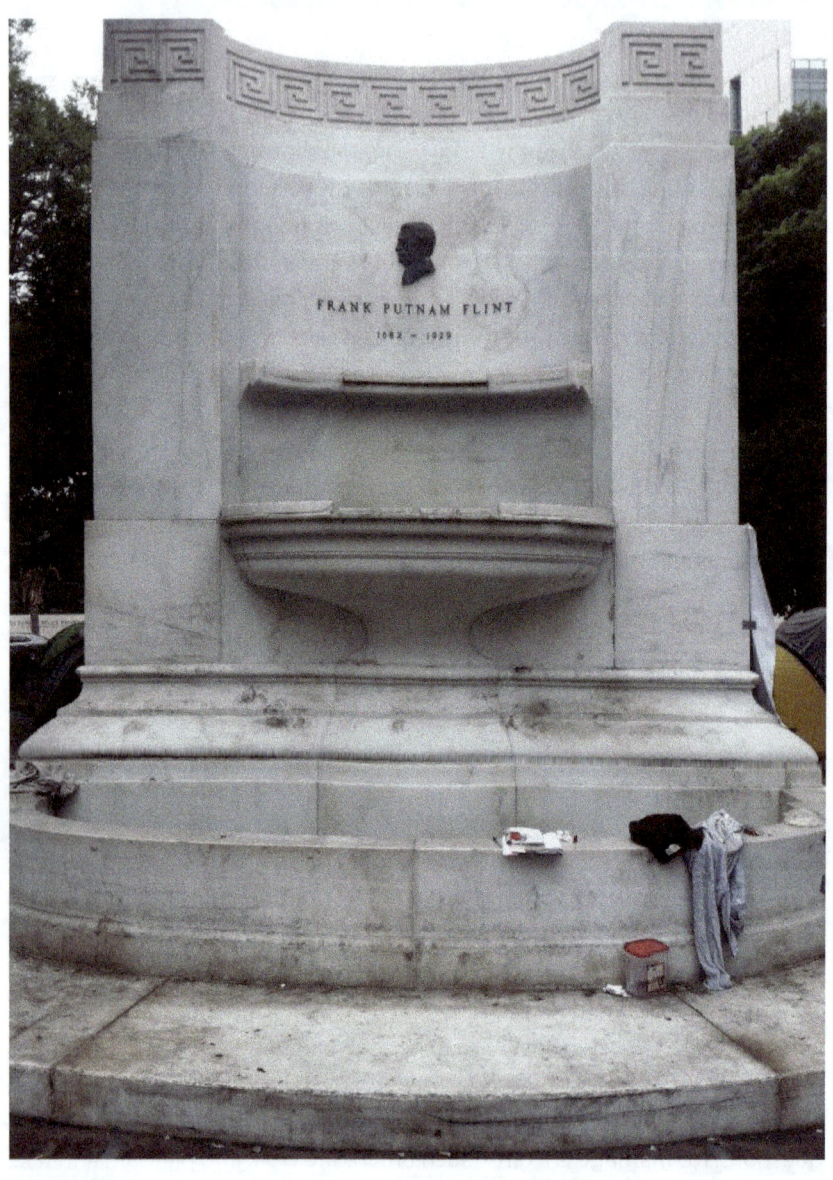

But back to our change in status and me finding my way: Recently, I have been reading about and talking with people about the Occupy movement. I have an admission to make—a queer admission, if you will—I am conservative and pretty reactionary politically, even while I am open and supportive of new ideas personally. My "real" politics are close to home, and my beliefs are in people. Big things are so distant that it is possible I react to feeling lost in the magnitude of policy questions by being conservative.

Despite my resistant nature, I have found myself drawn to the ideas and the feelings that emanate from Occupy, and especially from the Los Angeles branch and a group of artists and thinkers. I visited the City Hall camp, I spoke with friends who are involved, and I watched with tears in my eyes on that final day when the police and the mayor broke up and threw away the town that had sprung up on the lawn around the monument to Senator Flint.

Which brings me around to our marriage. I reject absolutely the terms set up by our larger culture for discussion of the question of queer, gay and straight marriage. I have learned from—or been reminded by—people like John Burtle, Adam Overton, Carol Cheh, Robby Herbst, John Barlog, and Ken Ehrlich that to have any substantive conversation about our culture and our community, we need to, as Lewis Carroll said in *Alice*, begin at the beginning and go on until we stop. I get the sense that we are nowhere near stopping.

So no, my friends on Facebook, David and I have not changed our status; rather, we have redefined our relationship according to our own terms, because the terms set for us are invalid.

Oh, and that town in the civic square that was wrecked by the mayor and the police? They can have it, trash that they made of it. The community that they sought to demolish is strong and is growing and will continue to grow as more and more people begin to question just what is right.

Published on January 3, 2012 by Geoff Tuck in Miscellaneous

A REVERIE

memories from an AIDS survivor, after the death of his friends,
inspired by a Pet Shop Boys song and a video by Brian Bress

"After being for so many years the life and soul of the party, it's weird…."

"I remember going to Pride after my longtime partner died in 1992. He and I had gone to Pride together often, often with friends. We were quite the scene. Haha, we'd be on roller skates in nylon running shorts; carrying cocktails and doing poppers; or in some kind of drag—modestly slutty or extravagant, as suited the person. We were fabulous. Now my partner had been gone for a year, and here I was, forty-something and going out thinking I was still twenty-eight."

The figure, clothed in anonymity, strikes a familiar pose. Once effective, embodying irony to separate him from the common crowd, now his clever angularity blends him into the furniture. At first unaware, slowly, he comprehends the disinterest of his audience. If he is noticed at all, it is with disdain. "Look at that troll cruising me." He changes his strategy as though this were a matter of fashion. Hah.

"Good bye. Is it magic or the truth, strange psychology or justified by the end of youth?"

"I parked my car near Santa Monica Blvd. Walking to the boulevard, I felt good; there were people streaming down the streets, it was sunny, the guys were beautiful. And young. I got a tingling at the back of my neck. Something felt off. No one looked my way.

"I got down there and I walked around, looking. The street was full. Summery boys in all their glory. A sea of them. Nobody that I recognized, no one that I knew. Oh. Right.

"Once in a while, I would see a familiar face, and their eyes stared outward hollowly. Old eyes, and confused. Even those I didn't know, I understood. I thought of the years we had spent partying, as though it was a right and not a luxury afforded by youth; I thought of our dead friends and partners: we couldn't anymore be the life of the party—we brought death with us. We brought history."

"Can you hear me, can you see me, am I really even here? I'm invisible. (I'm invisible.)

"It's too late to find an excuse, the party's over and I'm not much use tonight."

The patterned figure is not sleek or lithe—its costume is rumpled. It is that thing which stands out against its background, in this case of youth. In some cultures, such a mark is made to signify the target and the other. In the space of the screen, it is alone.

Quoted in italics are the Pet Shop Boys; in plain font, my husband.

Published on July 2, 2012 by Geoff Tuck in Reviews

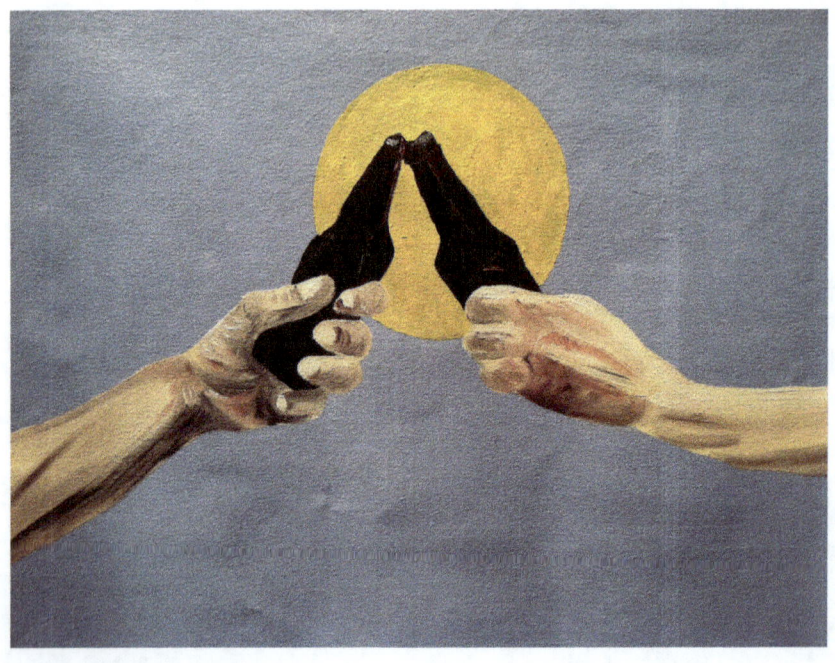

David Bell, *Summer Painting*
20 x 30 inches
Oil on canvas

LESS SUMMER, END
David Bell as Lucas Chaddwick, Jr.

A man hoisted himself up on a small ledge nearby the pool, but he wasn't preparing to jump. No, he was the host, finally stepping up to greet the crowd that had assembled from far and wide. Wearing a defeated expression, which seemed premature, he took a deep breath, raised his arms and spoke, regretting his words as they came falling out….

"Sorry guys, the cops just came and everyone has to leave or they're only going to come again." (Exhale)

Fortunately, these words were of no surprise to me. I was regretfully prepared for it ever since, less than an hour earlier, I had heard this preliminary speech while arriving:

"Shut the fuck up, you fucking hipsters! You don't fucking belong here! Get the fuck out of Silver Lake!!!"

"No, no, no, they're artists," I said unhesitantly to the man screaming down from his balcony, intensifying my stride toward the party, which I could already tell was going to be much less unruly than I would have liked. While rounding the corner, I couldn't help but wonder if the man raining such heavily abrasive, impassioned blows down upon arriving guests knew something I didn't about the attendees….

One thing I do know is that after a grueling, hot summer, art season has finally arrived, and the parties have begun to try to begin….

That night, they had come from all over. Many had spent the earlier part of the evening "embracing" Friedrich Kunath's take on Lacan's seemingly normal hair, or dizzying themselves at Susanne Vielmetter as Melodie Mousset recreated, through the use of the ceramic wheel, a feeling many of us incidentally were experiencing whilst driving in circles, searching for parking at Bergamot Station.

Upon entering the party, I realized immediately that the balcony critic may have had a point: perhaps none of these people really did belong there. Arriving empty-handed, I immediately made my way over to where I thought the drinks would be with the hopes of running into someone I knew who would be putting beer in the fridge, and coincidentally, there I would be standing. "You need one?" the acquaintance would ask unhesitatingly. "Ummm…sure, I guess, if you don't mind."

Making my way toward the drinks, I was easily brushed off by Davida Nemeroff, who stood with a group of friends in a conducive circular formation, and I didn't quite meet expectations in the eyes of Evelena Ruether, and why is it that every time I see Stanya Kahn in public I'm disappointed that she is not doing some random, crazy shit? Yet, as planned, immediately upon entering the atmospherically frat-y kitchen, Jan Tumlir, Guinness pack in hand, was quick to offer me a brew and continue on about his days as a marathon runner. "Yeah, cool, want to go have a smoke?"

It's hard to imagine that this environment could ever be anything but trite—I mean, it's purposely right out of a movie, a movie that only people from Los Angeles would watch, and perform, at the same time. I mean, if the most famous of visual artists in Los Angeles was at this gathering, she'd still be… well, *Almost Famous* (sorry). This party seemed to be a direct parallel to most art openings. If you arrive at a place that's heavily promoted as a "pool party," with artists being the majority of the people in attendance, then one would expect the pool to have everyone's attention, just as an "art" opening seemingly would place emphasis on the art and the artist and the viewers' engagement, outside of the desperate offerings of encouragement toward the art star of the evening, with words that hardly escape condolence, as the majority, gravitationally bound to the centerpiece, albeit through obligation rather than admiration, have hardly anything to express outside of misleading, congratulatory, non-critical sustenance.

Yet just when I thought it was going to stay overtly reticent, I caught a glimpse of the sun. Although, it was already dark and much too early for light, so upon second look, I realized I was merely staring at the tattoo in the center of Andrew Berardini's recently desert-tanned and all-of-the-sudden exposed chest. But perhaps his unveiling was the exact push this party needed. Before I knew it, the pool was no longer a threat, and people began to dive in; finally, the focal point was where it should be. One woman knew the *weekend* had begun, as she quickly took her pants off—shirt on, mind you—and jumped in, yet she was matched immediately when a young lady dove in in full 27/27 La Cienega attire, not quite realizing it was time to shed the costume. Perfectly timed, two beautiful blondes walked in, but I saw them edge toward the water, their eyes unavoidably fixated on the pool scene, and carefully, I watched and listened simultaneously to the one woman's lips, aimed intently on the pantsless swimmer below, murmur out the word "disgusting" to her friend.

I saw it all come crashing down just as fast as the first visible sign of hope had tossed off her trousers moments earlier, and as I looked up across the way, I saw the host about to deliver his surrender speech.

Published on September 18, 2012 in Additional writing by, Fiction, Lucas Chaddwick, Jr.

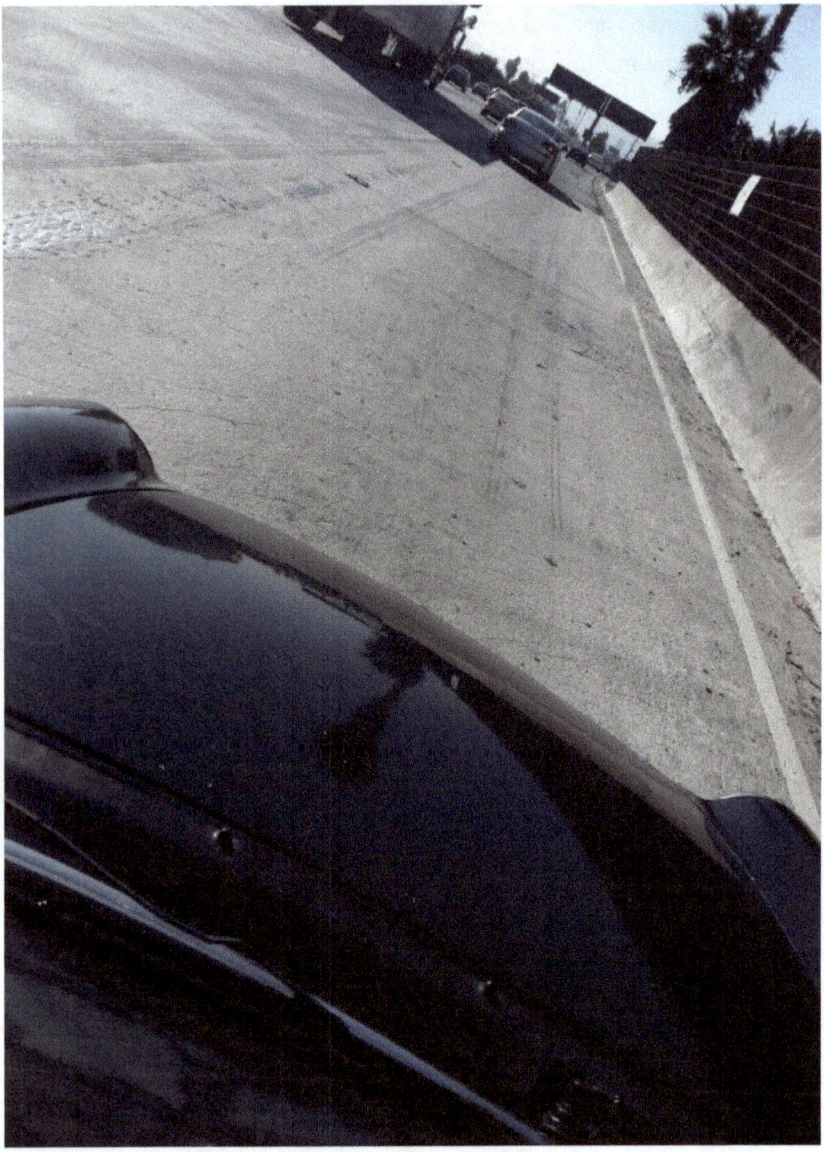

LAST NIGHT I WAS KIDNAPPED BY A MIDGET DRIVING AN ALFA ROMEO VELOCE SPIDER
an encounter with Calvin Lee

He bound me to secrecy—I talked most of the time we raced around the West-side. Telling stories of my own past, of crashing hotel penthouses, joy riding and lounging in pricey boutiques as though I belonged.

The Twisted Midget looked like a spy from the South China Sea. He claimed to be an artist—but I hear all the cool young CIA operatives are claiming to be artists nowadays. We went in search of celebrity prey—camera fodder—aquarium flakes for paparazzi-flash fish.

We strapped ourselves into a famous black roadster and departed the Clean Cave, his darksome underground motor port. Soon, we were roaring west on Melrose, him with his camera at the ready and me double-clutching, stomping the accelerator and gripping the wheel like a madman Morton Keepsneak: captive, collaborator, midget-artist-spy, joint-seeker(s) on this day for decisive moments when the stars align…with his lens.

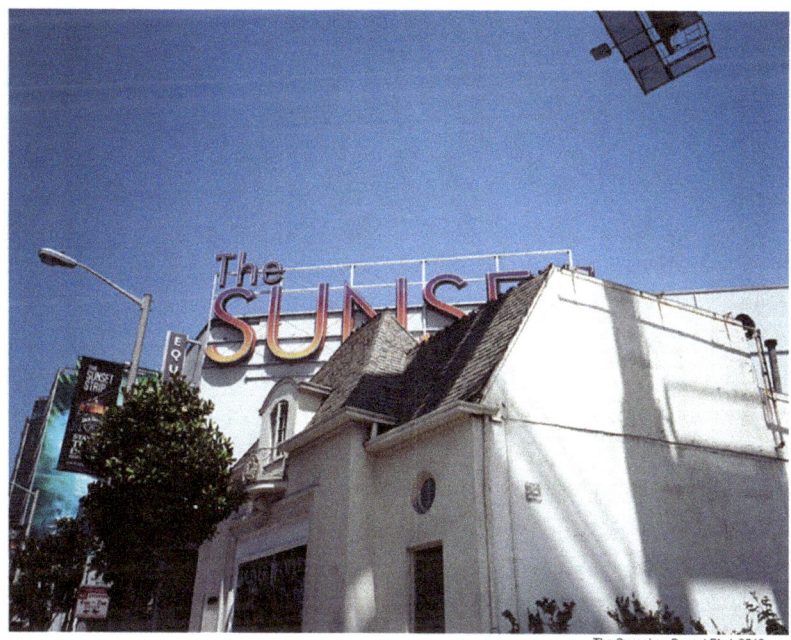

The Sunset on Sunset Blvd, 2010

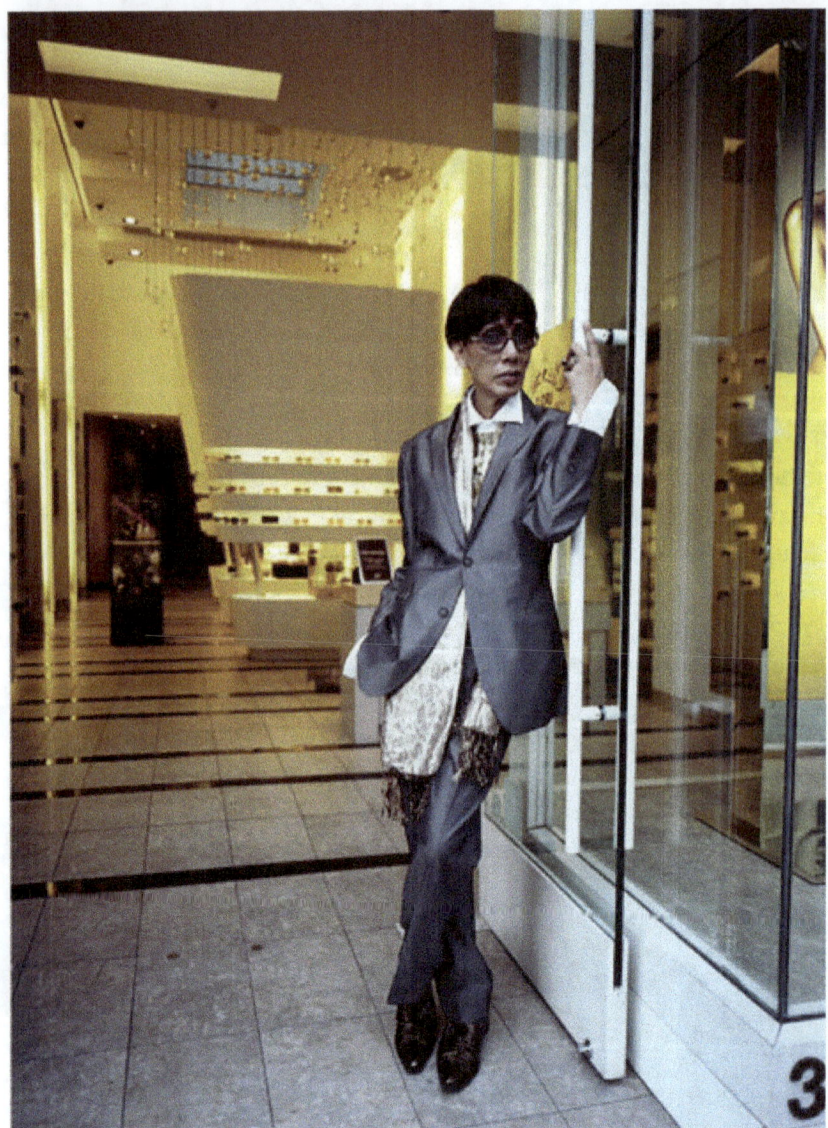

While it wasn't quite *Pretty Woman*, still, at one point Richard Gere commented to me, "Wasn't it Donald Duck? And weren't you at that party at Cap Ferrat? This is where I'll be for the next three months. I ate my lunch in five minutes: two egg yolks and a protein pill. I hear the pool boy…."

Teena Marie was on repeat all through the party (or was it recycle?), and Richard and Julia danced…no pictures, please. Let the lady have some space….

"Mine is bigger than yours," the guy with the big flash challenged an iPhone wielder.

We stopped first at Rodeo, and we strode, stalked and sauntered along a path from Missoni to where Giorgio used to be then back again. We veered to visit Larry at his lair on Camden, but it being Monday and not being as cool or as brave as we might, we chose not to pursue a visit and gazed instead at Therrien's work through the expansive street windows. I missed the drawings, which have been recommended by many whom I trust as being among the things to see this season.

The Beverly Wilshire welcomed us with open arms, champagne cocktails and hand-rolled cigarettes. Hernando Courtright himself might have orchestrated our welcome. Although my midget friend is unknown to many, in these elevated circles, his presence is felt to be necessary and his attention is cultivated. (Our Spy stopped the eager staff from doing as they did when Queen Beatrix visited and scattering daisies in our path along Wilshire Boulevard. Anonymity is his realm.)

Mystery surrounds him. "How do I get on his list?" starlets wonder, and budding heartthrobs beg him to point his camera their way, if only once. For this is what it takes in a shallow, insecure town where the signifier of a good image, especially one with legendary associations, is currency, is ne plus ultra, is one's calling card to fame.

Miley's Prius is so last year, isn't it?

We spoke of art and of artists, historical and present, of Cartier-Bresson, Atget, Weegee, Nan Goldin. We pondered the advantages and disadvantages of photographing another culture and photographing within one's own. Lighting a cigarette and inhaling deeply, he said, "Always be present, I tell myself. Go out, put my face in, take my camera, watch for Cartier-Bresson's 'decisive moment' (as an accident of photographic capture) and recognize its companionship with Barthes' 'punctum.'" Photography is like life in this way; being there is half the battle.

And then we saw Arnold and forgot all about our commitment to higher culture. Or perhaps we didn't. Perhaps this Spy's approach to celebrity is an al-

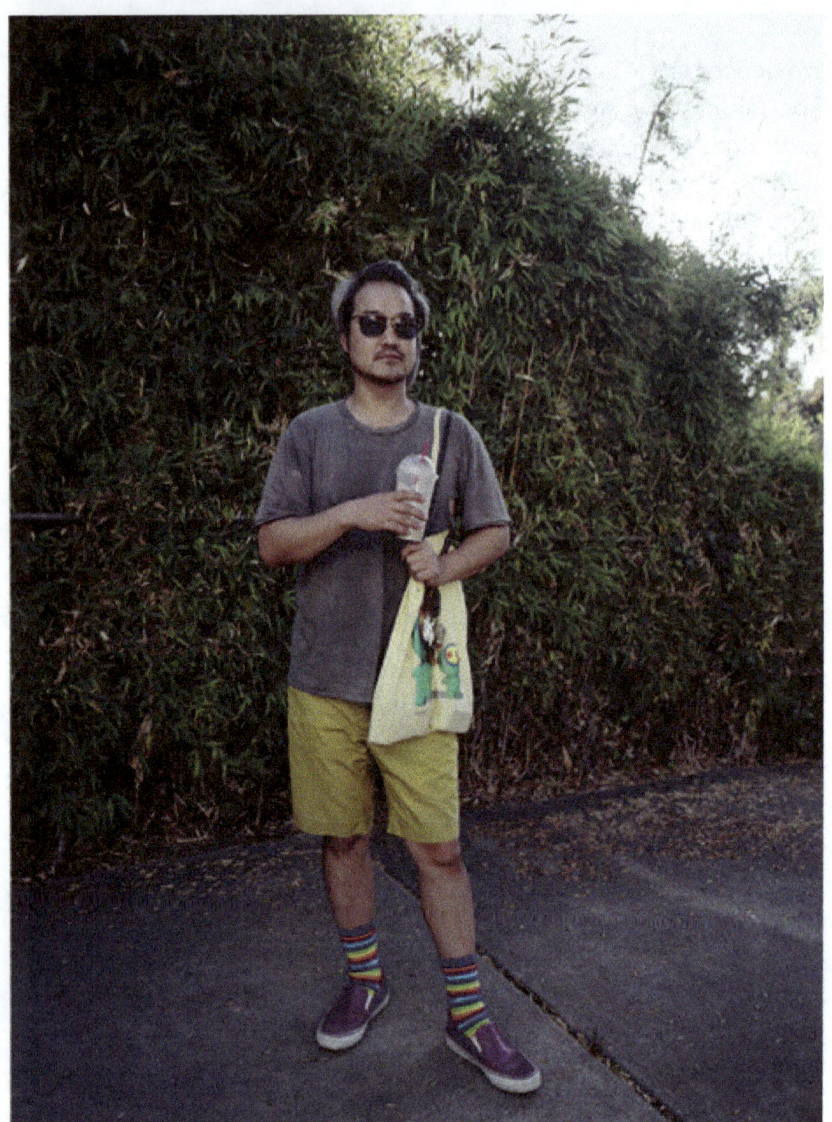

Forever Young Chung, 2010

legory, and the actions he takes—his manner of engaging with this other culture—tell a story about one's relationship to the art world, too. I have seen art
about art that is a lot less interesting than this, and I have rarely spent a more
engaging afternoon than this one, driving through all the various Golden
Gulches and Platinum Triangles in El Lay, scoping out stars, scheming break-
ins, talking and sharing an experience.

I wonder if art can be like this—a one-on-one thing? I think that it always is,
but rarely this clearly and with this much generosity and joie de vivre.

All photographs are by Calvin Lee, and are courtesy of him.

Published on October 12, 2011 by Geoff Tuck in Interviews and Conversations

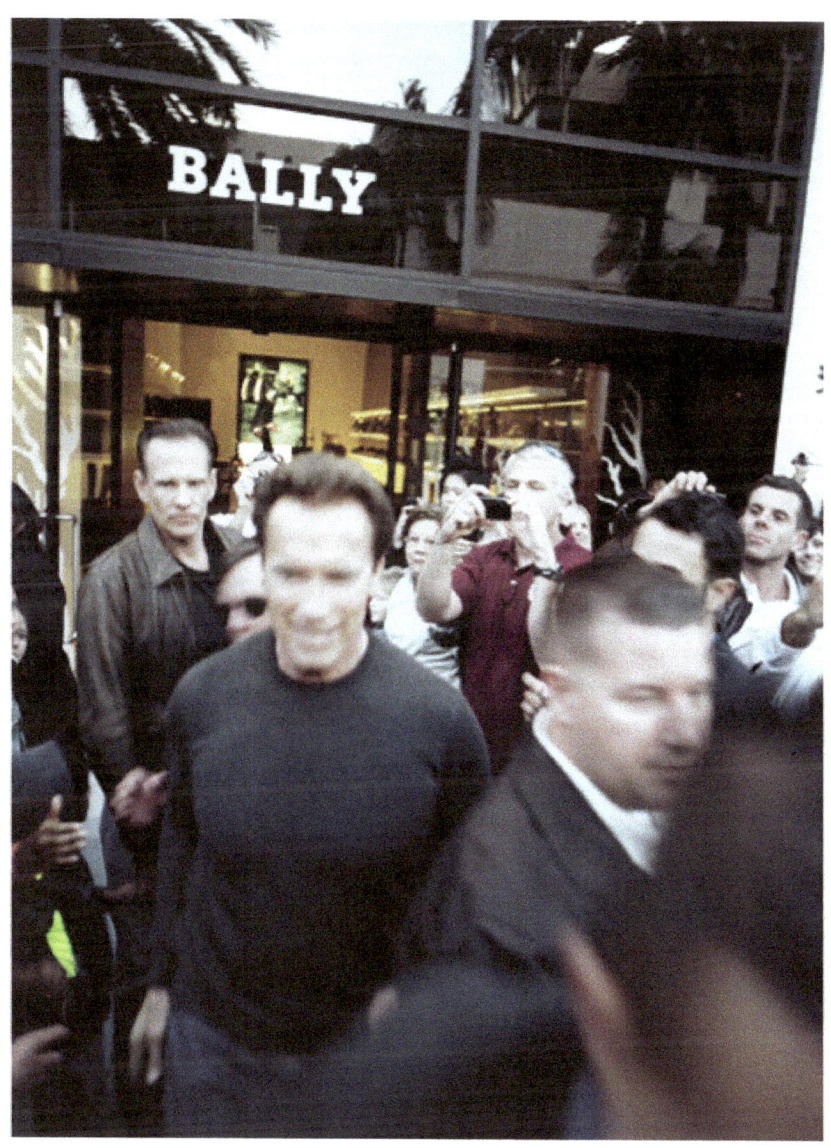

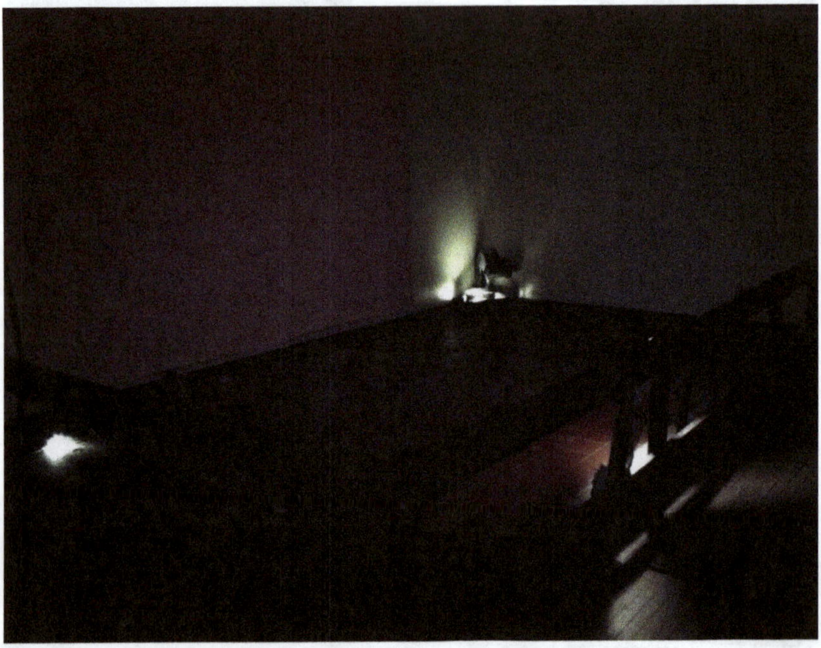

A PECULIAR READING
Latoya Raveneau

[DISCLAIMER: This is a work of fiction. Just as all my wine-embellished memories are.]

The sudden shift from the construction-site brilliance of the hallway to the comfortable dimness of the studio momentarily shocked my eyes blind. The few other people already gathered around the room seemed to seep gradually into existence, appearing first as little more than shapes, then apparitions, at last settling back into physical forms— some that I recognized immediately, though their faces were made nearly incomprehensible by the play of shadows.

As David—my friend and the evening's host—guided me deeper into his studio, I began to greedily assess my surroundings in a desperate attempt to silence the baseless anxiety that overtakes me whenever it comes to poetry readings. The ceiling was bare sheet rock, limned with off-shade paint and lined with wires. Several chairs and stools and wooden benches and other wooden bench-like things that might be used for sitting when the more normative sitting-type things ran out were placed around the room, along with a couch that took up most of the leftmost wall—there weren't nearly enough people present to warrant that many chairs just yet. At the center of the room was the most obvious and brightly lit fixture: a low brick and concrete stage, completely sectioned off from the rest of the space by a small wooden gate. At first glance, I was reminded of a playpen. And soon thereafter, a petting zoo. And soon thereafter, I apologized to David for not bringing any wine myself and promptly made my way toward the table with the bottles—the prospect of standing in that playpen was somehow much more daunting than any of the podiums of any of the readings I had ever been in before.

The calm, near-whispering interactions of the other people did much to settle me. After the second time being asked, I became swifter with a response to the question, "Are you a writer or an artist?" "Writer." Mostly true. It was too much work to explain that I had been both, that I continued to kind of be both, that I felt comfortable identifying as neither. As minutes passed and the levity and increasing volume of the conversations began to suggest that perhaps everyone was now present, or at least sufficiently intoxicated enough to begin the reading, our host mounted the stage and drew us all into silence again. I hadn't noticed when exactly it had occurred, but every chair and bench and bench-like thing had been filled sometime during my idle conversing.

The first person to read was the person I had just been speaking to—one Jonathon Hornedo, who I had never met before but who seemed friendly enough and introduced himself as a writer and a friend of David. He delivered a witty piece of prose that successfully managed to be just as funny as it was erotic. I was pleasantly shocked to see how eagerly people stepped up to read, each subsequent presentation unimaginably different from the last. At one point, writer Tracy Szatan tossed a metallic sheet of wrapping paper across the stage and positioned a lamp over it, reciting her open verse poem as she walked across the silvery carpet, light casting ethereally onto the walls beside her. At another, an artist whose name I was never to discover1 theatrically embodied the persona of an old woman, scribing rules for herself to live by in the sand of the desert (or the floor of the stage, as it were). Performance seemed to be the very nature of the evening, and when it came my turn to step into the playpen, I felt a sudden urge to dramatize my poems in ways I had never experienced before while reading them from a podium. As I watched the reading progress and was repeatedly stunned by the humor or thoughtfulness of the pieces, the separation of "writer" and "artist" lost all efficacy—surely Jonathan Tracy, an actor who gave a chilling performance of a short poem he had written, was just as much a writer as he was an artist. There was no prearranged order to the proceedings and no one keeping track of those who desired to read, yet the reading seemed to flow without pause as, one after another, someone stepped into the ring. It was at times difficult to tell what was planned and practiced from what was spontaneous word creation. I will never be sure if artist Ari Marcantonio staged his violent tripping into the stage for the sole purpose of reciting a poem about falling…or if the two events were a happy coincidence…or if perhaps he only created the poem as a result of the act of tripping itself. When at last the momentum of readers ebbed, our host, David Lucas Bell, returned to the pen and closed the reading off with an energetic "story," assembling the cast of characters entirely from the people he saw in the room. His performance of the space itself felt the most appropriate conclusion to the evening.

And here is the exact moment at which I had believed the reading ended. Good-byes and good jobs and we should get together agains all dealt with, I marched my way back to my apartment, thoroughly pleased by the evening and satisfied to have made several new acquaintances. But the next day, I was surprised to discover that one of the people I had "met"—one Jonathan Hornedo—was not in fact the person named Jonathan Hornedo, but instead a body double arranged to go to the reading in his place—that his entire existence at that time had been one grand performance…I began to consider the identity I had met—a stranger I will never meet again—and the certainty with which I accepted that identity as real, as what he claimed himself to be, nothing more and nothing less. All the people who had met me for the first time that night had accepted me with equal certainty—where did that certainty come from? Perhaps the performances that night had not begun only when we were made to enter the playpen and read, but from the very instant we had entered the room. Maybe from much earlier. Impossible to say when the performance began. Even now, I can't know if it has ceased.

[1] Tara Foley (ed.)

Published on April 27, 2013 *by* Latoya Raveneau *in* Additional writing by, Latoya Raveneau

LIZ GLYNN'S BLACK BOX

I got to Black Box early; the announcement said 7:30 PM and I was in the alley off Highland at 7:00. Alison was there already, along with Scoli and a few others who went inside the blocked door to complete their setup. A small group of us gathered in the unhealthy glow of a sodium street lamp, talking together about the same things any group of culturati would currently be talking about: Andrea Fraser's recent performance (good, very good), local press quotes from artist friends (inaccurate and misleading), the Welcome Inn SASSAS performances (running before, during and after the film we would see; some would make the trip to Eagle Rock and some would not), and the abundant pleasures of having an artist bar in Hollywood (excellent, way rad, blessings heaped upon Liz Glynn).

Inside, at the bar, the light glittering off Ivette's glazed jars of intoxicating infusions called to me—I sprinted, hungrily pushing my way through the crowd, and then I paid my money to the young barkeep, took the beaker in my hand and…with a grateful sigh, I fair sank into my melony vodka beverage the way a straight man might sink his face into the perfumed bosoms of a scantily clad dime-a-dance hostess. "Breathe deep the musky melon," I thought to myself. "It's the closest you're gonna get to a heteronormative experience in this lifetime" (fantasy, all fantasy).

Ivette Soler is a garden designer and consultant as well as a crafter of artisanal alcohol infusions. Call her The Germanatrix and find her here: http://thegerminatrix.com/. You may also find Ivette's infusions in the basement at Pepin Moore during openings. You may, and indeed you should. (Oh dear, of course Ivette is not of German descent. Germinatrix: say it, spell it, use it in a sentence.)

Tonight was the eleventh and final night of Black Box. Alison O'Daniel's film screening was on the schedule, Charles Gaines was set to play jazz, Karen Adelman would give two textually layered vocal performances—first upstairs in the attic to no more than ten people at a time, then my understanding is that Adelman would sing out of existence this temporary, memorable, and even necessary 21st-century speakeasy.

Ah, allow me to elaborate: Adelman would sing, Dawn Kasper would break down the shipping palette walls that defined the space, and Nancy Popp (possibly channeling Carrie Nation?) would take apart the bar. I wasn't present; there are certainly more details to be told, and probably facts vary from what I know, but all this questionability of the events surrounding Black Box is very much in keeping with the facts of its existence. Liz Glynn invited something like thirty or more artists to participate in the creation and interpretation of Black Box; the events of an evening were only to be learned on the evening by reading a blackboard near the bar—that is, one needed to attend to be certain what would be happening. Even Facebook and Twitter were not to be believed, because alcohol, traffic, mood and intuition each played strong parts as motivators and inhibitors of behavior and attendance for artists and for the audiences.

Black Box will be one of those things that grows over the years with each retelling of the stories. While I only attended a few nights of the events, I assure you that if you ask me next year, I will have been to many more—other people's oral histories will have joined with my own, and indeed lies I tell about it today will become part of those mutual oral histories. Next to a primary experience of an event, an imagined experience of something is the strongest memory available to us, and we can learn much from these imagined resources.

I think that Glynn counts upon this in her work. This artist not only draws upon mystery and myth—*Rome in a Day*, the Lincoln Heights pyramid scheme, her rebuilding and then burning of the Crystal Palace for the MOCA Engagement Party—she also creates unfoundable rumours, and she depends upon her audience to participate in the creation and distribution of the myth of Liz Glynn.

Twice, I have been blinded by this artist during a performance; twice, Glynn has removed from me any possible response to the question, "What did you see?" To misqoute Sgt. Schultz from *Hogan's Heroes*, "I saw nothing!" And that I saw nothing remains a powerful force in my memory, driving me to recall with my mind's ear hearing the self-serving ramblings of a minion of Bernie Madoff, to feel again with my hands of memory the sleek and strong feeling of a snake, to hear and taste again the crack of boiled eggs and the snap of Adam Janes' moonshine hitting the back of my throat as the sun set on the Eastside hilltop and the scent of wood from the palettes of Glynn's Lincoln Heights pyramid.

Last Monday, in the attic at Black Box, I recall the feeling of rich soil hitting my back as Liz Glynn buried me alive. "Just let me know when the pressure is too much," she quietly told me, as though the psychological pressure weren't already mounting unbearably. My eyes had been closed since before I climbed the stairs; the artist led me by my hand. Her actions were making me nervous and aroused in the way I had once been while investigating as a teenager with friends (after midnight) an abandoned ranch headquarters in the backcountry of Diamond Bar. Glynn's steady attention to the work of my entombing caused me to listen for human or other sounds—I suppose, seeking reassurance—and for some reason, I felt gratitude toward Glynn: as a burier of the means of reckoning, she is unsurpassed, and in that moment, I wanted to be stripped of reason by art.

I longed for the cool earth to cover me and calm my nervous fears. I struggled to maintain a detached intellectual interest while the clods hit my face: here I was, living an Edgar Allan Poe story, here, in Hollywood, near the source of so much in our culture (and in my own life). The flickering light of a million Hollywood movies, good and crappy, began here. I can imagine Kenneth Anger stalking these dark alleys; in a shop on this street, Richard Hawkins once did trade in the deviant paperbacks, star biographies and collectable books that began his career as an artist; from 1975 to 1985, I and a thousand other guys walked nearby streets at night, selling our bodies; and now a genius artist was burying me—did she care? Would it matter? When my head was finally covered and my face disappeared under earth, I wondered if she would "go all the way" and then walk off whistling and leave me. She whispered something in my ear that night; I can't remember the words, but I remember a delicious chill when she spoke to me and then continued her mounding of earth to cover my body.

Published on February 6, 2012 by Geoff Tuck in Reviews

DAN FINSEL—THE SPACE BETWEEN US

Dan Finsel is dancing; his feet do a ballet (they writhe like nervous, eager virgins) while his mouth directs his muse: "Spread your legs." His toes paint on the floor. "Now smile—not so tight. Tell me you love me. Say it." Is it shit or blood or paint that his toes and heels smear? Clay.

A sculpture asks, "Can I wait in the fireplace?" (Yes, sir, can I hide in your hearth, with its blowjob knee-hole eye-hole, at the very center of your heat? Can I?!)

Like Penelope and like Philomela (and like neither, for Odysseus is present, not absent in his exceptional perversity, and no one has been devoiced, although a rape—or two—may be taking place), Dan has woven rag rugs of inexpensive (and promisingly butch) tank tops and tighty-whitey briefs. These serve as blankets to protect his obsession from the floor, or vice versa. Resting on these are a table that supports one sculpture (a Minoan goddess or bastard Venus of Willendorf) and the body, the impression in clay of a months-long, torrid—if imaginary—affaire de lust.

A pineapple makes an appearance, and I am relieved. Two black-and-white photographs of this tropical fruit hang in the gallery, and I wonder(ed) why. The appearance is neither explained, nor is it given context in the twenty-plus–minute film. I think that pineapples promise wealth and welcome guests. I recall the sweet, hormonal scent of a pineapple left too long on a table in the summer, and my imagination conjures the sticky, tangy fluid that spills when I split this fruit and my eagerness to taste of its promise.

If one scene in the film does bring to mind *Étant donnés*, as the guard suggested to me, then when I think of Dan Finsel, can I hold at once in my head the roaring, gonadal monster of Picasso with Duchamp's sly, intellectual, and also sexy wit? And, thinking of Duchamp's sculpture with its closed door, through whose hole am I peeking when I view Dan Finsel's installation? That of his young muse? The artist, himself? Has Bataille's solar anus colonized my mind, and I see through this?

When I remember that they are acting, Dan and his friend, things become more interesting. I can imagine living this tale, but not making it up. I wonder how the clay feels in their fingers, and how it smells. The nice guard smells it for hours. The recumbent muse, or the artist, for they are indistinguishable, squirts oil on his chest like cum. "Touch me there." I want suddenly to touch, to sit on, to sniff the tank top and briefs material in the rugs—I look closely and note the guard watching me, incredulous. I fear that she may ask me to move, and so I do.

"What is the table about" she asks me. "Um, to hold it up?"

Postscript: those who read this piece early may note some revisions from the original. They are done, and that is that.

I extend my thanks to Dan Finsel. His work cannot be easy to make, for he is never less than present—even when he is watching himself be watched by us, as here, when under a greasy, matted wig, he glances out and catches himself when responding to his lover's urgings. For a bare moment, the veil dropped, and I saw Dan smile at his absurdity and at his shocking, debased, transcendent grace. Dan Finsel's willingness to arduously craft and inhabit for months a character and a history, and to then, amidst his passion play, to allow me the revelation of glimpsing the artist (the artist, did I say? Nay, the man, for "artist" is another of culture's imposed roles) at his work—all of this goes far beyond the mannered telenovela that is currency in high culture in our time. Thank you, Dan Finsel.

There are mushrooms that grow in Central California, after the last rains and the heat has dried the earth—baked it, really—at night; all at once grow fungi, thick, fleshy, white mushrooms. This growth is disturbing; it pushes aside the earth and cracks the clay-hard soil. In the morning, these mushrooms cover fields, fist-sized white horrors surrounded by miniature earthquake faults. This is beautiful and creepy beyond words, as are you, Dan.

Published on June 5, 2012 by Geoff Tuck in Reviews and tagged Dan Finsel

ALEXIS SMITH—MASCULINE FEMININE, DER ZAUBERBERG, ET ISADORA

Car le corps, c'est la maladie et la volupté, et c'est lui qui fait la mort, oui, ils sont charnels tous deux, l'amour et la mort, et voilà leur terreur et leur grande magie!

L'amour pour lui, pour le corps humain, c'est de même un intérêt extrême- ment humanitaire et une puissance plus éducative que toute la pédagogie du monde!
(Thomas Mann, The Magic Mountain, conversations between Hans Cas- torp and Madame Chauchat.)

I rely on a Wikipedia quote page, as I am not able to put my hands on my own copy of Thomas Mann's *The Magic Mountain*. This favorite paperback was a gift in 1979 from a lover (and, thrillingly to me, PhD candidate) who was nine years my senior and who, I recognize now, appreciated my native enthusiasm

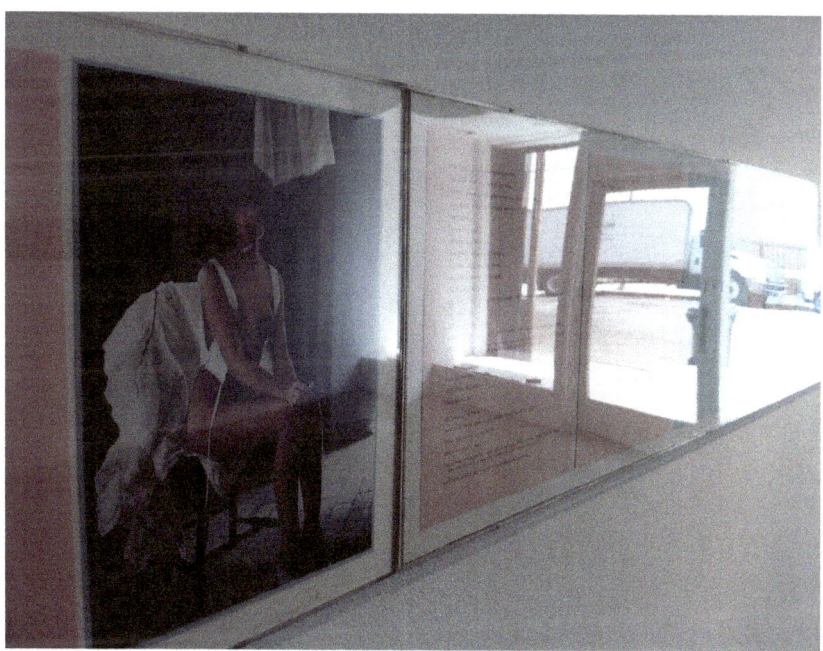

Alexis Smith *masculine / feminine* 1975-1976, reflection of Bernard Street

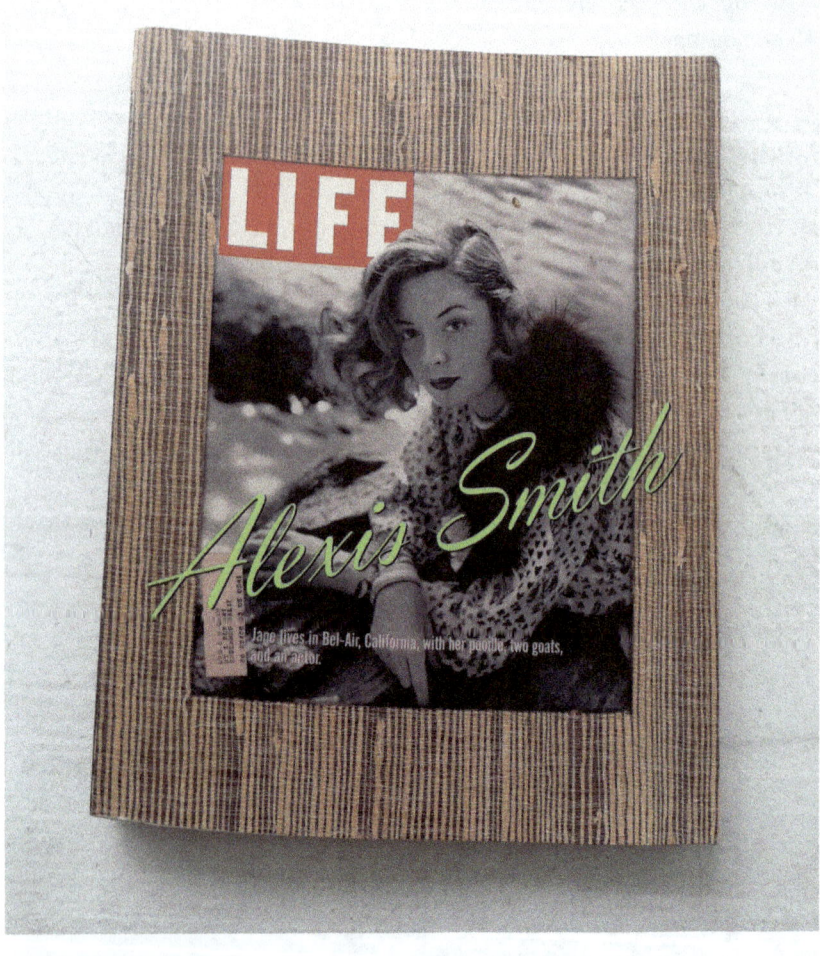

Alexis Smith

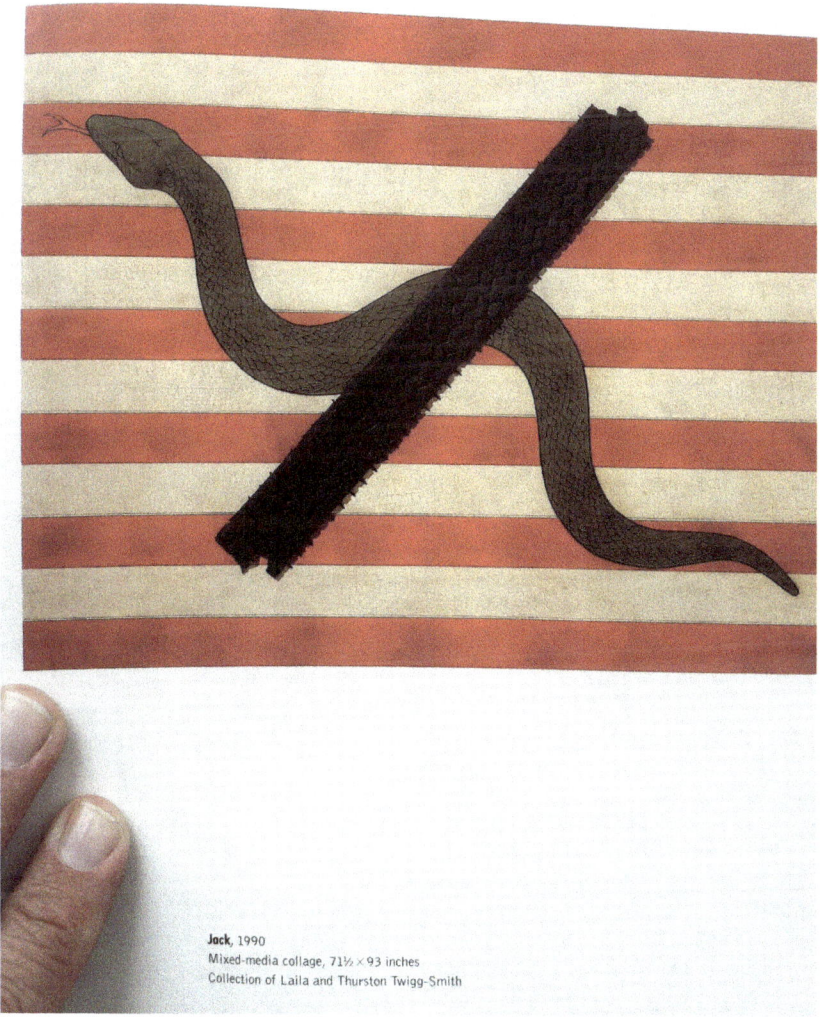

Jack, 1990
Mixed-media collage, 71½ × 93 inches
Collection of Laila and Thurston Twigg-Smith

From *Alexis Smith* 1991 Whitney Museum catalog available for perusing at Tom Solomon Gallery

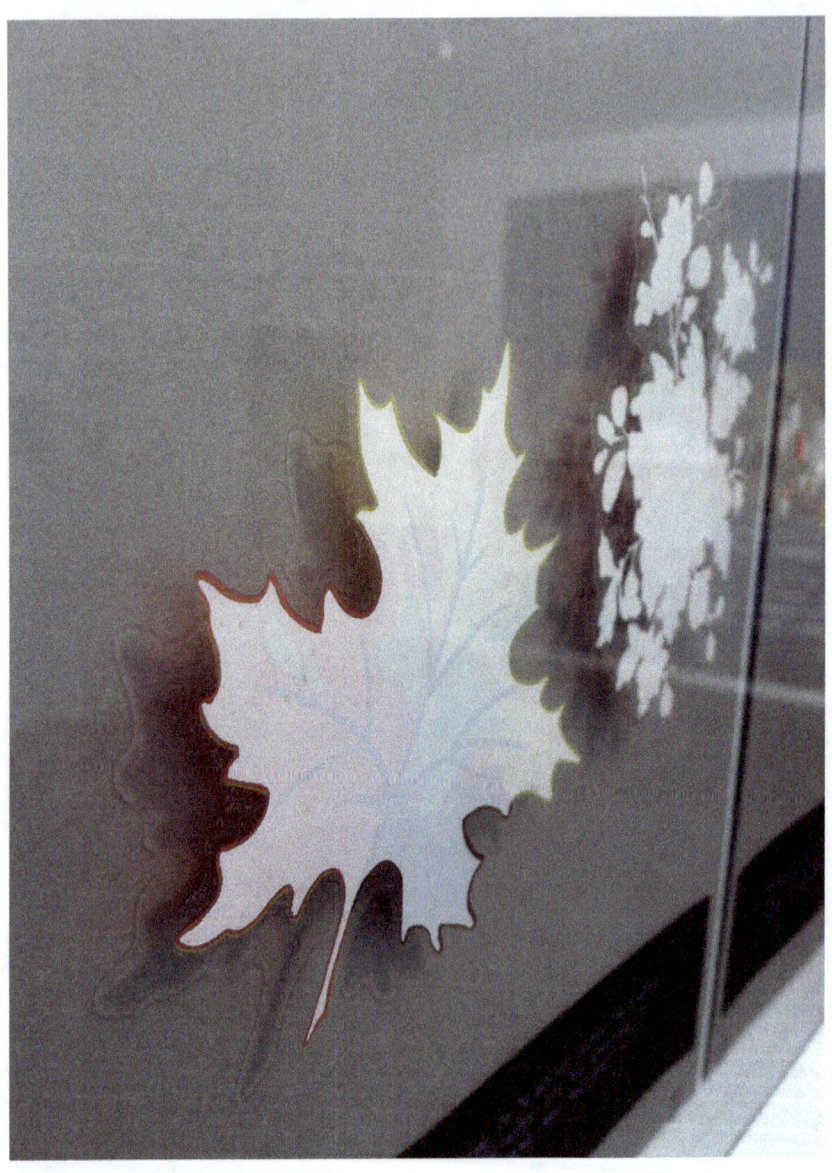

Alexis Smith *Silver Screen* detail

but preferred his bleach-blonde pseudo-punks to be more lettered. Thus was born in me, my friends, a culture-philiac. Thanks, college guy.

It happens that Alexis Smith's works in the current show at Tom Solomon are difficult to photograph. "But wait!" my more intelligent half says to me. "They're only difficult to photograph if you want to issue forth pristine images of idealized art objects."

It is as it should be: I find *Isadora* reflected in *Masculine and Feminine*; I see the world outside embedded in the presence of a young Chic magazine model; I stumble everywhere across myself.

Also, the state of these photographs represents perfectly my experience of looking and reading and skipping eagerly ahead, then skipping back a few panels to reread a poignant or poetic note. In this way, Smith's art resembles the cinema and literature from which she draws her power.

And isn't this just the way? The art in a thing flourishes because of—not despite—interruptions, errata and personal reflections. An artist making a thing aims and struggles toward…something. As she works, curious and unintended stuff presents itself and becomes part of the final piece. Her own treacher-

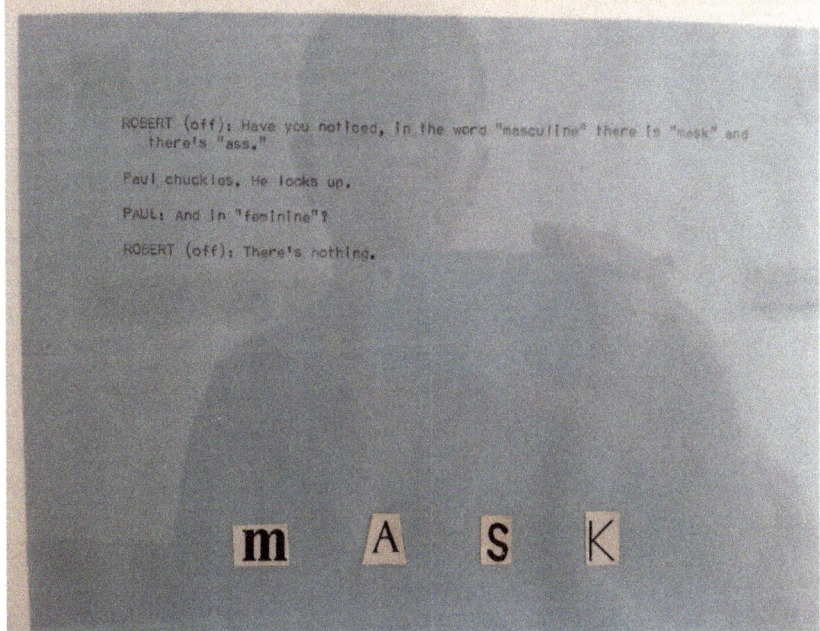

Alexis Smith *masculine / feminine* (and me)

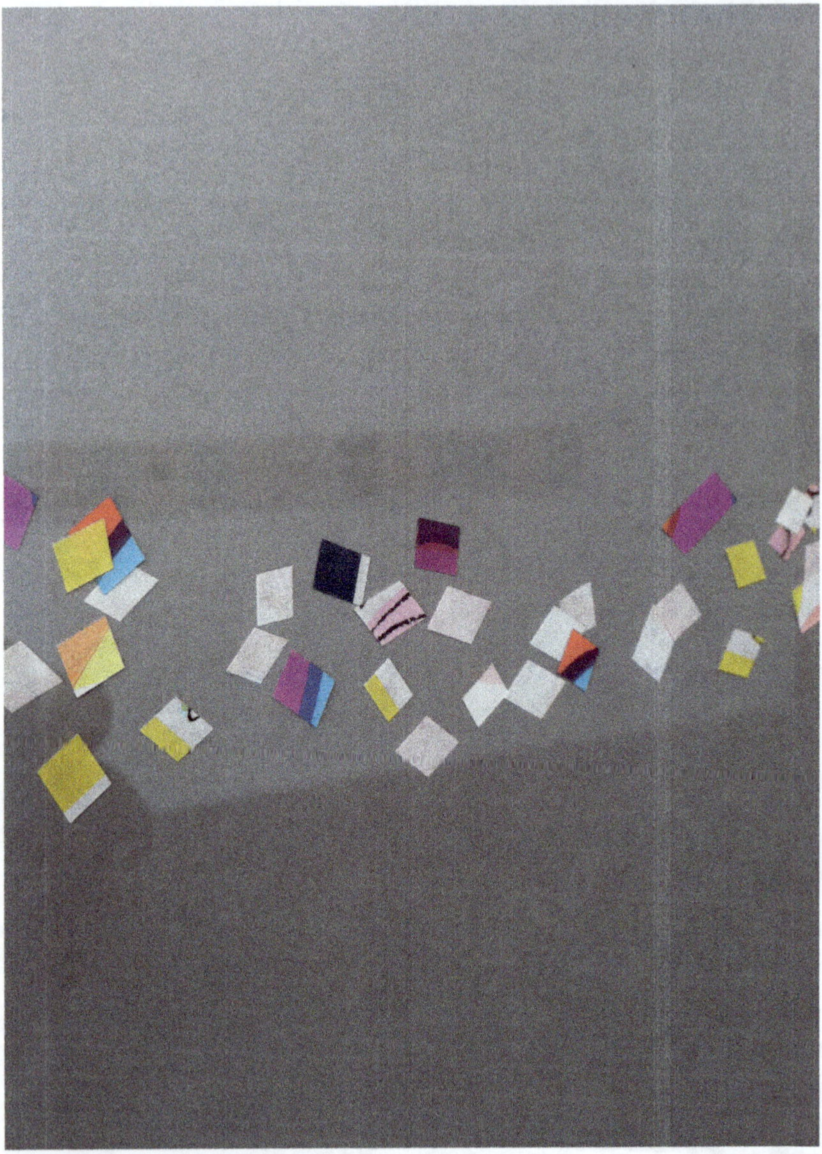

Alexis Smith *Silver Screen* detail

ous hand and her emotions may derail one plan, only to offer a looser and more nuanced trail for her to follow.

As it is with the artist, so it is with me: Stumbling over my own presence is, I think, how I become invested in the work.

In the case of the pieces exhibited in this show (*Silver Screen, The Magic Mountain, Isadora, Think* (a small sculpture that may be titled Think for yourself; I am not certain), and *Masculine and Feminine*), I kept recalling books I have read, movies I have seen, and partners I have had; the Montenegro quote that I use in a description of one of the "Isadora" photos is loosely translated from a 1970s television show about Duncan and her lovers. I have silently remembered the TV movie and this quote for 35 years now, and Alexis Smith managed with her art to unleash in me this memory and also everything that goes with it. (The long, shaggy, blue and green carpet on which I sat watching; conversation with my parents, who watched with me; our parrot squawking and talking in the background; and my Great Dane, Zeke, who lay with his head in my lap.)

And so, I had my own Proustian "madeleine" moment in a gallery in Chinatown. (Thanks, Alexis!)

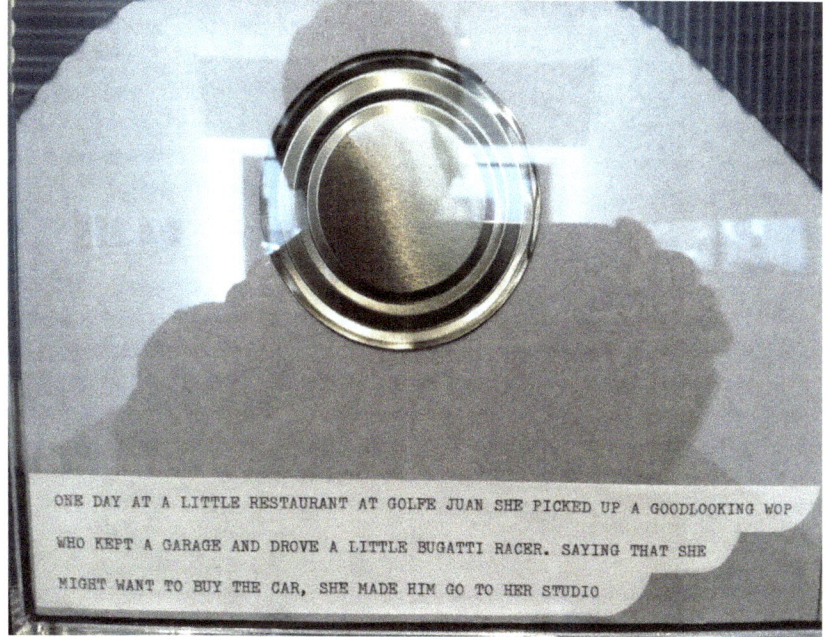

ONE DAY AT A LITTLE RESTAURANT AT GOLFE JUAN SHE PICKED UP A GOODLOOKING WOP WHO KEPT A GARAGE AND DROVE A LITTLE BUGATTI RACER. SAYING THAT SHE MIGHT WANT TO BUY THE CAR, SHE MADE HIM GO TO HER STUDIO

Alexis Smith *Isadora,* 1980-1981 detail (a good-looking wop)

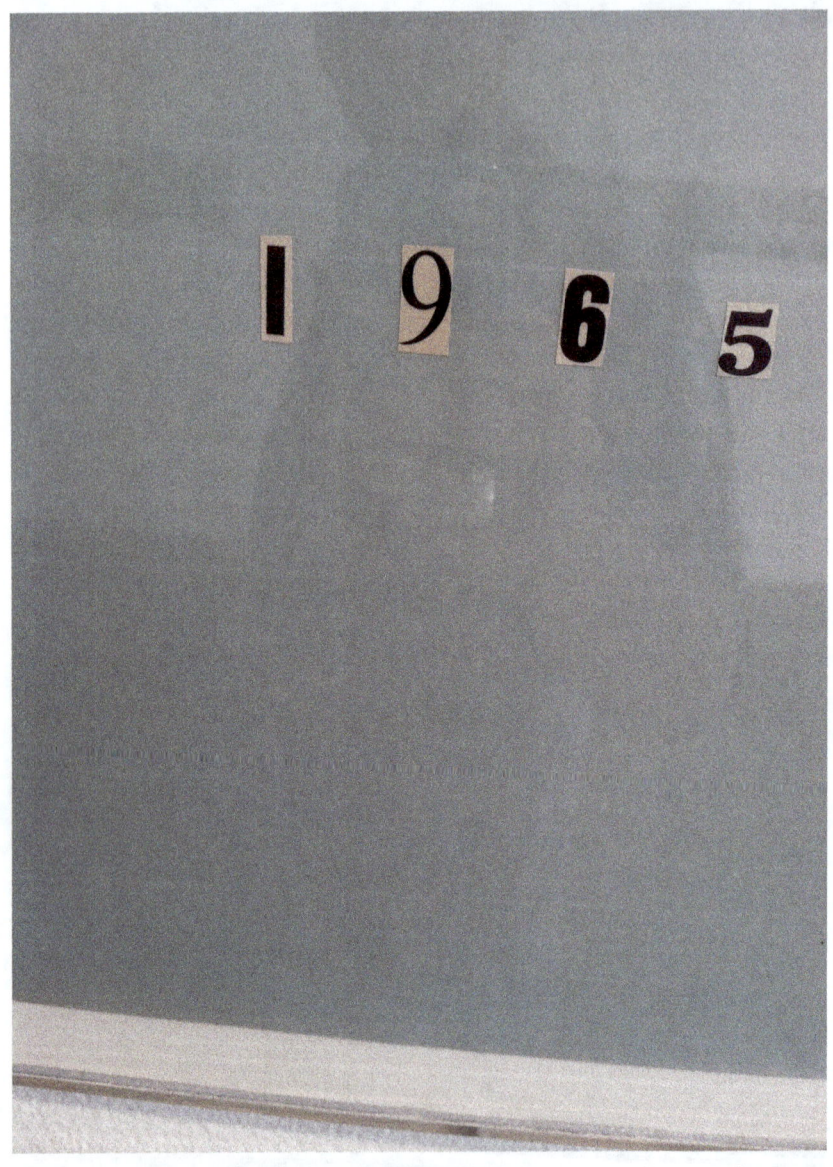

Alexis Smith *Masculine and Feminine* 1975-1976; Godard made *Masculine Feminine* in 1965

I asked Tom Solomon about the script that Smith typed on blue and pink pa-per for *Masculine and Feminine*. When I visited a second time to take pictures, Tom related to me that "Alexis reminded me (he said, blushing) of Godard's film *Masculine Feminine*, and of course the dialogue is clearly from that source. Funny that I should forget Godard…."

I like that Smith conflates Paul Newman with the Paul in Godard's film: imag-ining Newman in such a brusque, sexy and careless role is delicious. Smith relates the story of two male characters as they discuss strategies for—well, I guess they are trading pick-up moves. One approaches a woman in a café, asking to take a lump of sugar from her table. As our gentleman reaches, his fingers brush this woman's breast. He returns to the table, drops the sugar in his coffee and drinks, looking challengingly at his companion. His friend (ap-parently learning from his predecessor and yet masterfully upping his friend's ante) repeats this charade move for move, except that when the friend ob-tains his lump of sugar, he places it on his tongue, closes his mouth around it and…well, you get the idea. Hot on so many levels.

(And problematic: Can you imagine in our present day any man feeling able to touch a woman with such freedom? Can you picture a woman not feel-ing affronted? Were such actions invasive even then? Did this sense of entitle-

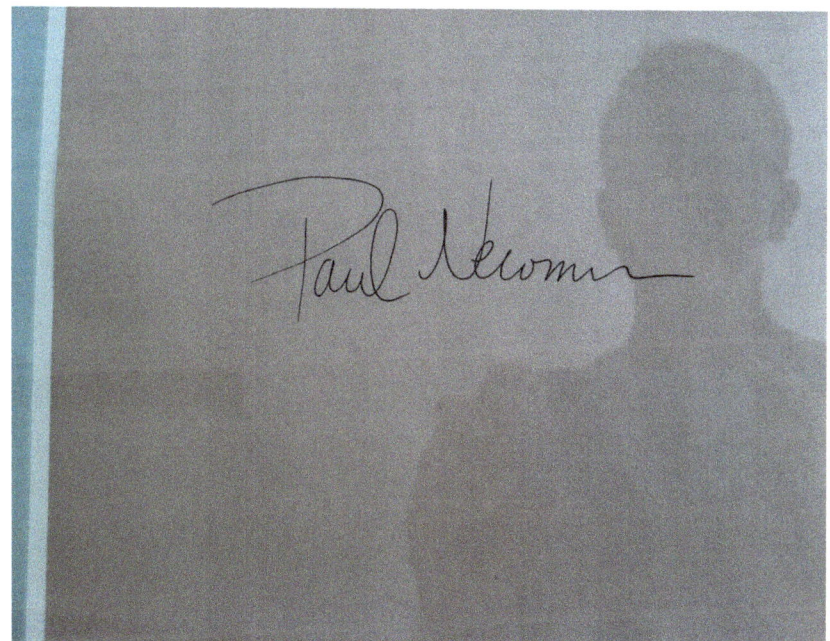

Alexis Smith *Masculine and Feminine* detail, as installed at Tom Solomon

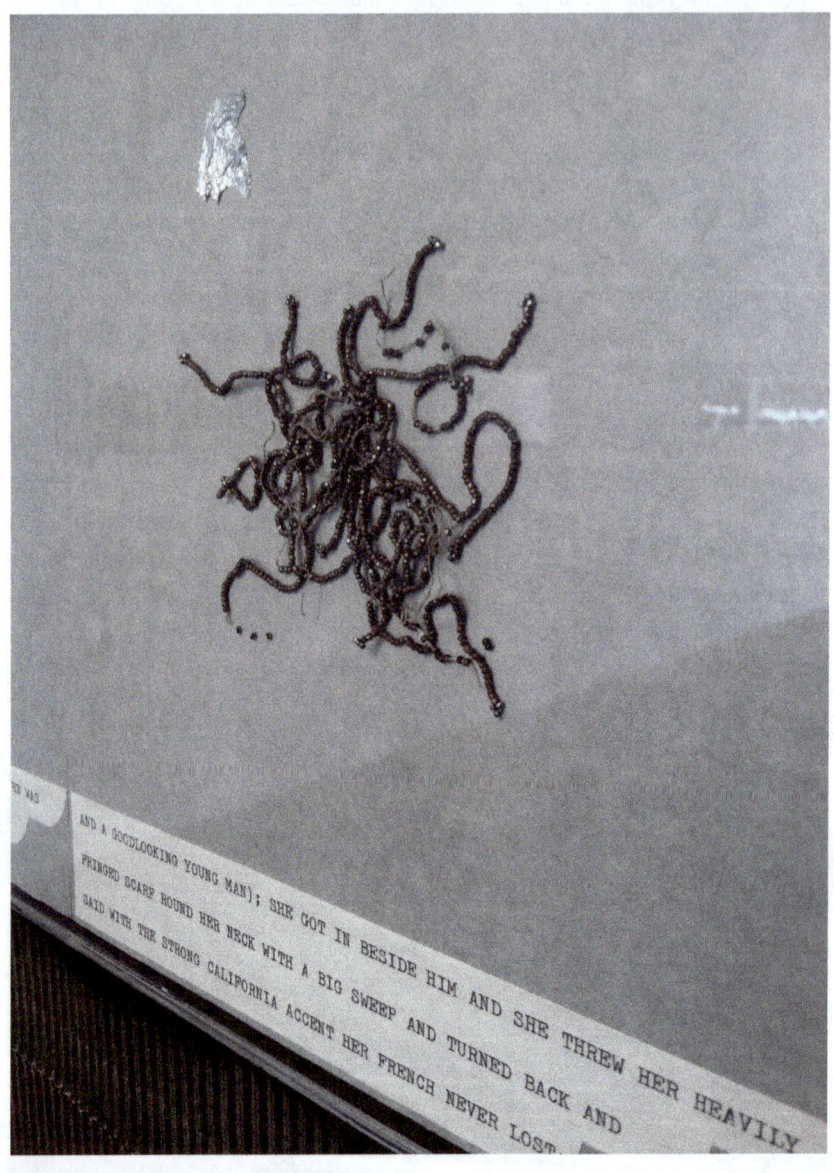

Alexis Smith *Isadora*, a glancing detail

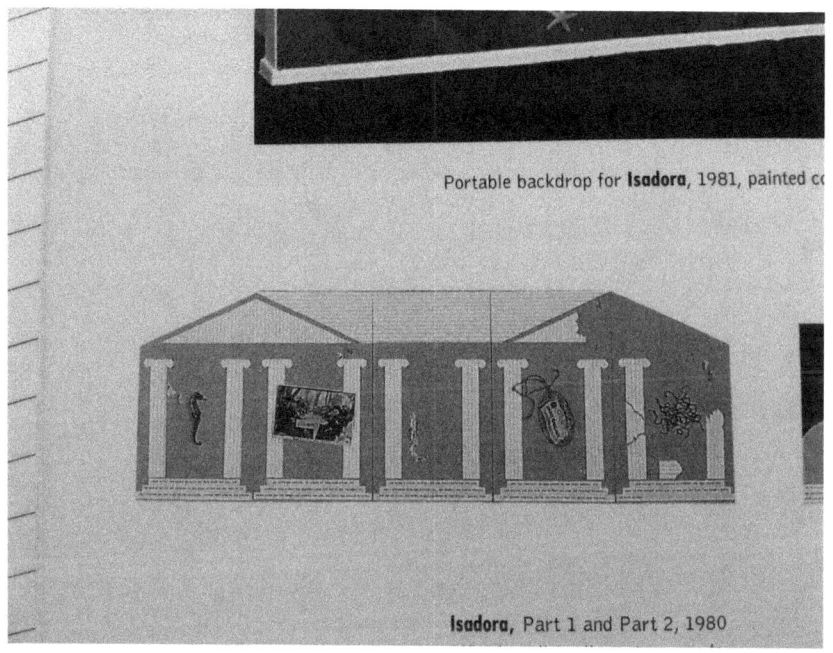

Portable backdrop for **Isadora**, 1981, painted c(

Isadora, Part 1 and Part 2, 1980

From the catalog *Alexis Smith* by Richard Armstrong for the Whitney Museum

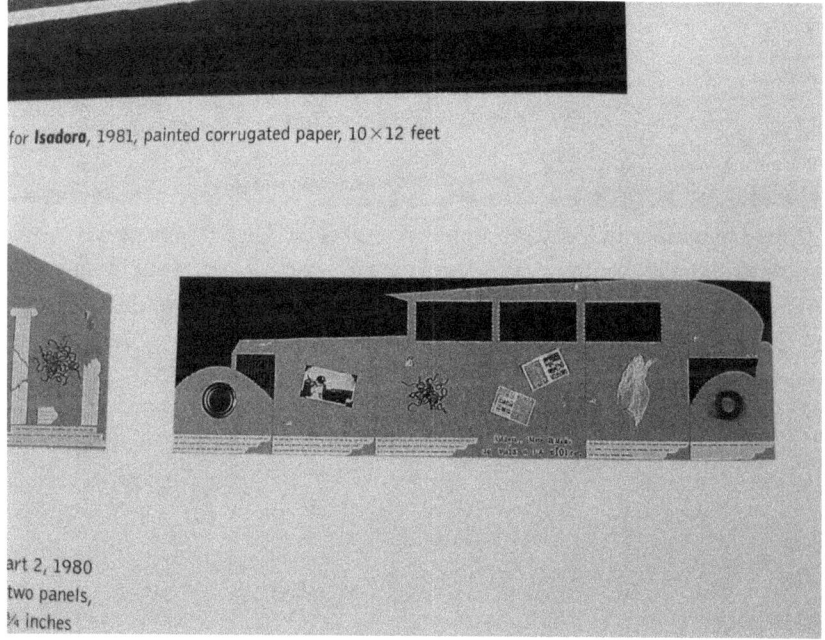

for **Isadora**, 1981, painted corrugated paper, 10 × 12 feet

art 2, 1980
two panels,
¼ inches

From the catalog *Alexis Smith* by Richard Armstrong for the Whitney Museum

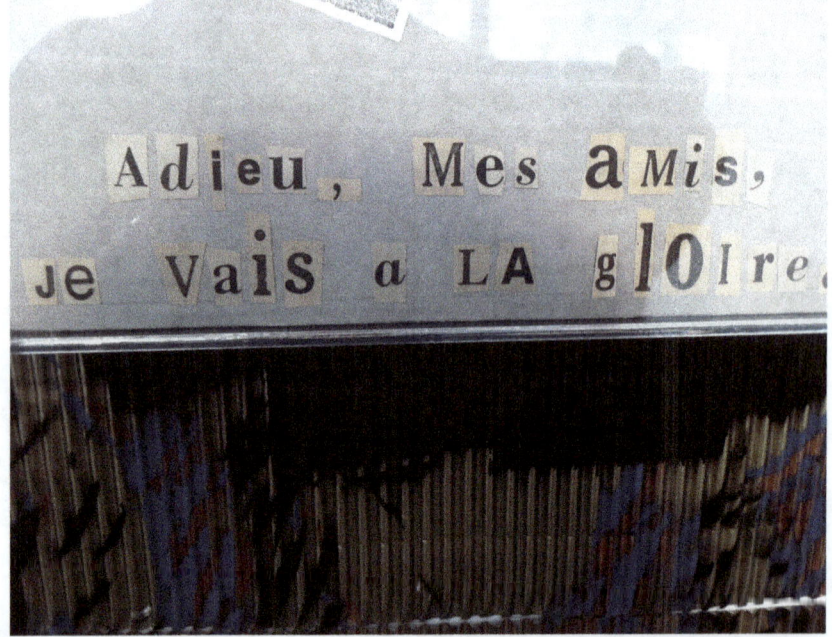

...thus spake Isadora Duncan—in her unshakeable California accent—as she continued her life journey in a Bugatti with a "good-looking wop." I remember him in the TV show as being from Montenegro, "Where," he told the dancer, "we fuck like tigers!" La gloire, indeed.

ment derive from a paternalistic and ownership-based society—even among French intellectuals? Are these thoughts examples of me straying from the artist's work, or am I having a dialogue with it?)

Alexis Smith's way with films, movie stars and with books feels risky and dangerous right now. She looks at her sources with the honesty of one who is charmed; her critique is subtle and is more a directed attempt to question one's own relations with the work and the world and with the originating films and books than it is an ironic statement about cinema or texts. I do not get a sense of distancing, or of coolness—rather, Smith is hot about the stories she loves, the characters she borrows, the narratives she repurposes and the movies in her dreams.

Respect is risky. You stake yourself on those things you value. People can see when you are in love.

All of you younger artists who read *Notes on Looking* would do well to visit *Alexis Smith: The Early Work* at Tom Solomon's. And then go back in your studio and risk something personal in the things you make.

A related anecdote: A dealer friend, while visiting a grad student's studio, listened in disbelief as the young painter told her, "Ugh, I don't want there to be poetry in my paintings!"

"Oh dear," says the fusty, middle-aged writer, "I beg to differ. You misunderstand either poetry or art."

Published on September 22, 2011 by Geoff Tuck in Reviews

REST AREA—DAN GRAHAM'S TRIANGLE BRIDGE OVER WATER, LAUMEIER SCULPTURE PARK, ST. LOUIS, MO
Aaron Wrinkle

Recently, while departing from the Los Angeles International Airport (LAX) to my home state of Missouri, I picked up my Dan Graham exhibition monograph from his well-deserved 2009 retrospective organized by the Museum of Contemporary Art, Los Angeles in collaboration w/ The Whitney Museum of American Art, New York. (An exhibition was also appropriately mounted at the Walker Art Center, Minneapolis, appropriate in that the artist has a long-time base of followers in the Midwest region.) Being that I was heading to the nature of the family farm, the generational acreage of my lineage, it only made since to reassert my attention to the chapter of Graham's writings in his "Garden as Theater and Museum." Although the farm is not a garden, theater or museum, the general notion of immediate nature akin to my family and the recent and partial placement of my own artistic ideas and practice to such an arena seems relevant here. With this said, I don't totally object to the possibility of viewing a farm as a garden, theater or museum. After all, all four of these contexts originate in and from nature. As I read through the artist's writings on the English garden's influence on the French's own appropriated English garden and the influence that literature, politics and theater had upon the creation of these sites of dwelling, leisure and recreation, I became restless, as usual. This is actually cheating the chapter, which also includes writings on Disney, Rem Koolhaas—Coney Island's Luna Park—and a great, almost romantic and historical exampling on the creation of the writer Rousseau's burial site. In short, Graham starts with the early model of the Arcadian garden and the evolution and happenings of the "garden" and its connections to creative culture, theatre, politics and nature. He follows up with the Baroque period and speeds up with corporate American theatre-ism found in the creation of garden-esque atriums in buildings, Venturi's hand in re-presenting Washington, D.C.'s original city planning in a public art work and of similar corporate frame workings of the garden in Europe. Finally, he reaches the European reality of the fair and of art experience as leisure and vacation, with families and children loading up in their cars and traveling to sculpture parks to view contemporary art. Ultimately, it (being the garden) always seemed to originate in relation to the familial or aristocratic and a tandem relationship shaped by government as an almost socialist model. Perhaps a context of art and life as a seemingly utopian experience, yet through the culmination of societal-political proportions involved, it would seem to be more about environments of multiplicity and even dystopia. Make sense? Dan once commented that he thinks I'm intellectually restless. This is true.

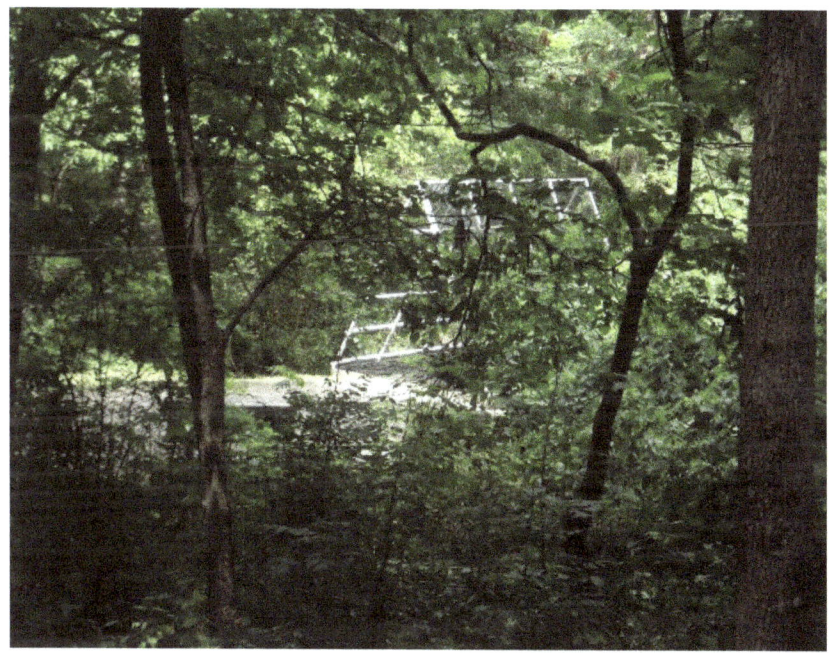

I began to flip through the chapter looking at images, eventually coming to plates of Graham's *Octagon for Münster*, his *Pergola Bridge for Clisson, France* (1988-90) and his descriptive reasoning and explanations pertaining to the history of these sites—supporting such structures' relevance for carrying out or creating them. The previous priming of the historical context shaping his practice in his writing really makes sense in the location of these pavilion works in their own time and place as well as today. Also, importantly, explained here is the artist's original proposal for the unrealized *Two-Way Mirror Bridge and Triangular Pavilion To Existing Mill House for Domaine de Kerguéhennec* (a chateau) in Brittany, France. The site of this original bridge proposal consists of a sculpture park on the grounds of an old familial estate configured within an old French garden that was converted into an English garden. Here, we see this cultural and regional transformation as vaguely mentioned above. Other elements found on the site were a surviving mill house and an old Chinese-oriented bridge, which the artist wanted to replace with a new bridge constructed from his now common two-way mirror and other corporate-oriented materials. These left-over elements on the property in fact influenced the proposal, as found in the roof form of the bridge and possibly the proposed converting of a bridge commented (not critiqued) on the site's own reconfiguring of cultural and/or regional motifs. This also can be said for the ever-changing history of the "garden" in general. In many ways, the proposal acted as an early in situ response or reaction to elements lending themselves to a practice relative to site specificity. In reality, Graham's pavilions' vortexual makeup almost always act as site specific in that they absorb the very site they are planted in, but it is important to acknowledge Graham's relevance in connection to the history of site specificity and artists that tend to get interpreted under the guise of "institutional critique"; specifically, the early site inventories of Michael Asher. In possibly a looser or humorous way, for the sake of writing about travel or the art fair, here, Asher's *Installation Münster (Caravan)* comes to mind. In fact, the two artists' practices coincided for the exhibition *Skulptur Projekte* (1987) curated by Klaus Bussmann and Kasper König (the exhibition was the second installment by these curators, coming after *Skulptur 77*, also in Münster, and the same year Asher picked his locations for his *Installation Münster (Caravan)*, Donald Judd and Claus Oldenburg also contributed to the 77 mounting). In 1987, Graham created *Octagon for Münster*, a pavilion consisting of eight panels of two-way mirror, a sloped wooden roof, a sliding door and a wooden pole in the middle of the structure supporting the floor (earth) to the roof. In short, the pavilion was placed in the middle of a tree-lined allée in an old park amidst the presence of preexisting pavilions, a university botanical garden, kiosks and even a palace. The positioning of Graham's pavilion acted essentially as an allegorical conductor in that it absorbed not only in production, but also in presentation the very essence of the history of the site pertaining to gardenhood (specifically English Baroque). It further commented, through its use of natural materials, on a step backwards into primitivism; and even further, through its use of two-way mirror, specifically comments on the surrounding contemporary city's corporate makeup of none other than two-way mirror.

The images accompanying this literary and visual scenario of *Octagon for Münster* and his *Pergola Bridge for Clisson, France* (1988-90), like images do, triggered my memory that Dan had created a similar work in my home state. This all struck a nerve. It supported my reasoning for taking the book off my shelf while packing my bag. It was clear to me on the airplane that I would drive across the state, visit the site and do this writing. It wasn't important for me to negotiate the gesture as art, as in a way, this was my Midwestern vacation. A middle-class vacation, if you will. I've still never been to Europe. It only made sense to travel and write about actions that supersede any meandering of if it's art or not. It's simply a case of an artist traveling and writing. I picked a bizarre way of starting out and found myself traveling alone. It was better this way. More importantly, this would be the first pavilion by the artist that I would experience firsthand.

After spending the week on my parents' farm in southwest Missouri on the outskirts of Springfield, the hometown I share with the likes of Brad Pitt and Bob Barker, I packed a bag of clothes and headed to Kansas City, where I had studied painting at the Kansas City Art Institute. Here, I stayed with my friends Neal and Lacey and their cats Mildred and Mr. Butters in their turn-of-the-century four-story duplex in the historic Westside district, with a special bonus to their hospitality always found in their dinners from the garden, Neal's bread baking and a huge record collection and library. One favorite in this area is Lou Reed's "New Sensations" track on the album of the same name, which I normally play at least 5 times over after a few beers or to introduce the drinking of a few beers. I realize this didn't happen this time, and we stayed primarily out on the back porch over conversation, Miller High Life, and a nice breeze w/ Mariah, Timmy and Phil.

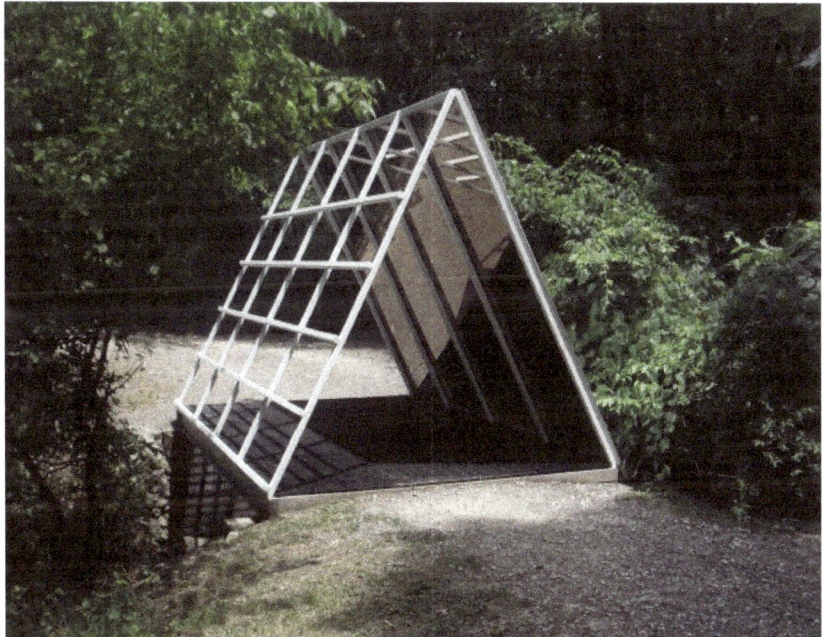

Previously, the sun had highlighted the back yard and the clothes on the line in a golden amber I haven't seen even in California. I was finally breaking out of an almost demobilizing neurotic and manic episode I'd been having for over a month with Maria as my witness, at least in Kansas City. Actually, she helped me end it. Even though I was aching to leave L.A. for a bit, I'd had to drag myself to the airport just a week prior. I hadn't felt this immobile since CalArts. We all talked about lots of things that night, and I selfishly talked on and on about the trip I would take the following morning. As Neal had looked through the Dan Graham book earlier in that evening in the front room, I'd flipped through an older Mike Kelley one that prompted a melancholic smile and feeling towards my studio in Los Angeles—towards Los Angeles in general. I was here to travel and write, though. It also got me thinking of what I wanted to do with all of those ball cards under the bed at my folks' house.... That was good. I needed to focus on a different outlet and take a needed break from what seems to be an overarching energy focused on what is success in L.A.. I admit it drains me. This inspiration that leads to the studio could wait for now, but sleep couldn't. It was already approaching 3:00 AM.

It was morning, and the sun blanketed the front downstairs library room. It was a lot brighter than the amber one from the sundown the night before. Being summer, I slept with only a sheet and pillow in a floral design reminiscent of Warhol. Mildred kept me company and woke me up by jumping on my back while the mockingbirds played rooster. It was 8:30 AM or so and approaching the upper 90s already. I was anxious. I shat, showered Bronner's style, brushed my teeth Tom's style (neither my own), grabbed some printing paper (not mine), a pen (not mine either) and left the house (I really came prepared). It was time to travel again. I grabbed a water and headed to the local snack shop, YJ's, for some fruit (a banana and an orange), said hi to my old professor Jack Rees, who was eating his breakfast in close proximity to where we'd once held a conversation on Max Jammer's *Concepts of Space* and the elementary foundations of geometry several years prior. I told David Ford—a local artist and owner of the café—I'd possibly be back through in the evening and he invited me over for a studio visit, wishing me a safe travel. The day would be packed. I was on my way.

St. Louis is a straight line from Kansas City on Interstate 70. The destination would be approx 250 miles and 4 hours later. I turned the radio on to hear Felony's "Fanatic," a fitting song for the trip and a great rhythm to approach the pavement regardless. It was a 96.5 the Buzz resurrection segment that wouldn't last much longer after the song, as once it got heavy into the popular music of '80s, I changed the channel for obvious reasons. Most music or creative things coming out of the '80s that I can appreciate relate more to the aesthetics of the '70s. Punk and pre-alternative seems relevant to my own interests. That and rap. Not thirty minutes into my trip, I began to question my driving for the first time alone to a city I've only visited not even the number of fingers on one hand. The last time I rode in a car on I-70 was to see Sonic Youth, Wolf Eyes and Hair Police in Columbia. On the way back, we listened to ...And Justice for All by Metallica. We stopped in a gas station in Booneville, to be called a bunch of faggots. I was wearing a Men's Recovery T-Shirt. My cousin Kristen once went to military school there. So this time, I drove, I peed, I drove, I peed, I drove and I arrived. I also stopped to buy batteries for my camera—my mother's camera—a Fuji.

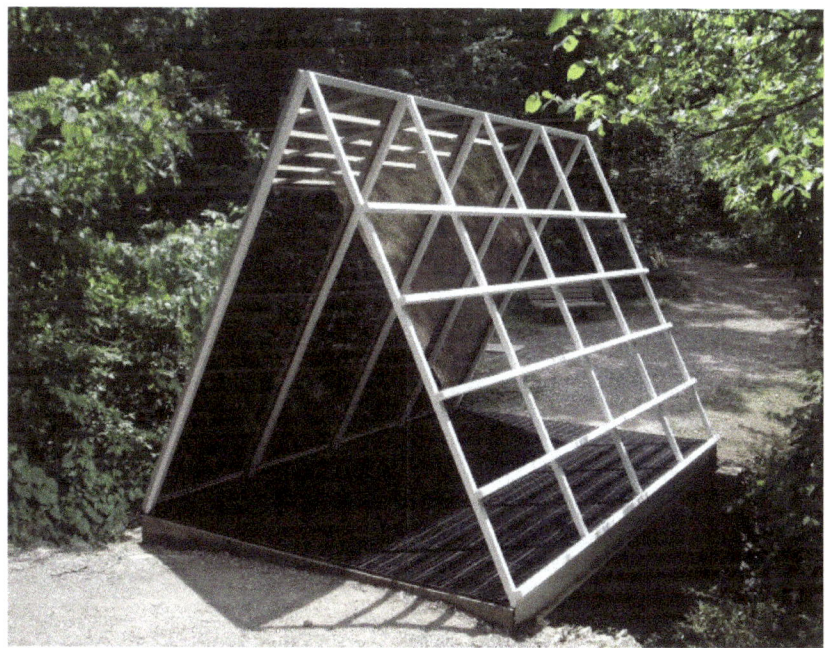

Laumeier Sculpture Park is located on the outer edge of St. Louis off of I-44 (198 miles west of the artist's birthplace of Urbana, Illinois, and 188 miles north of Springfield, MO) on 72 acres of the former land of the park's namesake, Matilda Laumeier. She donated the land to the county in 1968. Between 1975 and 1977, the artist Ernest Trova, via Pace Gallery, donated 40 works to help form the Park, and other donated works were later offered by Robert Morris, Alexander Calder and Mark di Suvero. The Triangle Bridge Over Water (1990) was part of the park's Ten Sites program from 1980-1990, a unique program that facilitated a collaboration between artists and the county's Trades people from the Parks Department. It was commissioned w/ funds from the Mark Twain Laumeier Endowment Fund and the National Endowment for the Arts. In 1989, the year before the bridge's installment, the park founded its first children's summer camp. Obviously, the new installment added a proven treat then, over time and now for children visiting the park, and as with most of Graham's structures, makes for great photo ops for couples and families.

After parking my car, I snapped a photo of a Harley-Davidson motorcycle with veteran-sticker–tagged helmets sitting freely on the seat. I then approached a man driving a golf cart, asking where to find Dan Graham's bridge work. He offered me a lift in the now 102-degree weather. I explained that I was visiting via Kansas City via Springfield via Los Angeles, my connections to Missouri, and that I know the artist. I jotted down the dates of the park's founding, inquired of the work's 1990 installation, and before I knew it, we were at the location, or at least right above it. He told me, "It's a steep incline to walk down, but you'll find it." I smiled and laughed inside and told him thanks! I didn't get his name, but I'm going to write a thank you letter soon. It was indeed a steep, concrete stairwell with long black handles that wound down a hill that turned into a beaten-down dirt path with wildflowers and surrounding woods. The structure began to reveal itself midway. A child might think there's a house down there. It felt very "Hansel and Gretel." I could see its peak. Its 2-decade-old white frame was still quite stark for the mostly dual palette of green and brown found in these particular Missouri woods. The sun sparked off the structure. The sun was a spotlight in this garden of a museum. I once joked that I thought Dan's pavilions were the perfect culmination of two of his past relationships. It wasn't meant as a cut down, obviously, but more so an appreciation for Dan possibly acknowledging his influences subversively. Actually, the artist has never been one to hold back from admitting influence or admiration for others, or support for that matter. Basically, it was that Dan borrowed a general aesthetic from Smithson through glass by replacing it with corporate two-way mirror and reconfigured Flavin into the sun that shines upon his works. I must say that the full credit goes to Dan, and not on a whimsical or even absurd observation, but more so the very fact that his pavilions are proof to the evolution of art in general (this isn't an academic approach (Neither Dan's to his work, nor Wrinkle's to observing his work. Ed.); it's strictly natural—almost scientific and/or supernatural). Knowing that Dan's generation despised Duchamp, it can safely be assumed that such a natural and elemental shifting upon, say, the view of fluorescents being replaced by the sun can be spouted. It is my opinion that Dan's work is the perfect example of a capturing of the everyday activities of humanity and materiality, specifically in relation to art and nature and more specifically in the hybrid,—non predictable experience that is offered by Graham's work in Laumeier Sculpture Park, as is offered above. It's alive! In Dan's own words—*"I'm skeptical of models that implicitly recognize the world as it is."*[1] Sometimes, these activities of production, thinking and viewership are captured literally through documentation, and sometimes not. Whatever the case, a pavilion on its own does this: It sits there; it participates; it has a conversation with nature (which is anything *but* natural), with kids playing; it might even reflect a police car with sirens flying by—ultimately, it reflects the societies surrounding it. It is this that is in complete alignment with the evolution of the garden, museum and theatre. This is not sociology, but rather a culmination of varying humanities. With this said, I find the *Triangle Bridge Over Water* and its placement at Laumeier Sculpture Park to be a very important work in relation to Graham's "Garden as Theater as Museum," and although some may argue that the second French site that was realized (*Pergola Bridge for Clisson, France* (1988-90)) makes more sense to the original proposal (*Two-Way Mirror Bridge and Triangular Pavilion To Existing Mill House for Domaine de Kerguéhennec*), not only in its location, but in its regional posterity—I propose that the Midwestern placement in relation to the sculpture park, the existing homestead of Laumeier, along with other architectural structures, including a country-style bridge honoring a bird sanctuary, makes more sense in alignment to the original proposal. But what also stands out to my personal experience is how photographic the work looks. Aside from the fact that the thing is alive in all that it does, it really just feels like a great snap shot from a distance. Maybe I'm biased on a best-case scenario, or maybe this is a question for the artist and a needed visit to the French location on my part. Whatever the case, the book-to-life experience feels somewhat 1:1.

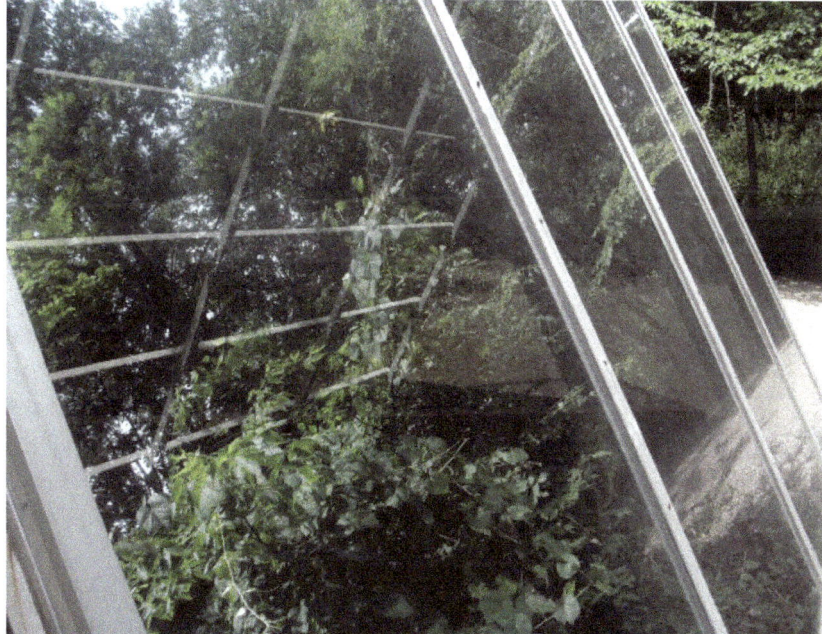

The dirt path has now turned into a curvilinear gravel one surrounding and defining the perimeter for *Triangle Bridge Over Water*. There's a faux wood bench to the right, but I walked into the work, took in a few glances and, for the moment, opted to sit in the middle of the structure instead of on the out-side. It was a place to rest and a place to write. (The last time I had been to a rest area or park in St. Louis was speed-induced, as I recall an old friend losing his knife in a game of throwing it at a tree while another drew blood and pushed it back in, while a possible cheating couple on their lunch break fornicated on a park bench.) The thing about nature is it is always reminding and revealing, especially when you come from a place with a lot of it. It's not always good. A lot of times, it is weird, but this time it was pleasant. Actually, this time it was great (Laumeier Sculpture Park).

I began to take note of the elements making up the work and their and the work's overall collaboration with the nature surrounding it. The bridge's make-up consists of two large concrete walls placed on each side of a cavity where a spring exists, runoff from two large drainage pipes. The structure is reflected in the shallow water below and, in the current climate, looks similar to a sheet of glass laid flat across the earth (this is very interesting in relation to the properties along the streets to the park where the water comes from, as low-tier corporate buildings with two-way mirror glass line them). Sitting atop this common support system for bridges are three high black beams, a black metal grate-like frame acting as the surface you walk on and over and through which you can look down into the space below (both the original proposal and Brittany work had two-way mirror flanking the grate walkway, whereas the St. Louis work is solely the black grating). There's some minor flak-ing of the paint on the edge of the black edging, revealing an orange primer, and some small cobwebs also exist. Both entry and exit sides are flanked by age but still very sturdy approximately 8×2 raw unstained wood pieces/base-boards. On the south side, four large sheets of two-way mirror extend from one edge. The sheets of glass are seamed and held up by long industrial and flanged like aluminum struts and held in place with a few replaced bolts that are raised and octagonal in shape and mostly secured by the original rounded Phillips-style heads (the cross kind) that are now rusted. It all makes sense the way it is. The cycle makes itself. No need for restoration, but fix anything that might jeopardize the standing of such a structure, this being a very common view in the likes of repairing things in this part of the country with work skills originating from the Great Depression.

On the other side, a 20-panel frame and grid (equilateral to the two-way–mir-rored one), akin to an open garden trellis or lattice for vegetation (English ivy) to possibly run up, supports the north side. It's very Sol LeWitt. The trel-lis, built out of approx. 2×2 cubed welded and painted white steel beams, is

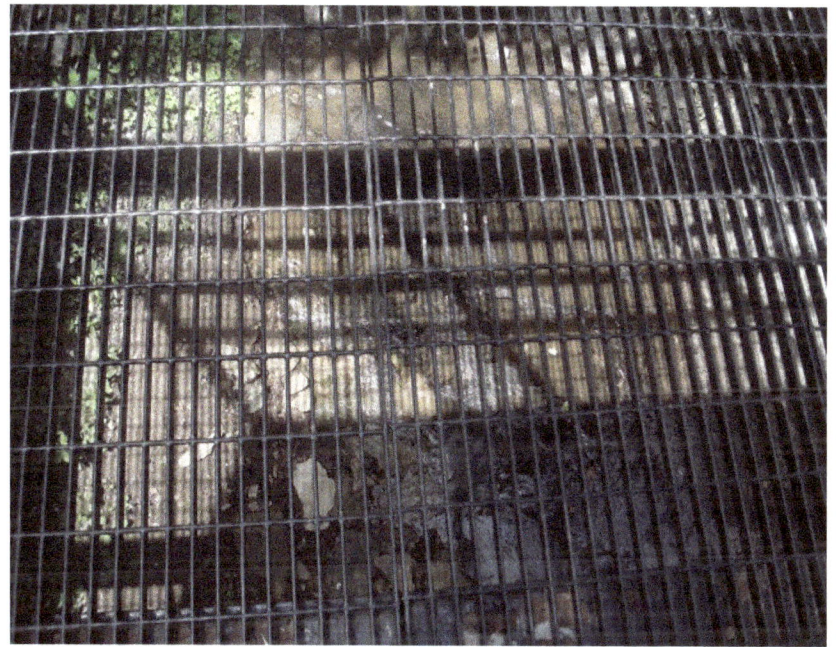

currently and has presumably been empty and is patinated with a couple of runoff rust drips right at the seams. It has been sweating. A similar description, aside from the mentioning of somewhat arbitrary disrepair, supports my St. Louis experience and findings as stated by Graham on the Pergola Bridge—*"My Two-Way Mirror Pergola Bridge from 1988-'90 consists of a 4-meter-long equilateral triangle bridge, one side two-way mirror glass, the opposite side an aluminum lattice planted with climbing vines. The spectator can walk through the triangle over a water canal across an open steel grid."2* Although the setting of the French work is probably and arguably a more desired setting by many, as its location is more grandiose, it is obvious the two works share very much in common in their production and placement in nature. More importantly, the grate-like walkway relates to Graham's original proposal for *Two-Way Mirror Bridge and Triangular Pavilion To Existing Mill House for Domaine de Kerguéhennec*, more specifically in that it is based off of the French use of similar materials in their vents found in the Paris Metro. (*"The bottom of the triangle—the walkway surface—was to be the steel grating with an open square grid, the same surface used for Paris street air vents over sewers and the Metro."*)3 Grating was the first word that came to mind as I took my notes on the Bridge's materials. Visually, the grate is very optical and another example of a practical material used by the artist to lend itself to something other than what it is. Importantly here, it reverberated—focused upon the visual vibrancy of a Bridget Riley painting in monochrome, of course. More importantly, it was a pluralistic suggestion on post-minimalism. Aside from these assumptions, as usual, Dan's referencing to materials and site is right on and strangely very specific. This can also be said for the general make-up of the surrounding nature found in the water and foliage of greenery. This thing is alive in nature, as indicative of its general make-up and the aforementioned rustic patina, the peeling of paint and, I now remember, the fogged-up glass. It has become, if not already in the beginning, part of nature. Actually, the nature surrounding Dan Graham's work is something I don't believe to be written enough about aside from the artist's own words. People tend to get caught up in the corporate appearance, which is hilarious in that the very material Dan is referencing or possibly critiques, people generally fall in love with. This is all fine, but I suspect that the greater relationship found in the work is of hybrid if not of multiple sensorial relationships between humans, objects and natures. However, maybe it is the fact that these works can be viewed anyway one likes that make them so special—and for that matter, by anyone—and I guess in some cases there isn't literal nature at all.

Back to the site—the non-presence of ivy running the trellis is replaced in the reflection of nature upon it in its reverse, as the grid acts as a window in to normal viewing as well as in its reflection found in its reflecting counterpart (the four panels consisting of two-way mirror). As a reflecting image or reality, the grid juts out, appearing as a propped-open window in its two-way mirrored counterpart. This is actually what happens when you create an equilateral triangle that is reflective on one side, meaning it pulls the overall form up to the reflecting surface, essentially suspending the object partially in midair. At least visually, it appears that way. It is a kind of geometric substantial magic, a weightless pendulum. The setting of this thing is appropriate and fitting, even if strangely literal for the imagination of a summer window opening. We had a place we went to as teenagers that we called trip land. We played baseball with hedge apples. I ran through a Sol LeWittian landscape of multiplied grids being chased by a Doberman Pinscher. On another occasion, a friend humped a tree, shaking its leaves, as another threw a cinderblock through a large black corporate window. In nature, anything can be seen and can happen. I glance through the trellis to find a woodpecker and three squirrels running up a tree in the nature surrounding the trail. They are real! I turn around to see my own morphed projection and reflection onto the two-way mirror. I'm not on anything. It is true; Dan's works are of psychedelic relations. No drugs needed. Extra priming might make it more intense, though. Everything is still moving for me. It's similar to my father's copy of the Byrds' *Greatest Hits* album, which consists of an overlay of psychedelic foliage transposed onto the band members' images. This connects to Dan as well. Dad is ten years younger. Good early music taste, though. Another tangent but, in my opinion, which many may disagree, the Stones were actually punks in a good way. Punk goes back to blues and jazz and even further into ancient tribes. A somewhat more recent pop cultural example coming to mind is the Predator's appearance in the jungle as it dives in and out of combat, blending itself into nature. What I was trying to say is the Rolling Stones were an early punk band, but became popular.

A tour is approaching. It is the man who gave me a lift. "You found it," he declared to me and the group with a friendly gesture of his hand to the work. He then stated, "And here we have a friend of the artist." I'm on the stage, the bridge. I'm wearing rose-colored shades. I step out onto the path. He asks, "How do you know the artist?" I explained the gallery I once ran and the fair conversation, Dan's generosity in conversation and ideas, but more importantly the conversation began to act as some kind of a locative performance between myself, the two docents and the three couples riding in the empty golf cart I had rode in before. What I mean is we began to talk about the work. I realize when I say performance, this sounds as if I'm describing it is an artwork. I must stress I don't view this as such. I think it is safe to say I share Dan's distaste for such institutionalized conversational gestures of, say, Tino Sehgal. The only thing else I could say is, "Yes, this is a great location for this work." The man exited the cart and stepped into the bridge. As I followed him in, he said, "Tell Dan that on tours, rambunctious kids always go to the middle, see their reflection and calm down, and it really takes to them." I acknowledge the site's great ability to possibly do this for anyone and the funhouse nature and corporate joke as well. I also say there could be a good Frank Lloyd Wright joke in here somewhere, with this quasi-architecture over water. The female docent goes into her tour speech, declaring, "This is a perfect place where nature just melts." The tour is wrapping up their viewing of the bridge. As they leave, the man energetically says, "Only a friend of the artist would be caught viewing the piece in rose-colored shades." I explained I was born and raised in Missouri.

After the tour left, I decided to snap some images through my rose-colored shades of the perimeter and even of the bridge. I must say, I didn't experience the work with my shades on, but the remarks by the tour guide prompted production. I wrapped up my tour of the piece as well. I made two passes in and out of it. As I reached the top of the stairs, I glanced down at the peaking roof again. The brush was making noise to my right by way of a chipmunk. I snapped a photo and walked away.

Although I visited Laumeier Sculpture Park to view *Triangle Bridge Over Water*, I wasn't necessarily traveling to see art. Actually, I was trying to escape it temporarily. Out of respect for the park, I walked around, and the land, its history and installments are impressive. With this said, I'm not disrecognizing Dan's work as art or even the importance of a park I will most likely visit again, it's just that sometimes we just need a place to rest. I guess I should pack my bags. It's time to go back to Los Angeles.

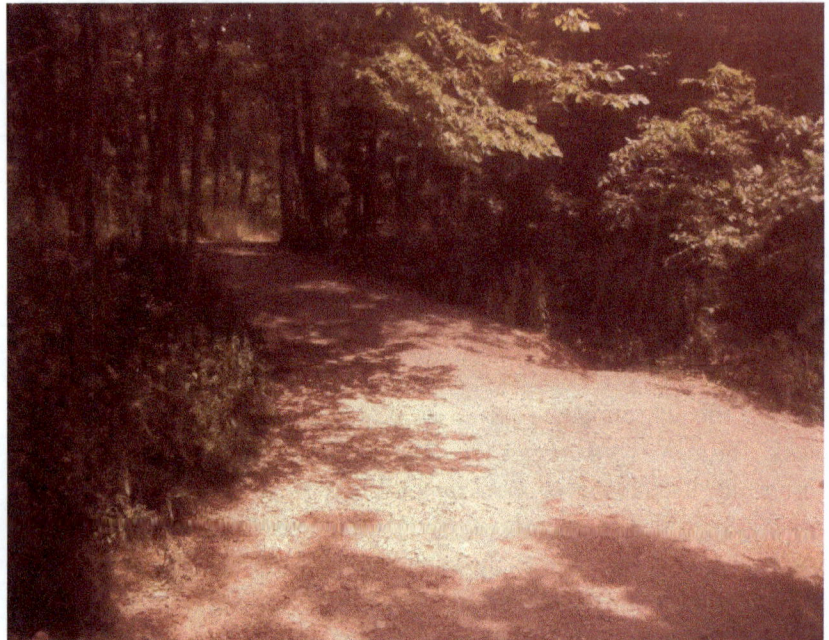

Photos in this piece are by Aaron Wrinkle.

[1]Back of Book Caption, *Manga Dan Graham Story*, Fumihiro Nonomura and Ken Tanimoto, tenpo-press
[2] pg. 252, *Dan Graham Beyond*, Simpson and Iles, Editors, Museum of Contemporary Art, Los Angeles, The MIT Press
[3] p. 253, *Dan Graham Beyond*, Simpson and Iles, Editors, Museum of Contemporary Art, Los Angeles, The MIT Press

Published on June 30, 2012 by Aaron Wrinkle in Aaron Wrinkle, Reviews and tagged Aaron Wrinkle, Dan Graham

RICHARD JACKSON, A BOOK AND MY BROTHER

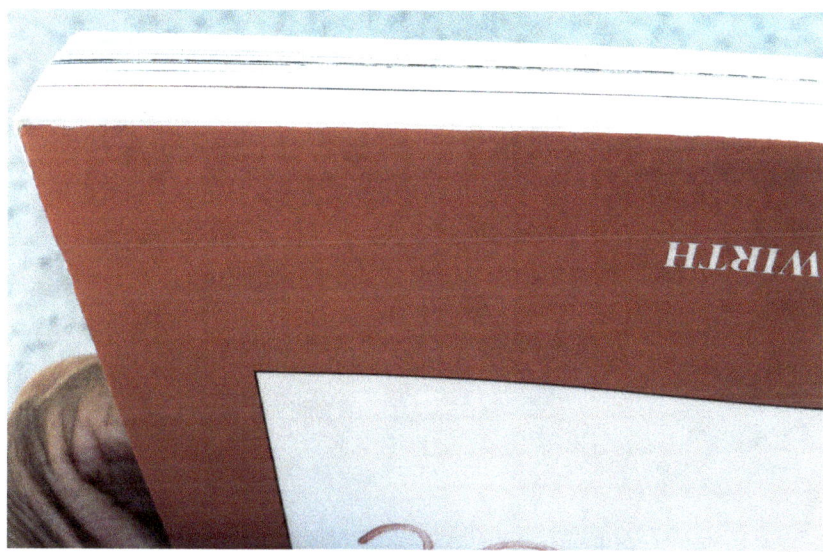

(August 27, Parkfield) The edge of Richard Jackson Deer Beer, 1998 Galerie Hauser & Wirth, Octagon Press

(August 27, Parkfield) It occurred to me that I might photograph the perimeter of the book

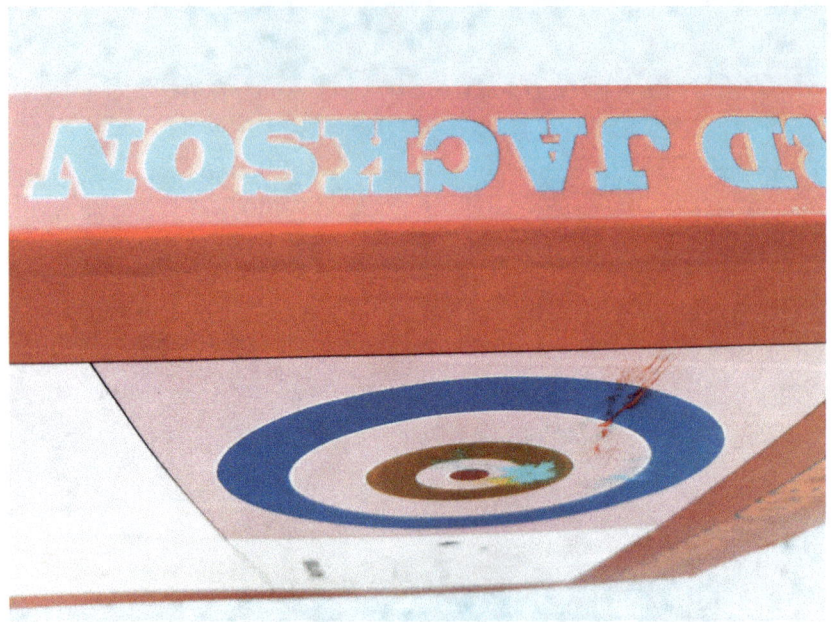

…and thereby capture its contents.

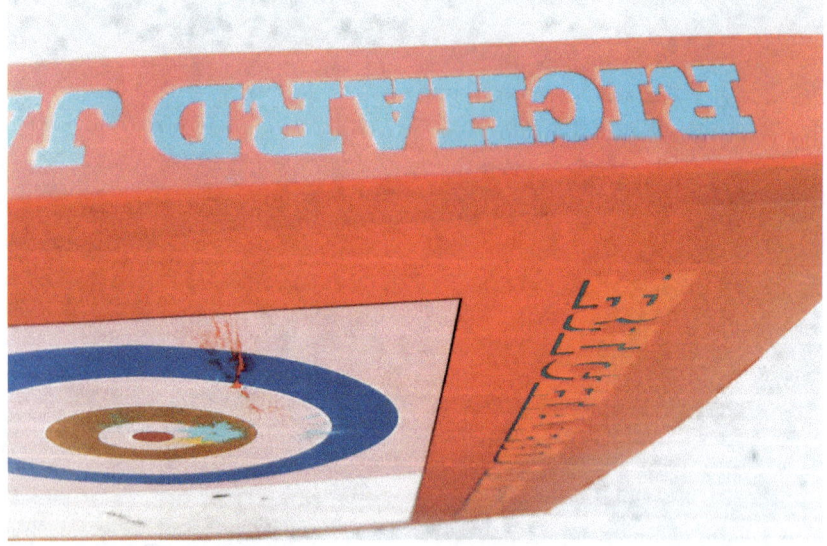

As is often the case, my plan became a struggle to learn my tool—for this project I had an iPhone 4 camera

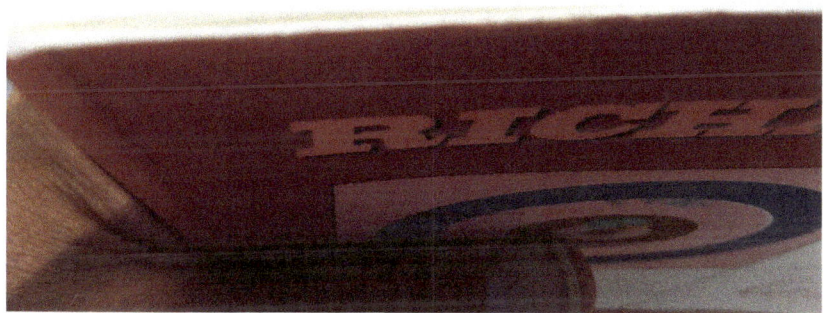

…which, I learn, wants to focus on what it recognizes—in this case, the text, rather than the book's edge. (I use what tools and materials I have at hand. Together, these inform the work and shape my ideas.)

(August 27, Parkfield) At the inn by the pool, as with the preceding and following photographs.

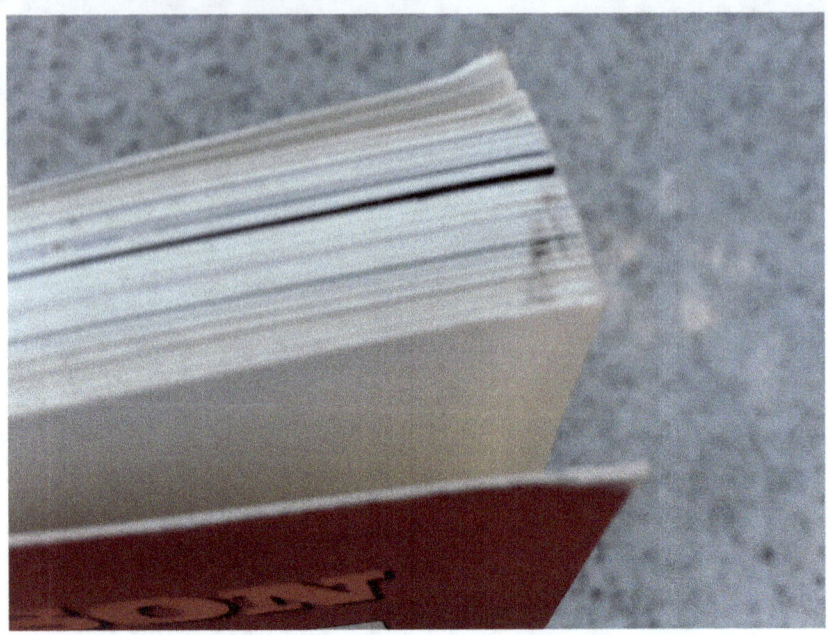

Or maybe it was on Sunday, August 28th? Now I wonder…. The temperature was 105 that day, and I drank a lot of beer.

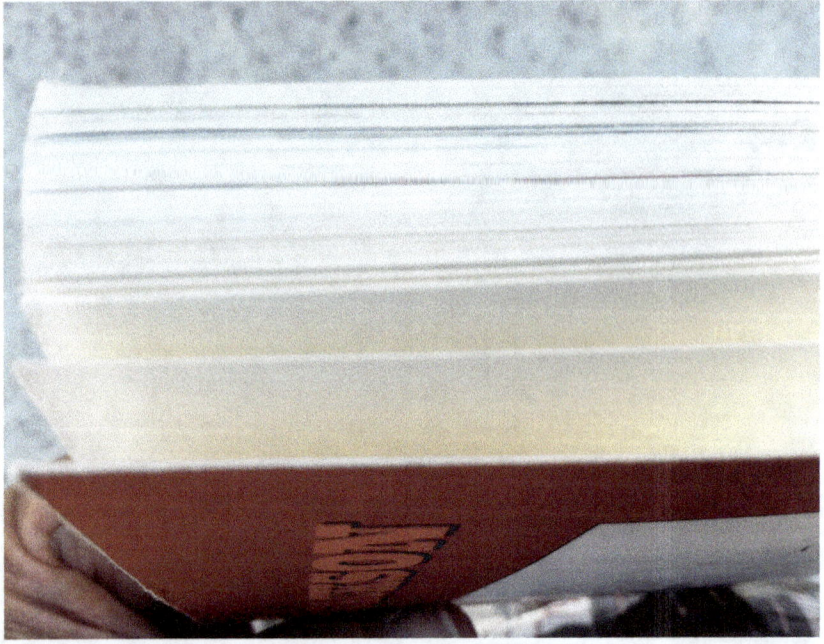

Pressed, our text is, between my chest and my belly: my brother's book, my hand, and my body, in David's shirt—there is more to be done with books, my friends, than simply to read words on pages.

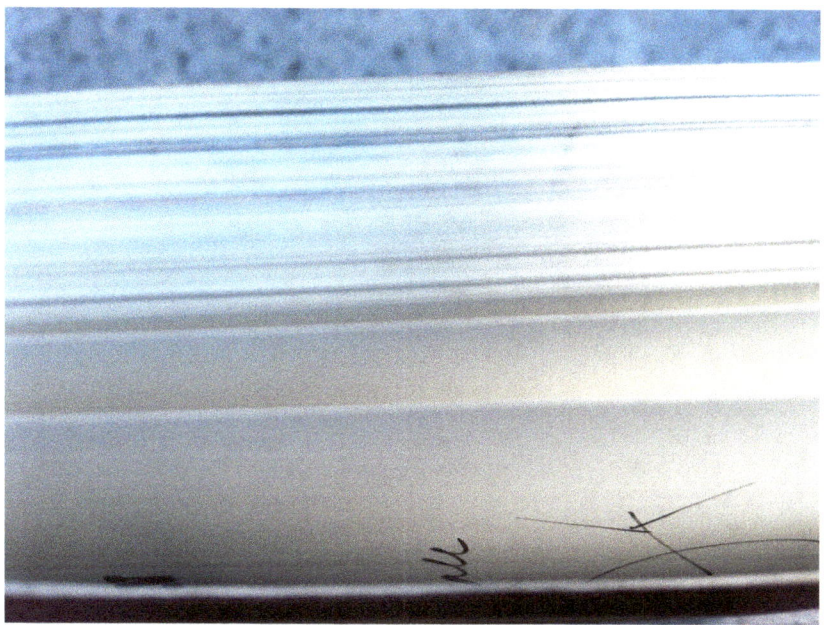

The catalog is inscribed by the artist with drawings of a deer head and a beer bottle. "Dear x" it says, "Thanks for all your support." A cupid heart surrounds the head and the beer.

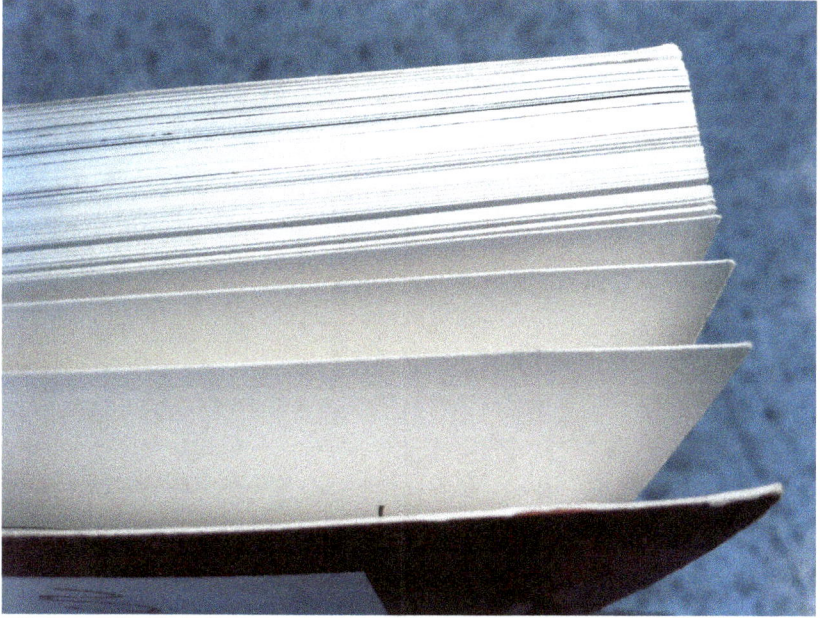

Finally, a crisp picture of the lovely pages. This was my original intent in picking up the camera and approaching this object—to capture the nature of this area of a book. I like better what has happened. So much for original intent.

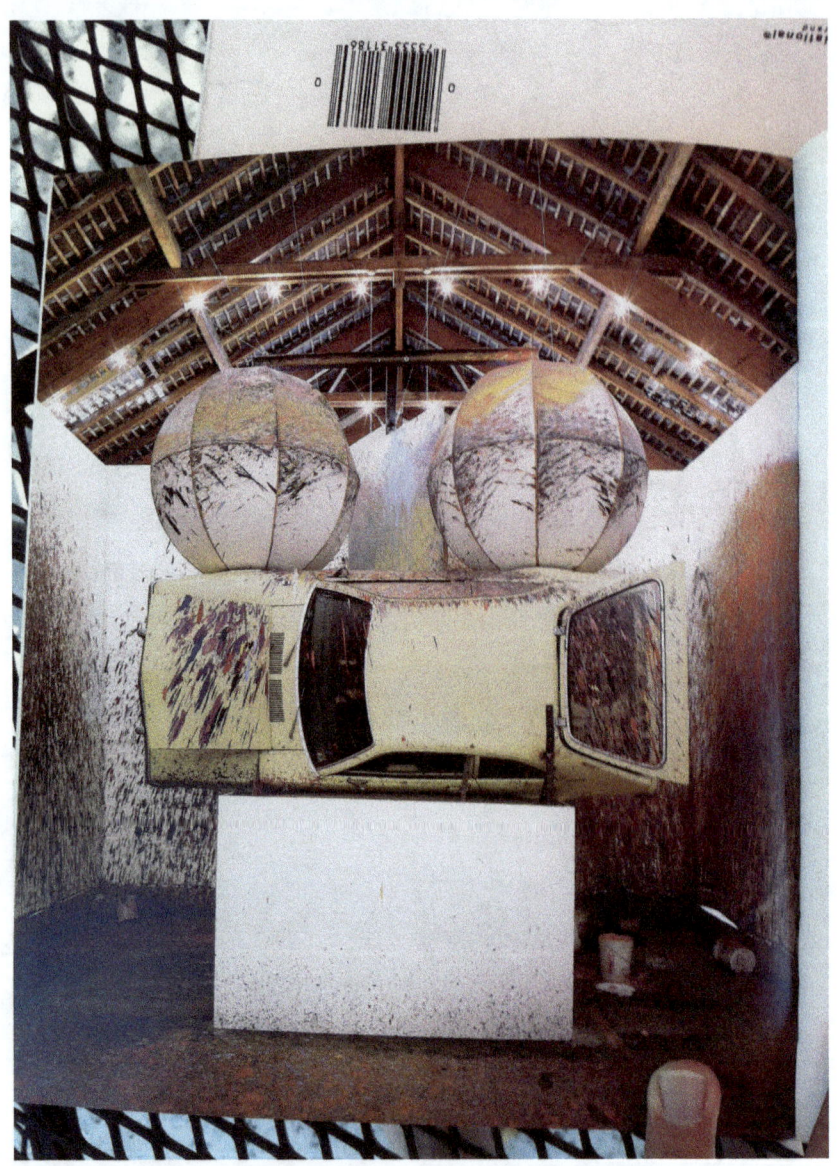

Richard Jackson, *Painting with Two Balls*, 1997 Ford Pinto, Metall, Holz, Leinwand, Acrylfarbe, 609.6 x 109.3 x 609.6 cm „Holderbank", Kunstausstellung Holderbank, Schweiz (page 131)

I wonder whether Richard Jackson's use of a pale yellow Ford Pinto in his 1996 action-sculpture-painting-installation *Painting with Two Balls* has any reference to Jason Rhoades' 1994 piece, *Swedish Erotica & Fiero Parts*?

I understand that the older artist was a mentor to Rhoades, and that Rhoades, as a much-lionized young artist, championed Jackson's work. So there is an acknowledged connection between the artists. The catalog's writing on *Two Balls* doesn't mention Rhoades' *Fiero*; in the discussion among Jackson, Alberta Mayo and Hans-Ulrich Obrist, *Two Balls* is presented as a response to Jasper Johns' painting of the same name. (For what it's worth, may I point out that Jackson's balls are much the bigger pair?)

On YouTube, there exists a video about Richard Jackson that, in a cinematic way, takes one through what must have been curator Harald Szeemann's process of discovery: seeing the piece first in the artist's studio and being charmed and amazed, then through its installation at the Biennale in Lyon, where Richard Jackson poured gallons of paint on his balls, climbed in the open hatchback of his sideways-mounted Pinto, and ran the engine—spraying paint "all over the painting, the balls and every fucking thing," to quote the artist. In the final section (good God, stay around for this!!!), the nice people at the Manitoba Museum add the music of Vangelis from *Chariots of Fire*. How audacious and crazy is that?! You will squeal and love this manipulation of your emotions. You will cheer our hero, Richard Jackson. Finally, you will laugh at the entire adventure and at your part in it. Yay. Plus, the Swiss present this object and performance in a highly clinical fashion. Jackson must have had a part in this—men in crispy white coveralls looking like NASA clean room workers, shiny ladders—all great stuff.

My older brother Mike loaned this book to me some six or seven years ago. Or rather, Mike brought the book with him to my house when he visited and, in that way that family members have, he left it for me to look at. Time went by, and I never returned it. ("Hey Mike—I'll be done with the book soon, I promise.")

Deer Beer has become a sort of totem to me for my older brother. Seeing Richard Jackson's book around my house connects me to Mike even though we're—well, we're not estranged, really. Our relationship is more like an archipelago. My brothers and sister and I are close and are very aware of each other, but there is a bit of ocean around each of us. This bit grows and shrinks with the slow tide of our lives.

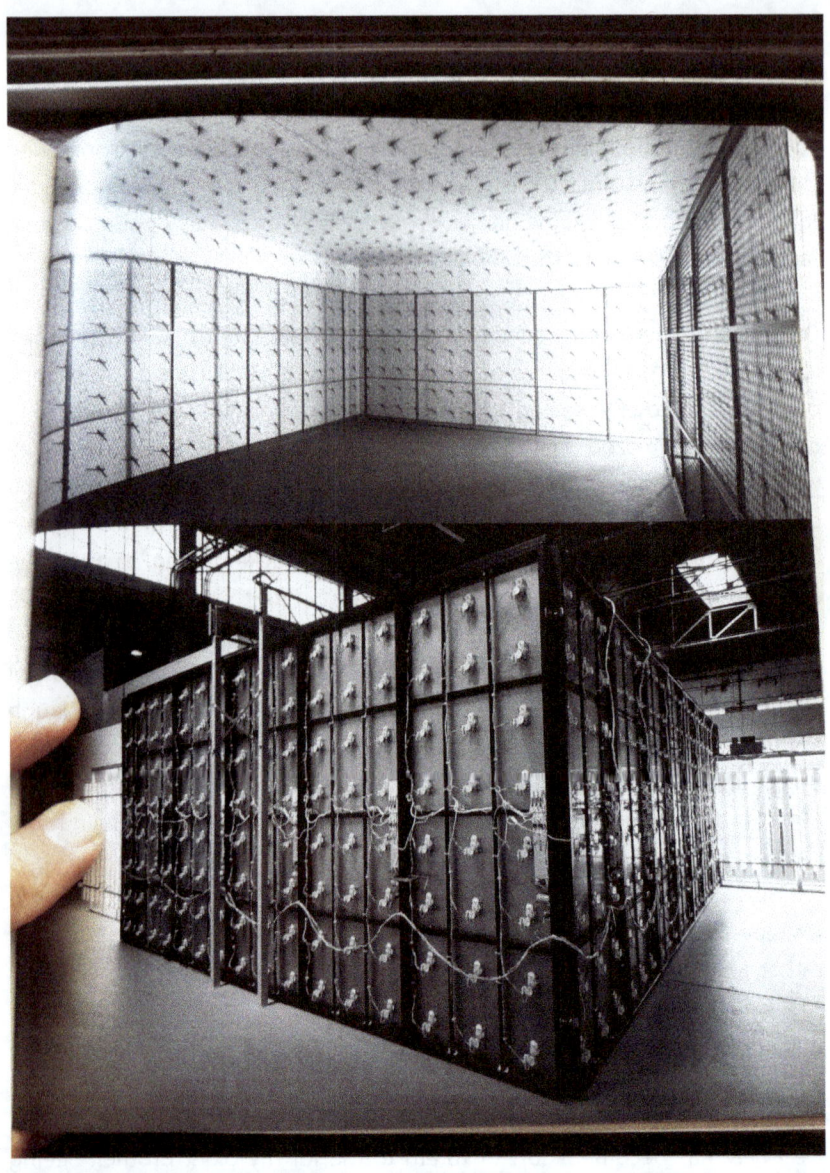

You see, my brother is friendly with Richard Jackson. They go hunting together, they drink beer, and they camp. As I understand it, Mike built Jackson's studio, as well as the studios of other important and famous artists. (My brother is a carpenter by calling, formerly as a trade and now as a hobby.) Richard Jackson's 1998 catalog is the point where our worlds, Mike's and mine, cross and meet. Because of this meeting of worlds, I'm recently finding myself faced with young artists who furrow their brows at me and ask, "Are you Mike Tuck's brother? I worked with that guy in Richard Jackson's studio. He's cool!" Given my presumption of remove from my family, this is unsettling, yet also very thrilling—I am proud of my big brother, with his skilled hands and easy way with people, and I am proud that I look good in his eyes for my accomplishments in the art world.

Each of the several times Mike has talked with me about Richard Jackson, he has mentioned seeing *1000 Clocks* at MOCA in 1992. Mike's face lights up and he gets a far-away, storytelling look in his eyes. *"I walked in, Geoff, and on every wall and on the ceiling were clocks,* (now Mike is gesturing, as though pointing out these clocks to me) *each one ticking, each keeping exact and exactly the same time. Click, click, click…."* As he finishes with the "clicks," my brother trains his eyes on mine, driving home the magnificence he saw and the mind-altering amazement that he felt at that time in 1992 and still feels today. My brother has a wizard's probing grey-green eyes and rather heavy brows. While powerful, his gaze is also gentle, and when he holds me in it I cannot and I do not want to look away.

Quoting briefly from Richard Jackson in *Deer Beer*, pages 19 and 21. (By the way, I find that the catalog Richard *Jackson Deer Beer* is available from Hauser & Wirth.)

"For me it is important to make it all by myself because I don't have a lot of good ideas and I think most artists don't. Executing the idea is another way for me to think of the next project. The labor is another element in the work, the amount and the scale can also be overwhelming. 1000 Clocks, *which was one of the later big ideas… people weren't aware at all that I made every single clock. It is part of my reaction to the 1980s, when art became so corporate and so collective rather than an individual activity. I am not as much interested in what a group of people can do inasmuch as an individual can do on their own. It is easy to have ideals when you are twenty years old but the job is to maintain them in the face of temptation."*

„1000 Clocks" entstand kurz bevor der Künstler 50 Jahre alt wurde. Die Arbeit wurde vom Künstler bezahlt, und jedes Teil ist von Hand gemacht oder zusammengesetzt. Es dauerte fünf Jahre, bis die Arbeit fertig war, finanziert wurde sie durch seine Arbeit auf dem Bau. Eine Arbeit über Zeit, die die Zeit während der Entstehung der Arbeit dokumentiert.

Gezeigt wurde sie in „Helter Skelter: L. A. Art in the 1990s", völlig außerhalb ihres Kontexts. Es war das erste und einzige Mal, daß sie zusammengesetzt wurde, daher gab es keine Abbildungen davon im Katalog. Es wurde nichts über diese Arbeit geschrieben. Sie wurde schlecht präsentiert. Fehler des Künstlers.

"1000 clocks" was made by the artist just before turning fifty. It was funded by the artist and every part was hand made or assembled. It took five years to build and was funded by working a construction job. A piece about time, documenting the time during the making of the piece.

It was shown in "Helter Skelter: L. A. Art in the 1990s," completely out of context. It was the first and only time it was assembled, describing there were no photographs in the catalog. Nothing was written about this piece. The piece was badly presented. The artist's fault.

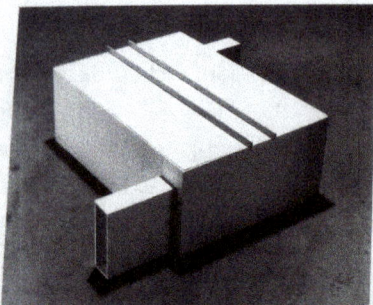

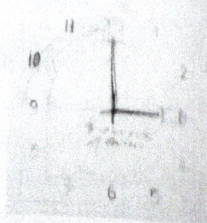

Ohne Titel 1987
Modell für 1000 Clocks
Karton, Leim

Untitled 1987
model for 1000 clocks
cardboard, glue

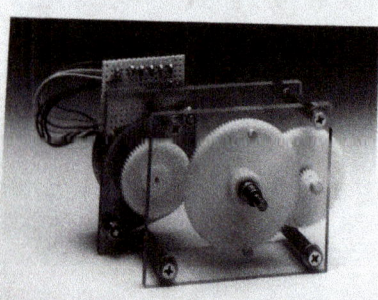

1000 Clocks 1987–1992
Stahl, Aluminium, elektronische Teile, Leuchtstofflampen, Ölfarbe
304.8 x 1097.3 x 914.4 cm

steel, aluminum, electronic parts, fluorescent lights, oil paint
120 x 432 x 360 in.

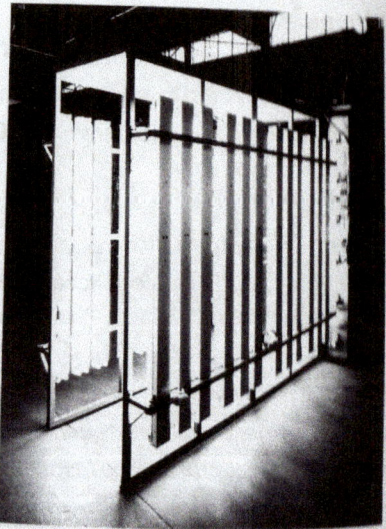

„1000 Clocks" entstand kurz bevor der Künstler 50 Jahre alt wurde. Die Arbeit wurde vom Künstler bezahlt, und jedes Teil ist von Hand gemacht oder zusammengesetzt. Es dauerte fünf Jahre, bis die Arbeit fertig war, finanziert wurde sie durch seine Arbeit auf dem Bau. Eine Arbeit über Zeit, die die Zeit während der Entstehung der Arbeit dokumentiert.

Gezeigt wurde sie in „Helter Skelter: L. A. Art in the 1990s", völlig außerhalb ihres Kontexts. Es war das erste und einzige Mal, daß sie zusammengesetzt wurde, daher gab es keine Abbildungen davon im Katalog. Es wurde nichts über diese Arbeit geschrieben. Sie wurde schlecht präsentiert. Fehler des Künstlers.

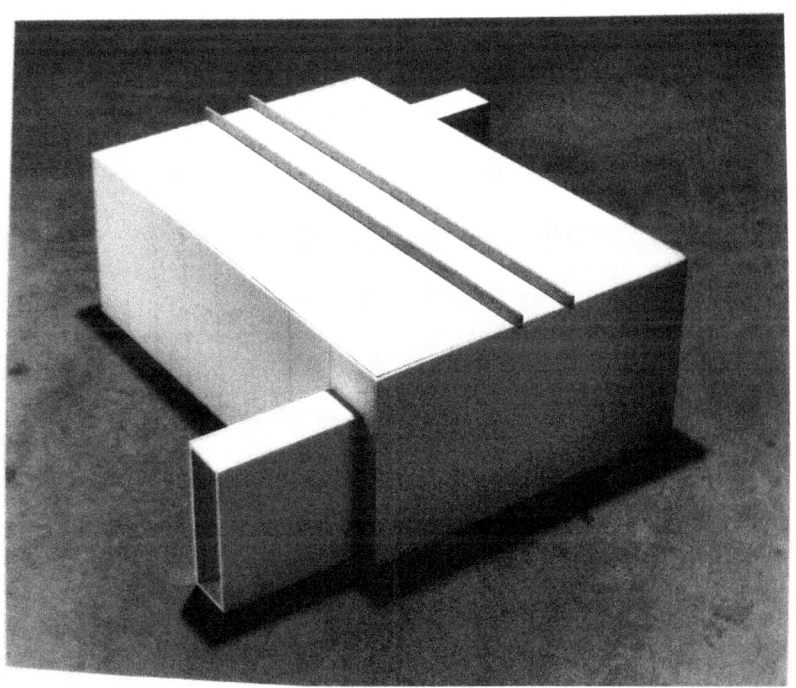

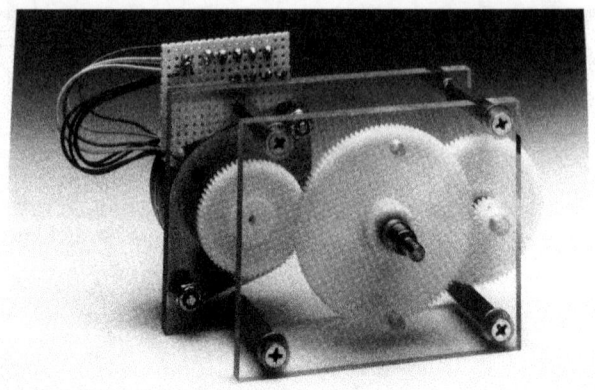

1000 Clocks 1987–1992

Stahl, Aluminium, elektronische Teile, Leuchtstofflampen, Ölfarbe
304,8 x 1097,3 x 914,4 cm

steel, aluminum, electronic parts, fluorescent lights, oil paint
120 x 432 x 360 in.

50 Jahre alt wurde.
, Teil ist von Hand
ahre, bis die Arbeit
auf dem Bau. Eine
ing der Arbeit doku-

e 1990s", völlig
ige Mal, daß sie
ungen davon im
ben. Sie wurde

"1000 clocks" was made by the artist just before turning fifty. It was
funded by the artist and every part was hand-made or assembled. It
took five years to build and was funded by working a construction job.
A piece about time, documenting the time during the making of the
piece.

It was shown in "Helter Skelter: L.A. Art in the 1990s," completely out
of context. It was the first and only time it was assembled, therefore
there were no photographs in the catalog. Nothing was written about
this piece. The piece was badly presented. The artist's fault.

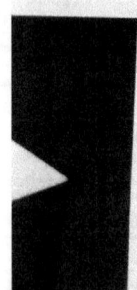

Ohne Titel 1987
Modell für 1000 Clocks
Karton, Leim

Untitled 1987
model for 1000 clocks
cardboard, glue

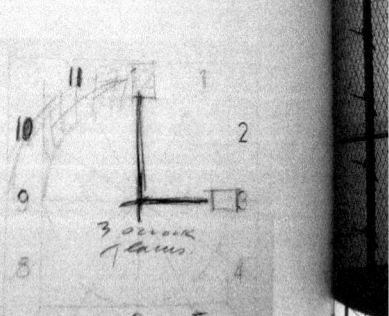

And later, in response to a question from Alberta Mayo about Jackson's transition from thinking about time in his work to using clocks in the work:

"Yes, however, the other event is thinking about turning fifty and thinking about time from that perspective. So there's 1000 Clocks, *a piece involving time made over a period of time documenting the process. The piece took five years (1987-1992) to make and, as the others, was all done by myself. It's a piece about spending time, making time and thinking about time."*

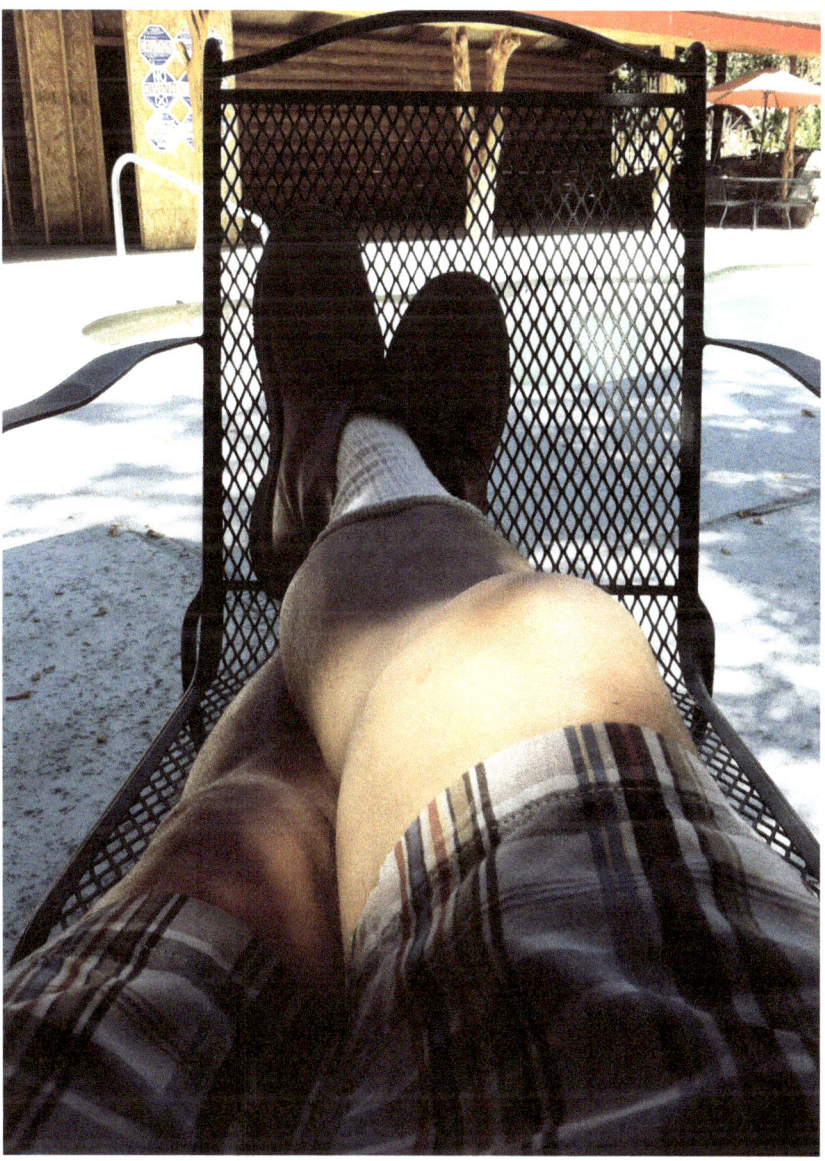

Richard Jackson would as likely as fail the Swiss soldier's "obligatory shoot" for he is a passionate game hunter – and a beer drinker, as his neon message "deer beer" clearly proclaims. Those who encounter him find him in firing position. There are cynical hunters – my English teacher at high school belonged to this category, always bad-tempered in his green felt kit whenever his instinct collided on Wednesday and Saturday mornings with the timetable – and intent hunters, noiseless, waiting, stalking, tracking, waiting. The shot through the shoulder to the heart is not placed in a bout of hunting fever but with the existential and artistic nature of a huntsman. When Richard Jackson, who as a boy hunted with his father the "sly black tail deer," fixes his gaze on his opponent, sees through him and penetrates him with a "tremendously" clear eye, at the same time laughing heartily and astutely, one can imagine the way in which he moves in the "hunting field" of art. From his knowledge of "hunter" Jackson, Ed Kienholz has distilled the following maxims: "One learns to foresee one's own needs - and to calculate them." "The powers of endurance are for the most part a matter of attitude." "If something has to be done, then do it. Begin at the beginning and see it through to the end." "It is important to understand the absurd aspect of life from a lofty standpoint and, if possible, with humour." [1]

Edward Kienholz „Für Richard Jackson" in: Katalog Galerie Maeght, Zürich, Juni bis Juli 1981

David and I spent the afternoon by the saltwater pool in the remarkable town of Parkfield. The V6 Ranch, from whom we rent a bunkhouse for our visits, is isolated and beautiful for it, and each detail is attended to with the care that an artist might bring. Everything fits, even the saltwater pool and Jacuzzi, without detracting from the honesty of the experience. While we were at the pool, and in between my photographing sessions with the book, a young friend named Sean, who is native to the small town, regaled us with tales of hunting pigs in an unusual and alarmingly romantic-sounding fashion. He sort of acted it out for us, his skin and bathing suit wet from a recent backflip into the pool, a beer held in one hand and his imagined homemade fighting tool (a spear) in the other—laughing and chugging, pulling back and pressing forward, until he and his dogs (two—an "ass" dog and a "head" dog) ultimately prevail over the mythical-seeming wild and angry 400-lb. beast.

I share with you curator and catalog essayist Harald Szeeman's observations on Richard Jackson as a hunter and as an artist.

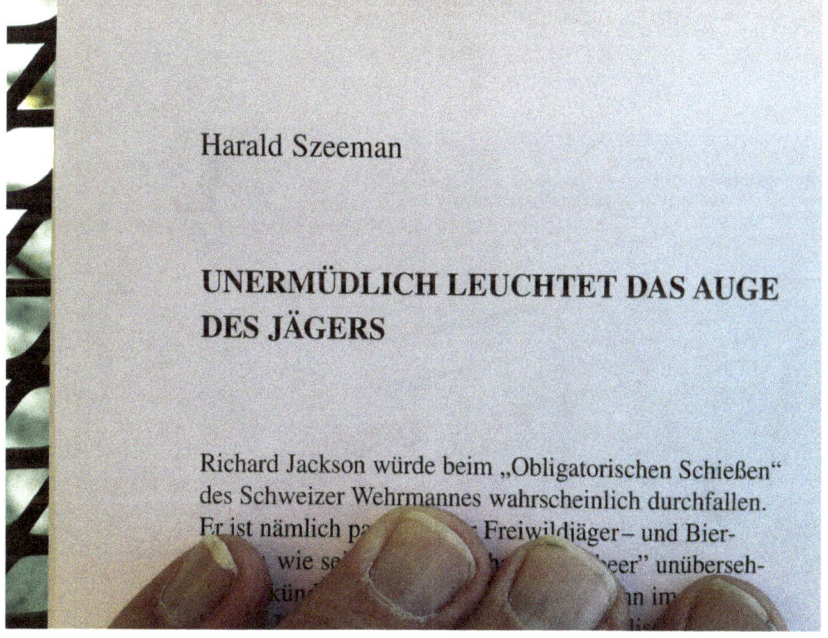

Harald Szeeman

UNERMÜDLICH LEUCHTET DAS AUGE DES JÄGERS

Richard Jackson würde beim „Obligatorischen Schießen" des Schweizer Wehrmannes wahrscheinlich durchfallen. Er ist nämlich p̶   ̶ Freiwildjäger– und Bier-   wie se̶   ̶ ̶eer" unüberseh-

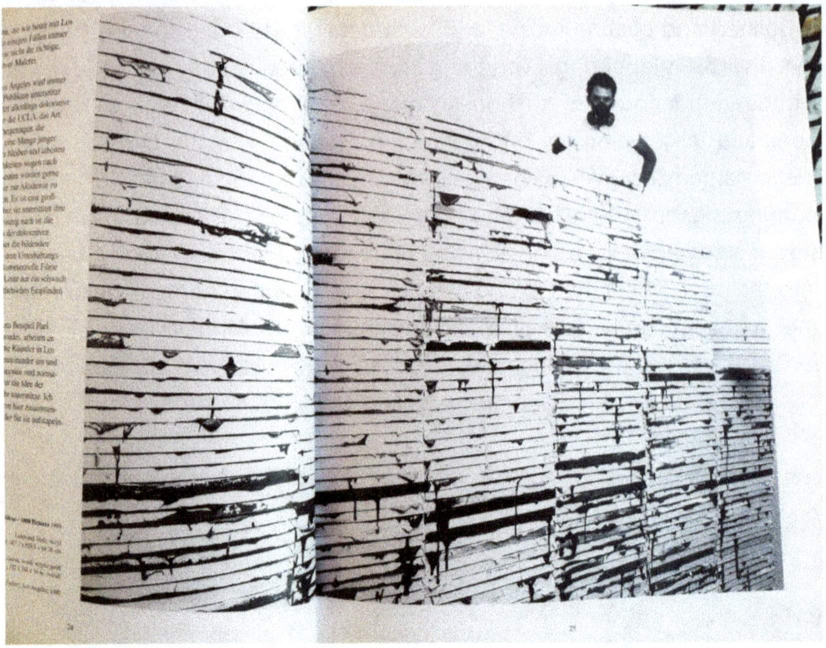

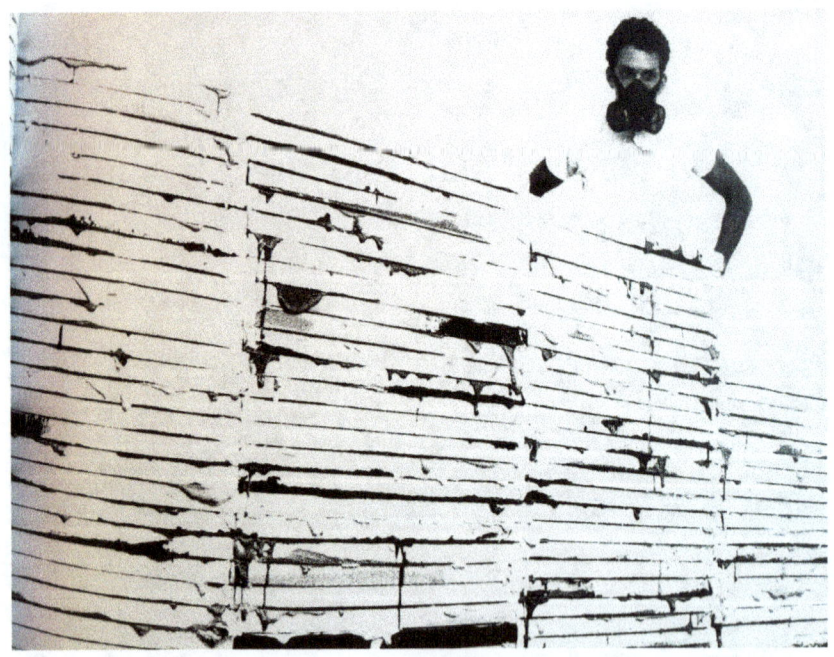

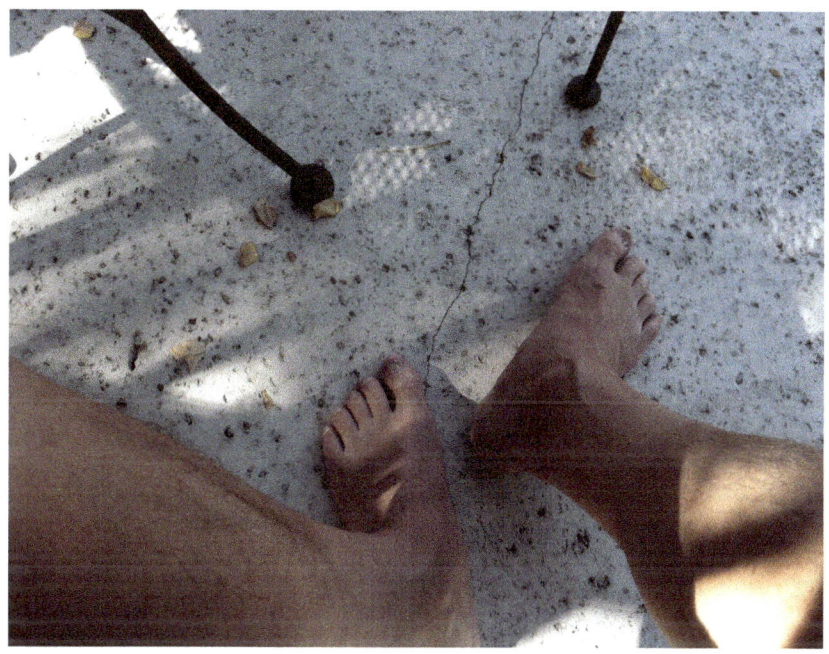

Big Ideas—1000 Pictures, 1980, is pictured to the left and on the following page; or rather, I have re-pictured the image in *Deer Beer*. God bless Rosamund Felsen. This exhibition was 31 years ago.

To me, these images present our hero as a young stormtrooper for a pure art, having just assembled and ascended the mountain of his early triumph and now gazing upon us from above like, well, Apollo on Olympus, or maybe Prometheus on his rock.

In the evening, when we returned to Blue Oak Camp, I switched from quaffing beers to sipping Parkfield-modified Manhattans for cocktail hour: pour any rye or bourbon, add sweet vermouth, rocks, two cherries and a squeeze and twist of lemon, stir and enjoy with cooling air and the sound of bees, cows and birds in the surrounding hills.

At the big outdoor table, I had my insight about yellow cars, and I figured out how I could begin writing about Richard Jackson and compiling the many photos and videos I had just made. Life is good when I can remind myself to find a first question and then to bring in whatever connection to the art that I have, even a very personal and seemingly extraneous one.

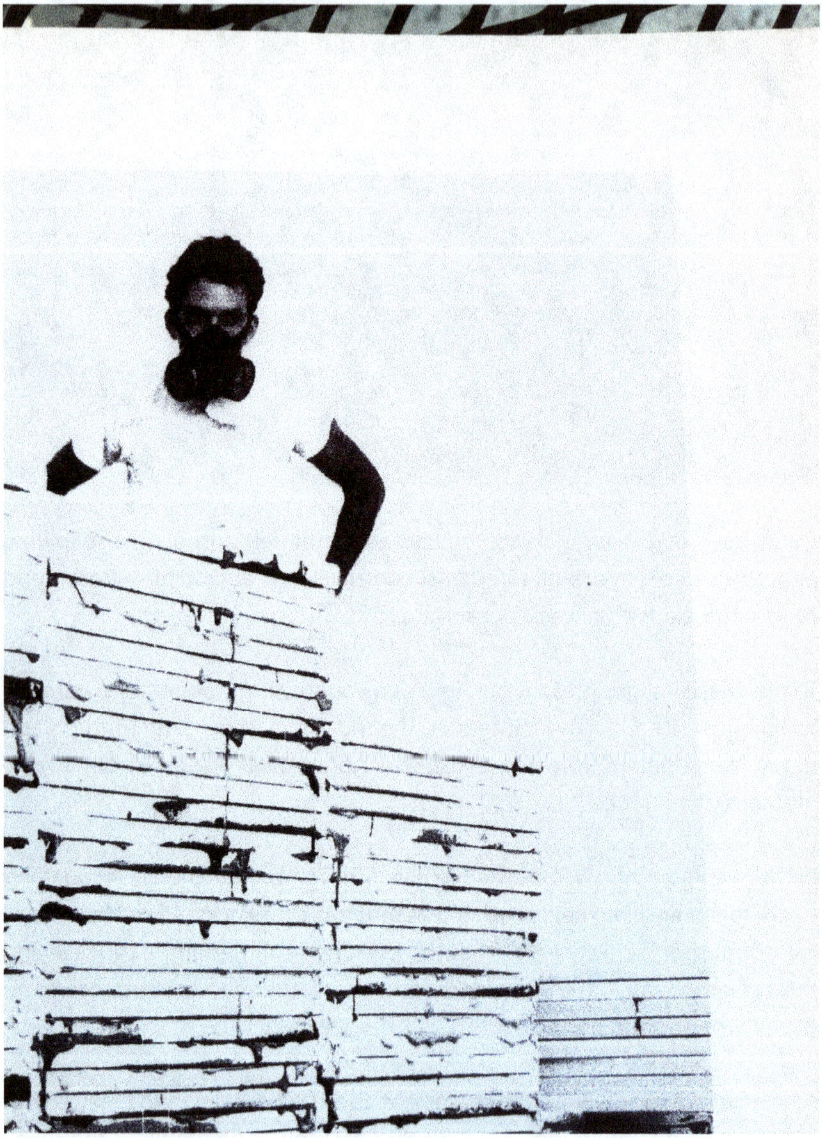

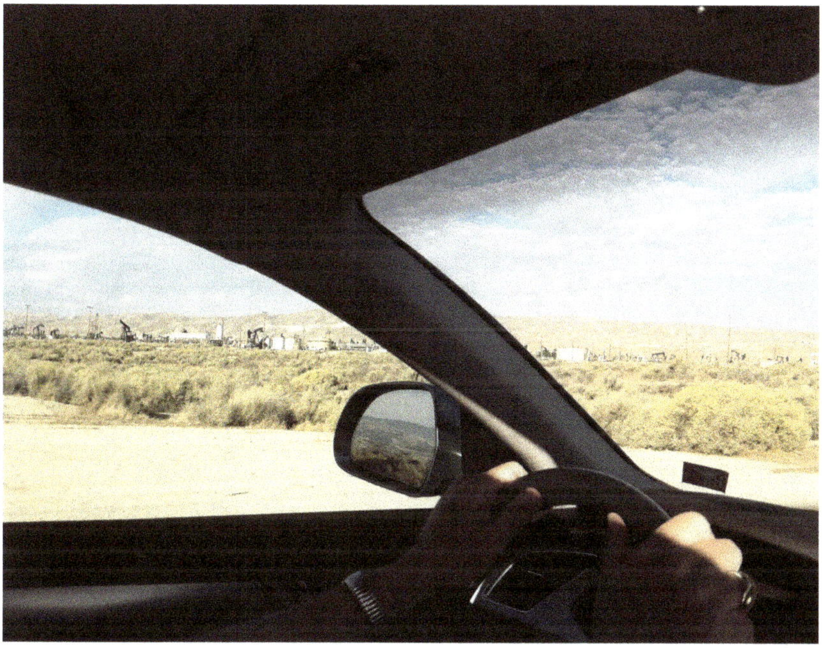

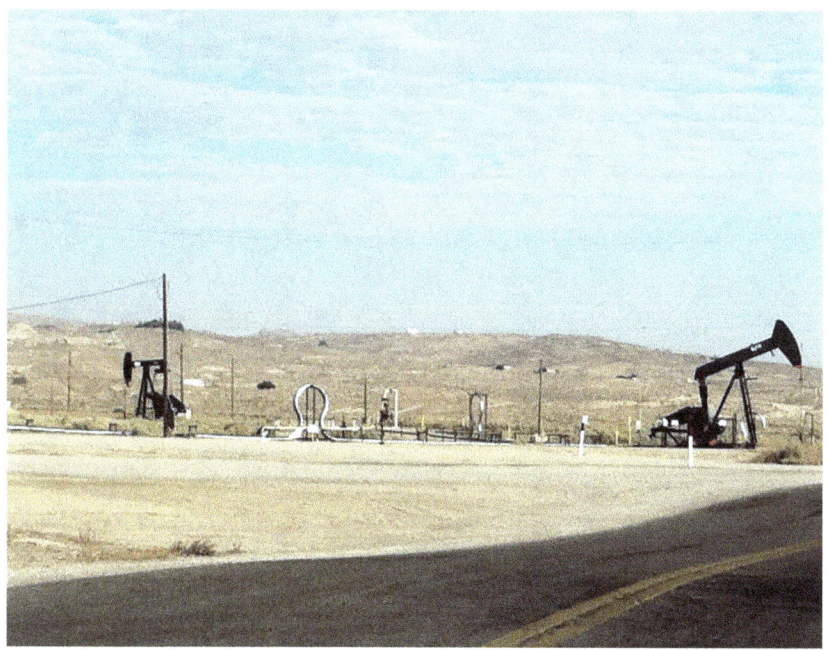

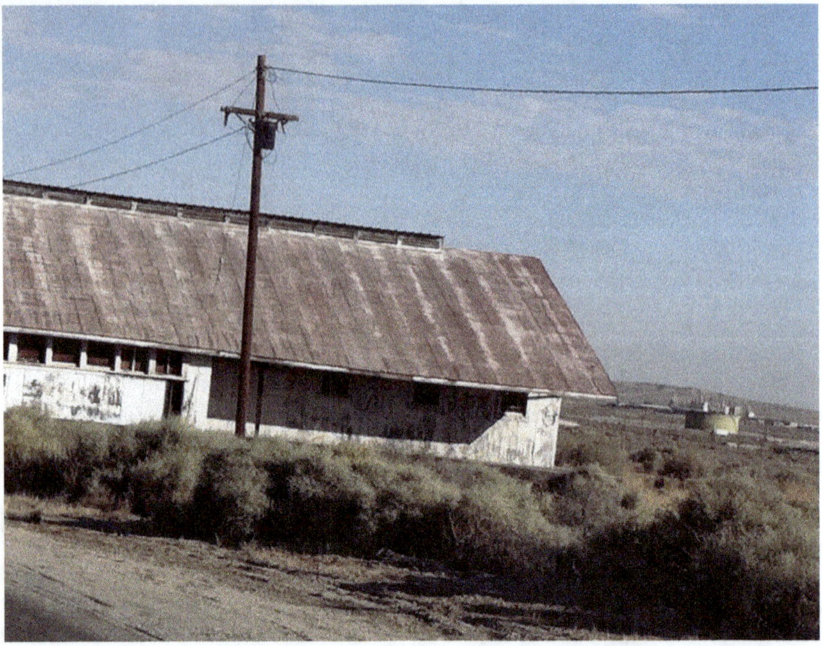

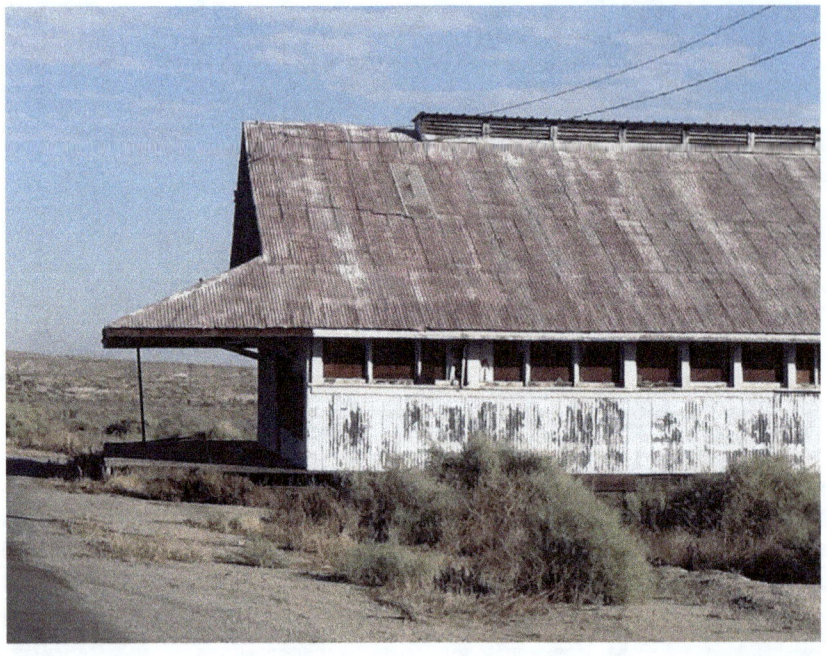

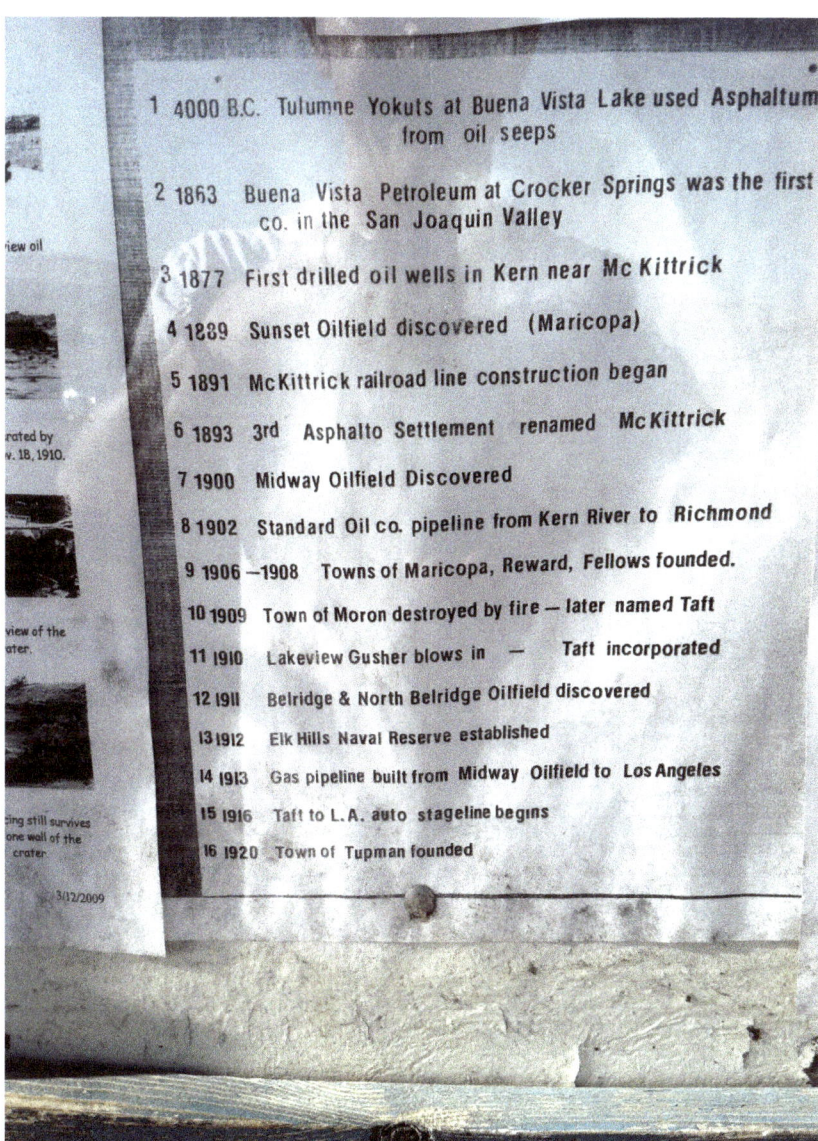

1 4000 B.C. Tulumne Yokuts at Buena Vista Lake used Asphaltum from oil seeps

2 1863   Buena Vista Petroleum at Crocker Springs was the first co. in the San Joaquin Valley

3 1877   First drilled oil wells in Kern near McKittrick

4 1889   Sunset Oilfield discovered (Maricopa)

5 1891   McKittrick railroad line construction began

6 1893   3rd Asphalto Settlement renamed McKittrick

7 1900   Midway Oilfield Discovered

8 1902   Standard Oil co. pipeline from Kern River to Richmond

9 1906 —1908   Towns of Maricopa, Reward, Fellows founded.

10 1909   Town of Moron destroyed by fire — later named Taft

11 1910   Lakeview Gusher blows in —   Taft incorporated

12 1911   Belridge & North Belridge Oilfield discovered

13 1912   Elk Hills Naval Reserve established

14 1913   Gas pipeline built from Midway Oilfield to Los Angeles

15 1916   Taft to L.A. auto stageline begins

16 1920   Town of Tupman founded

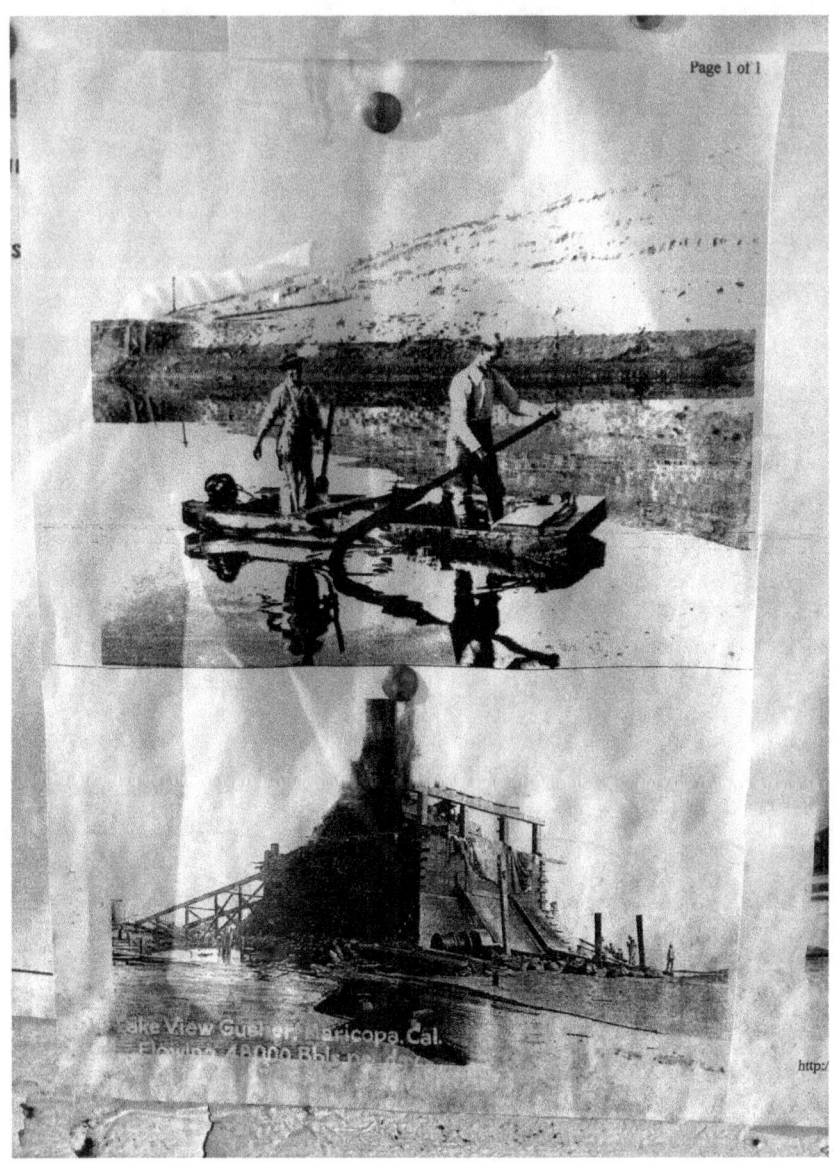

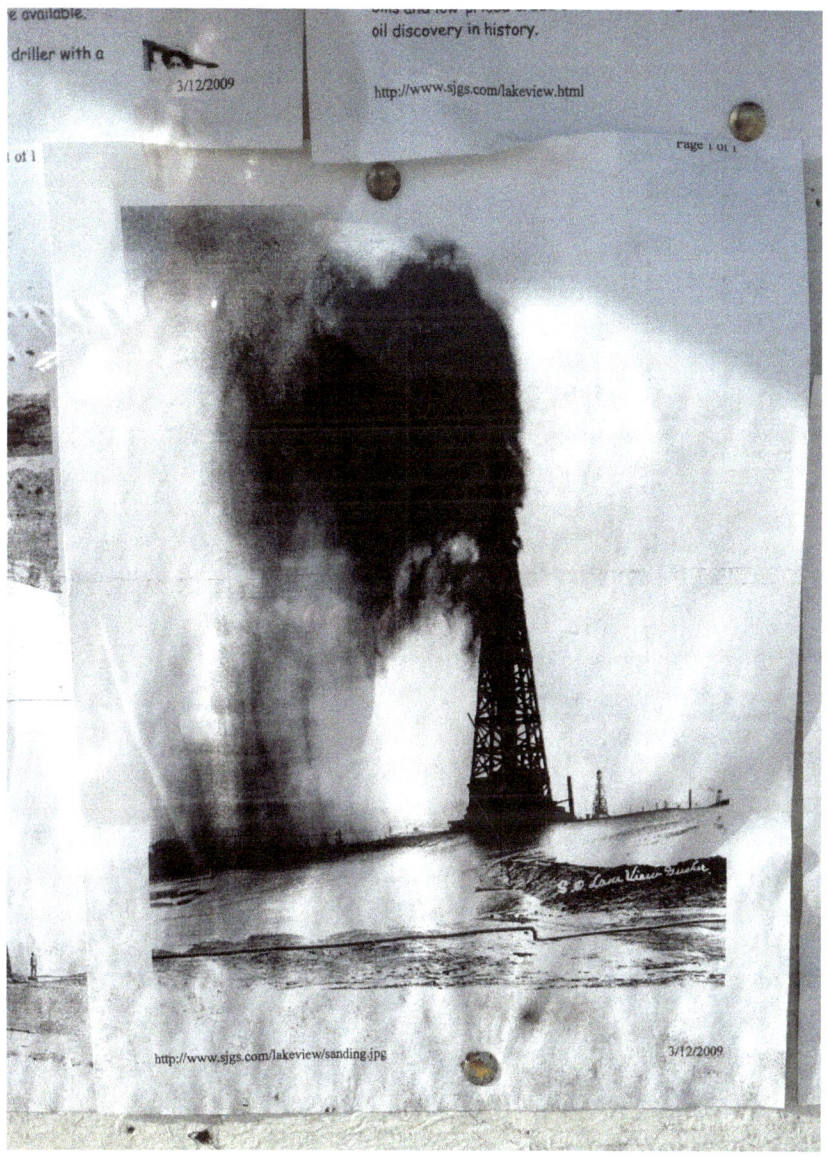

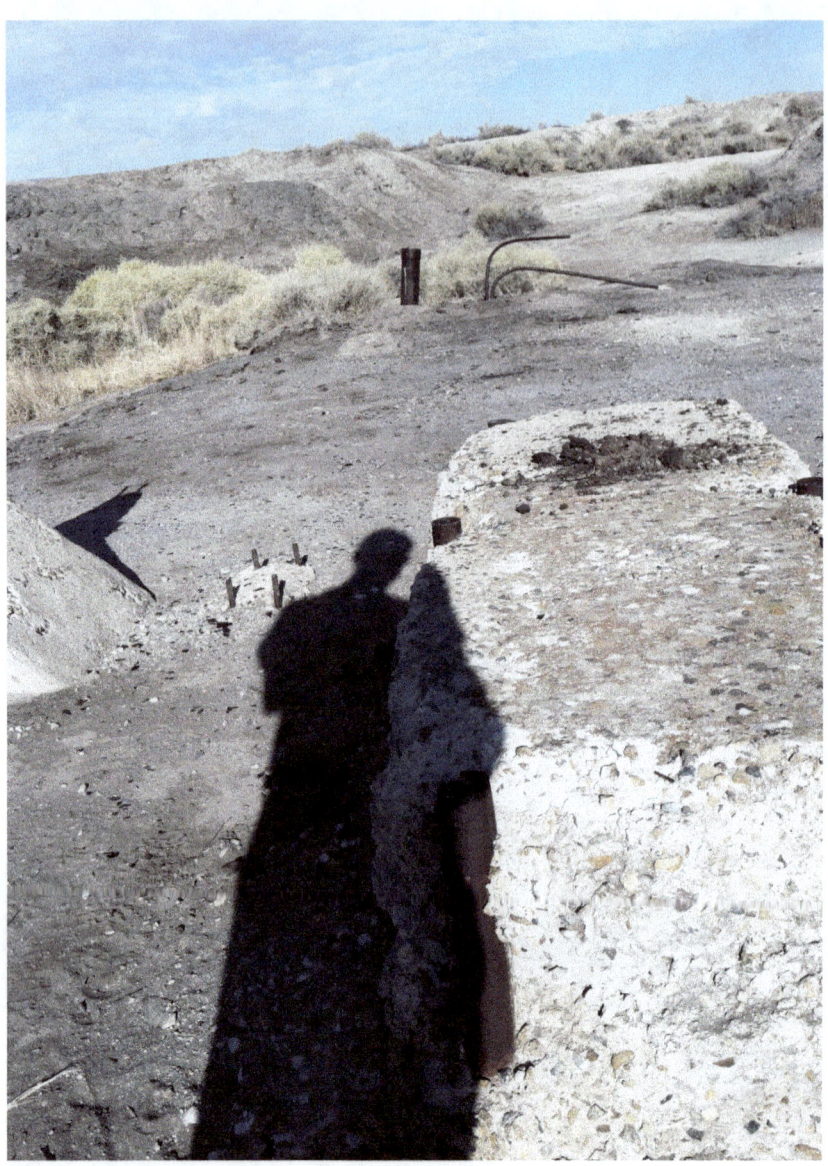

Part of any trip to Parkfield is the path that we take. Our route changes every time, as there are many highways between Los Angeles and this central valley in the middle of our state. For this late August trip, we drove over the Grapevine, then turned left at Hwy 166, spending our first night in Maricopa and visiting nearby McKittrick at dawn.

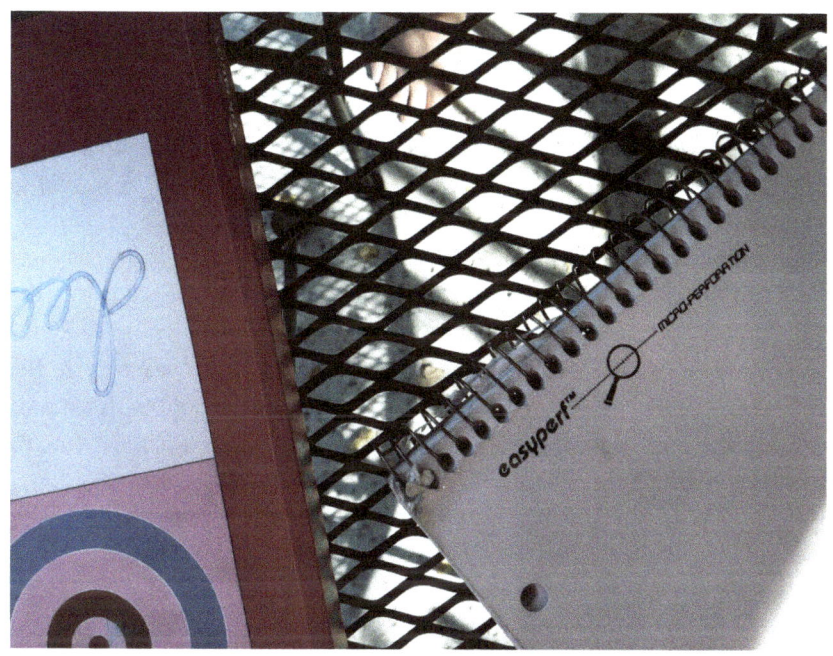

What remains of my family have many mystical tales of my paternal grand-father wildcatting for oil in this region, and each time I visit, I commune with his spirit and with my father's spirit. They are both long gone and they did, as we all eventually must, leave many questions behind. As David drives and as

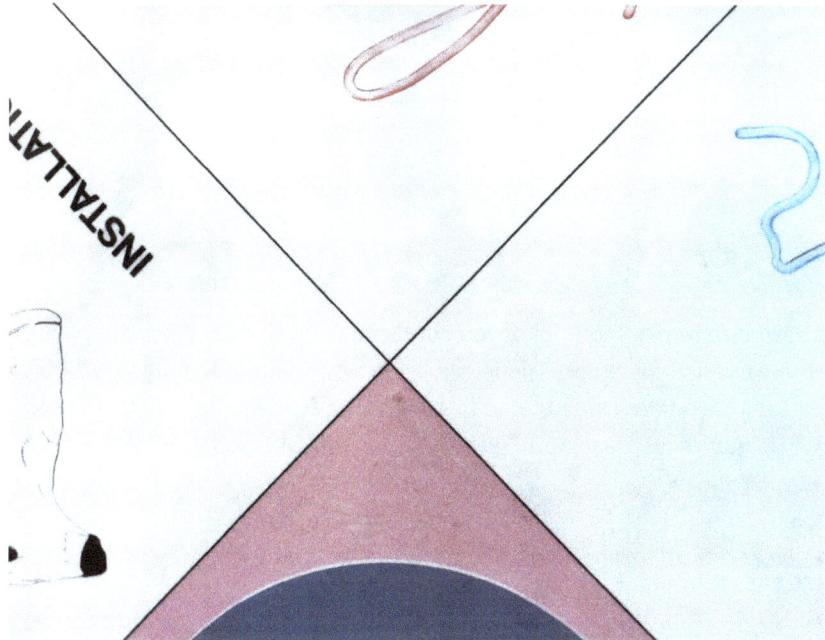

we walk, I wonder, and I think, and I remember, and the landscape feels very much like home to me: It is lovely and barren and marked with pumps and wells; it is exploited and forgotten, and men may note of it only what they can make use of—but the land remains, and when attention is paid, it amazes with its beauty and generosity.

We continued north on Hwy 33 to Coalinga, and then back down and west on the 198, a narrow, winding, and precipitous ascent then decline into the beautiful Peach Tree Valley and finally, through San Miguel and on to Parkfield. Over the past twenty-four hours, we had driven nearly 400 miles to arrive 190 miles from home. Along the way, we cast off everything but our five senses and the moments we were to spend together, and on this trip, the moments we were to spend with Richard Jackson and with my brother.

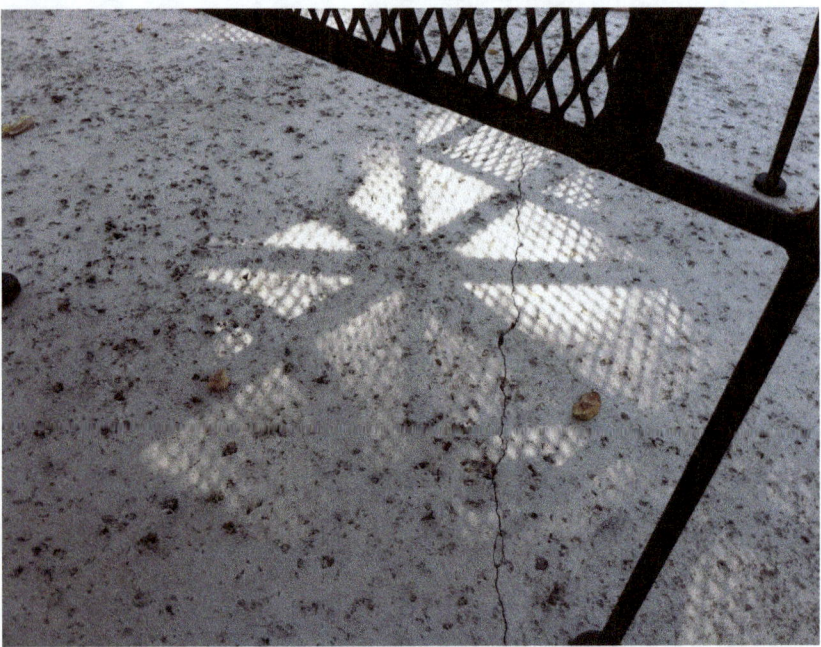

I hasten to remind you that if you contact Kunstgriff Bookshop, the publication representatives for Galerie Hauser & Wirth you may purchase *Richard Jackson. Deer Beer*. (Note that in trade terms, this would be "Galerie Hauser & Wirth (ed.), 'Richard Jackson. Deer Beer', Cologne: Oktagon, 1998, ill. (exh. cat.)" Buy it if you can.)

Published on September 6, 2011 by Geoff Tuck in Wanderings

YORK CHANG: FROM THE PARKFIELD REVIEW #2
York Chang

I wasn't sure when Gustavo Raynal first showed up at Parkfield, but I remember when I realized he was there—like suddenly hearing a car alarm that had been going off for hours. The last time I saw him was at a Pettibon opening at the old Regen Projects, when he got thrown out for pissing on the door to the director's back room. A friend at *frieze* magazine told me Raynal was fired from the staff there last year after he slipped a pornographic piece about the editor-in-chief's husband into his regular column. At Parkfield, when I saw him walking towards the showers, holding a bottle of either bourbon or tequila, I realized someone had made the horrible mistake of inviting a visceral realist to the camp—they're all extremists and reactionaries, so contrary to the quietly generous and open gathering that Geoff and David intended for Parkfield. But there he was, the founder of visceral realism, and everyone was too polite to tell him to leave until it was too late. Until he got into a shouting match with an artist about whether it was *Night Gallery* or *THE Night Gallery*. Until he capsized a paddle boat in the middle of the Parkfield lake, nearly drowning a painter who shows with ACME. After dinner, Raynal threw rocks in the campfire and began raging at people about things I can't remember exactly, don't quote me, but something about how Rimbaud was *"the shit,"* or that Baudrillard was a one-trick pony, or how Deitch could potentially be a zombie, I'm not sure. Late that night, a few of us were sitting outside of my cabin to watch a freak lightning storm in the sky, and we noticed Raynal standing on top of the table in the middle of camp, waving a long metal pole in the air, as if asking to get struck. Later, when he thought no one was looking, he seized someone's horse out of a trailer by the rope and rode into the night. A police detective called me weeks later and asked me what I saw. I told them that I was alone walking to the showers when I saw him take the horse in the middle of the storm. I don't know why, but I didn't tell the detective that, in the moment after he leapt onto the horse, I saw Raynal lit up by a yellow flash of lightning, caught frozen in mid-air at full gallop, careening towards the dark mountains which framed the camp, with the momentum of car crashes and tumbling glass. I never saw Raynal again.

Reprinted from the Parkfield Review #2, 2011-2012

TO THE LIGHTHOUSE—SOUTH OF THE CHICKEN STATUE ON BROADWAY

Is it about looking and that inevitably when we do, we reach beyond ourselves?

Is it about finding in others things worthwhile to support and so finding oneself strengthened?

Is it about asking questions of what we find, holding a mirror up to the person who makes—and to the thing made?

What if we determine that the only way to create the world that we want to live in is to live as though it already exists?

What if belief can be a tool for artistic inquiry—belief in possibility as a natural fact, faith that the people with whom one engages in this inquiry may also guide one?

What if art is a social union and not a placeholder in a sterile intellectual environment?

What happens when eleven artists come together who, through their ongoing practices, engage with other artists, create challenges to the social status quo and who, by their actions, help to create the world in which we work?

What if they have fun doing it, and so do you?

Come To the Lighthouse on May 19. Have more fun than a body should be allowed.

To the Lighthouse is an exhibition at JB Jurve with:

DAVID BELL
JOHN BURTLE
YOUNG CHUNG
ADAM FELDMETH
DANIEL LARA
CARRIE MCILWAIN
DAVIDA NEMEROFF
IVETTE SOLER
GEOFF TUCK
ALEXANDER WOLFF
AARON WRINKLE

With an in-play contribution from
ANDY ROBERT

Published on May 8, 2012 by Geoff Tuck in Miscellaneous

Thanks for spending some time with *Dreamscapes of Los Angeles*, the *Notes on Looking Reader*. This book is a selection of articles, stories, considerations and conversations from the website *Notes on Looking*. Visit notesonlooking.com.

Yours,
Geoff Tuck

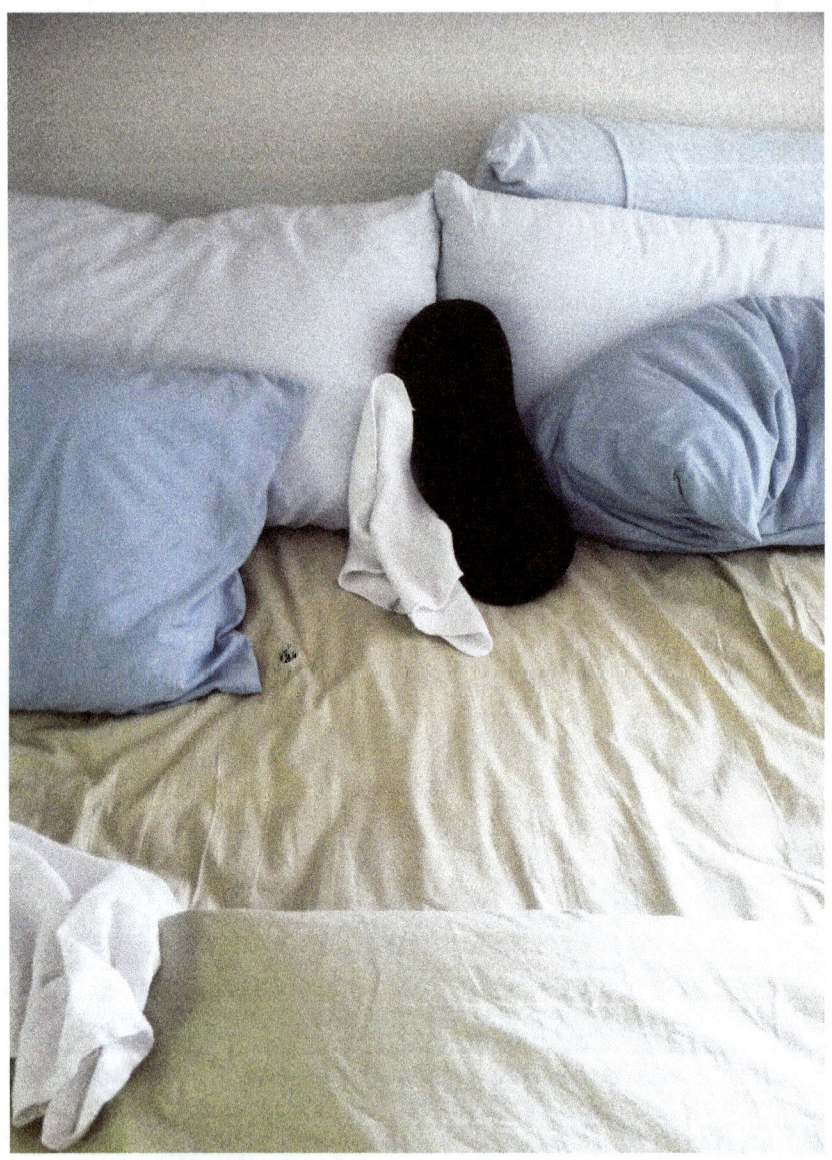

The End

POSTSCRIPT

Dreamscapes of Los Angeles was originally published in July of 2013, for the group exhibition *Nowhere to Run, Nowhere to Hide*, in a limited edition of twenty-six copies. In this new edition of *Dreamscapes*, which is published after the exhibition has taken place, I offer you documentation of the exhibition, as well as a correspondence with architect Alex Gross, in whose building, called *The Funny Pit*, the exhibition took place.

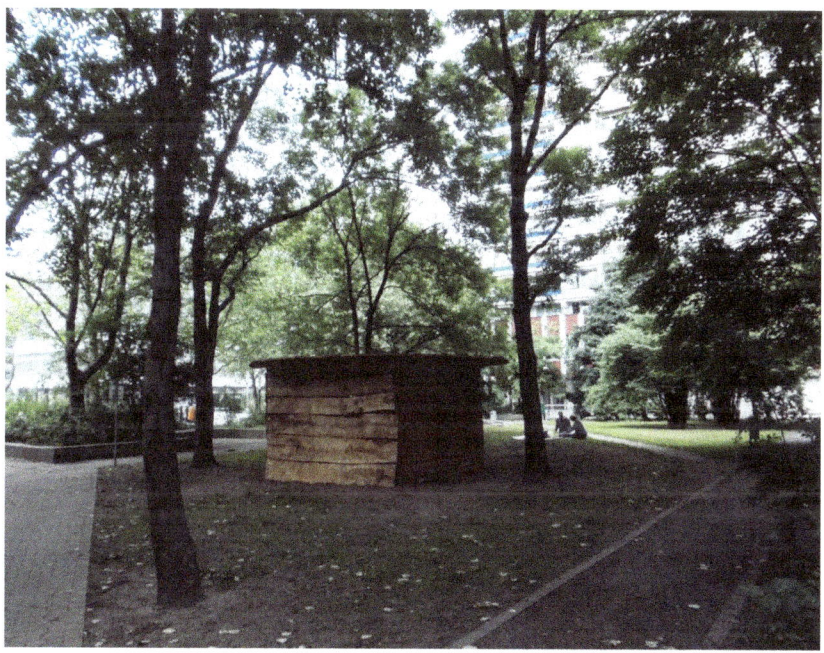

Dear Alex,

I'm writing to thank you for making the wonderful space in the park, *Die Lustige Grube*. I was there on August 9 and 10, when I presented a show, *Nowhere to Run, Nowhere to Hide*.

Your hut has a magical quality of existing partly in another time. The wood construction recalls to me what little I know of ancient history of the German peoples: that instead of building with stone, as did other early civilizations, the Germans built with wood—having it easily at hand. In my mind, for I have an active imagination, I created a story of trees felled one thousand years ago, and hulking timbers hauled by leather strap and hand to a clearing where they were hewn into shape and built over a little pit. (Then my mind wandered off into Valhalla and Wagner, and I decided I better stop.)

In my memory, sitting here now in Los Angeles, I can see from the open door of your hut the great apartment block that gave your site its name of "pit," and so my fanciful narrative from ancient history speeds forward to the post-war time when those buildings were built.

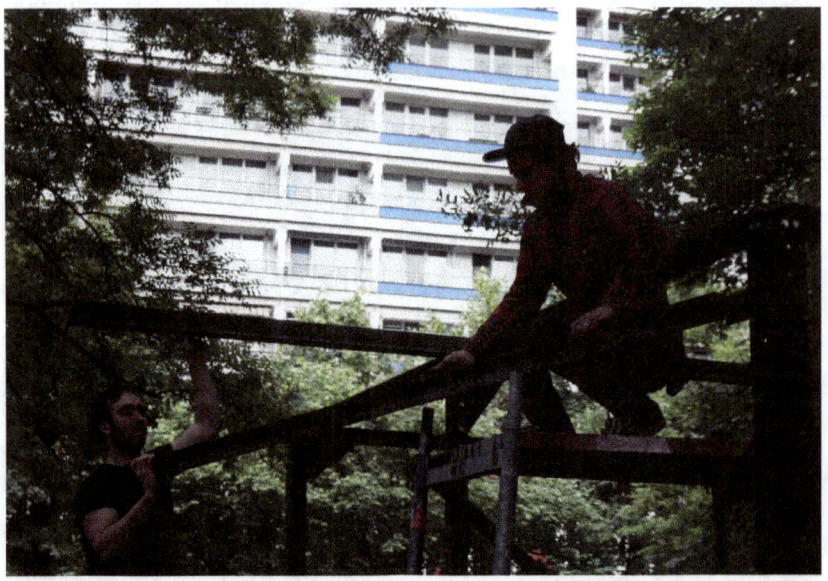

If I consider that your hut was built in this summer of 2013, and the logs were certainly milled this year, and if I also then consider that you hope to re-build *Die Lustige Grube* someday—perhaps at a festival—then the "out of time" nature of this project at this site is manifested clearly, for your building encompasses several eras—and the future!—and it exists in the modern German capital, surrounded by new (and old!) capitalism and by the remnant of capitalism's counter, and is inhabited by the very polyglot denizens of that city. Well done, Alex!!

I also must also tell you that as the Berlin sun sets, golden light reflects into the hut in a most pleasurable manner!

Will you tell me of your thinking in the design of the hut? And also will you explain the pit to me? I understand you were not able to dig into the rocky soil to depress the interior floor. What was your goal for this planned depression?

I also appreciate the roughly hewn nature of the planks, and the cracks that appear between them!

Architecturally, is this project a rebuke of the insubstantial nature of much contemporary building, and also of the machine made-ness of buildings today?

I do not know much about your practice. I do know that you teach. How does this project fit with other projects you have undertaken, or projects have planned?

Were you able to engage in critical discourse with the architectural community in the city? The project seems to rise to that level, one would expect some interest.

I am yours Alex,
Quite sincerely,
Geoff

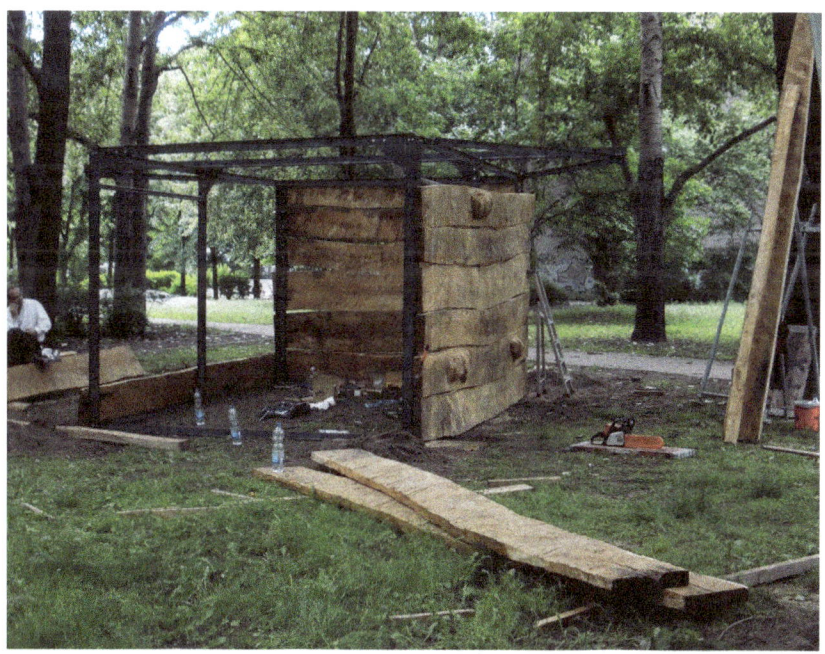

Hi Geoff,
I like your own interpretation of the set-up a lot, and would just like to add some of my own thoughts, ideas and research regarding the project.

I started the project 2010 with the title *The Funny Pit*, it was mainly planned as an art-installation consisting of a dug out hole in the ground and a simple architecture. I am a little obsessed with earth and mud.

My question during that time was: in which way does a haptic experience, in this case, walking in the mud, change the way architecture is perceived. The act of walking in the mud seemed neither active or passive, but it seemed to create some sort of an inner space, maybe triggered by a "muddy thinking" in the sense of R. Smithson.

My first experiments with mud led to the construction of Swamp Thing in 2009 for Transmission Gallery in Glasgow. (www.grossalex.de/swamp-thing/). The spectator was slowed down by a square field of mud underneath a shiny, plastic structure. *The Funny Pit* (*Die Lustige Grube*) is a continuation of these ideas with the intention to create more participation and also to offer other artists a field of experience outside the restrictions of the white cube.

To be able to realize the project, I joined forces with the Berlin non-commercial art space Infernoesque, to curate and invite interesting artists and conceive the funny pit as their/our new gallery space.

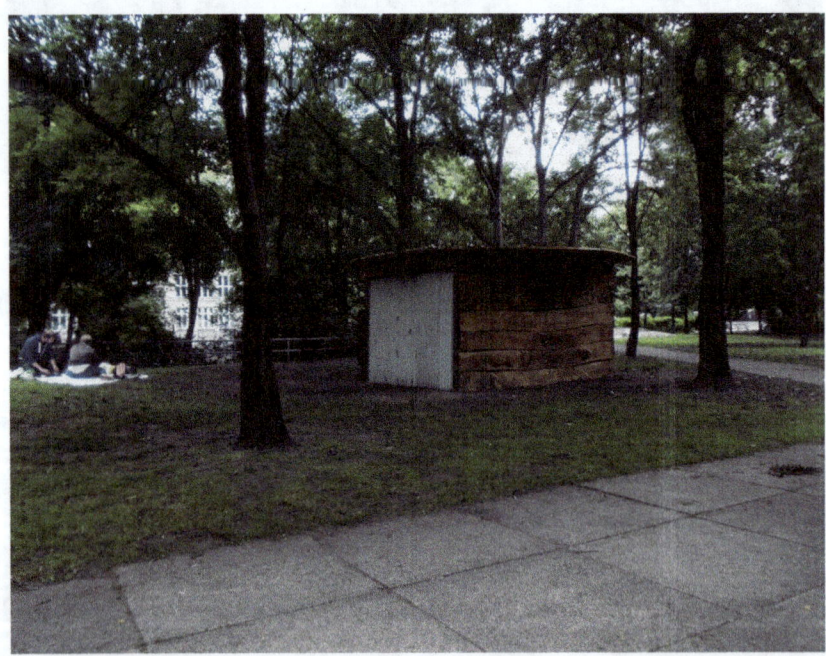

The Infernoesque Project Space (Gerdes, Weiss, Schmidt, Mields/Gross) functions as the transmitter between the space and the artists. Another factor of the work was the site. It took me half a year to find somebody who wanted to host the project. The glorious times of free wastelands in Berlin are definitely over. Finally the WBM housing company got in touch with me through their cultural manager Mr. P, who was such a great support. I was looking for an abandoned park or wasteland adjacent to a '60s social housing complex. I wanted to have locals involved into the project. The site at Leipziger Strasse was really nice. (This stretch of Leipziger Strasse is in what used to be East Berlin, and the apartment block dates from the GDR Era.) When I saw it first it was winter and pretty grim. Grey sky, blue architecture, no leafs, low life, dog shit. It was perfect, I am a big fan of John Waters movies. I had a meeting with the council of the housing estate and I was really happy that they were interested, I think they were really longing for a positive new momentum to kick in. I hope we could provide that during this summer.

By the way, the motto to the project is: "A dialogue between people and architecture." For me the funny pit is already that, some kind of a mixture between a person and a house. (This is not a scientific text). And if we follow Georges Batailles' thoughts, than people are just "an intermediary stage within the morphological development between monkey and building." (1929)

I recently rediscovered the writings of Georges Bataille as source of inspiration. Most of his ideas, for instance about his materialism of the lower than low and his idea of a process of the informe (formless) seems to me more relevant than ever. I started writing on a thesis that is concerned with examining something I would call a formless architecture, architecture that is being hit by the process of the informe. I don't really know how to get deeper into detail without becoming boring. When a woman during one of the shows asked me why there are those chiseled bumps in the wooden boards, I said: "because I read too much Bataille".

I really wanted to dig the pit, so to have a more extreme experience, but this wasn't allowed; the environmental Commission forbid it because of the roots. But maybe I can do it when I show the work again. I do think this *Funny Pit* has architectural relevance. There are many projects, especially in Berlin, dealing with similar issues. For instance Leerstandmelder and wasteland-twinning dealing with abandoned sites, there are even architects that try to put the ideas of Bataille into architecture (of course they fail). But I think that's worth trying. So I hope I can realize more projects in this direction.

Hey Geoff, thanks for coming over and doing a great exhibition,

Cheers,
Alex.

Nowhere to Run, Nowhere to Hide

Making art requires the translation of an idea—consciously or unconsciously—away from an unmediated expression of self and toward an externally determined presentation.

But, currently, I see conditions in the contemporary art world requiring that the authentic self, the spirit of the artist's idea, must remain largely undercover—or negotiate itself out of existence.

Yet, as in the words of Martha and the Vandellas – sometimes there is nowhere to run, and nowhere to hide; this imperative to dissemble can be problematic for an artist who is trying to maintain the germ, the spirit, and the rebel that is central to their art.

Everywhere I go

Your face I see

Every step I take

You take with me, yeah

I know you're

No good for me

But free of you

I'll never be, no

Each night as I sleep

Into my heart you creep

I wake up feeling sorry I met you

Hoping soon that I'll forget you

Nowhere to run

Nowhere to hide

Got nowhere to run to, baby

Nowhere to hide

Nowhere to Run, Nowhere to Hide is:
David Bell, Anthony Bodlović, Asher Hartman, EJ Hill, Brianne Latthitham, Paul Outlaw, and Geoff Tuck

The exhibition is at (a summer-long series of exhibitions in Berlin organized the members of Infernoesque and curated by international artists).

The exhibition hours are Friday and Saturday, August 9 and 10, Friday from 6pm-10pm, and Saturday from 1pm-7pm.

On the lawn, under the trees, in the park at Leipzigerstrasse 40, Berlin.

Performance by Paul Outlaw, written and directed by Asher Hartman, Friday at 8:00 PM and Saturday at 3:00 PM.

The scene: a semi-private park fronting on iconic Communist-era apartment buildings. The park is inhabited by office-workers taking lunch, neighborhood kids playing games and sneaking beers, dog walkers, and local street people. Members of these disparate groups sometimes do, and sometimes don't pay attention to the goings on in the newly-built hut in their park. During the weekend of *Nowhere to Run*, members of each group took part in the festivities, and helped with the show.

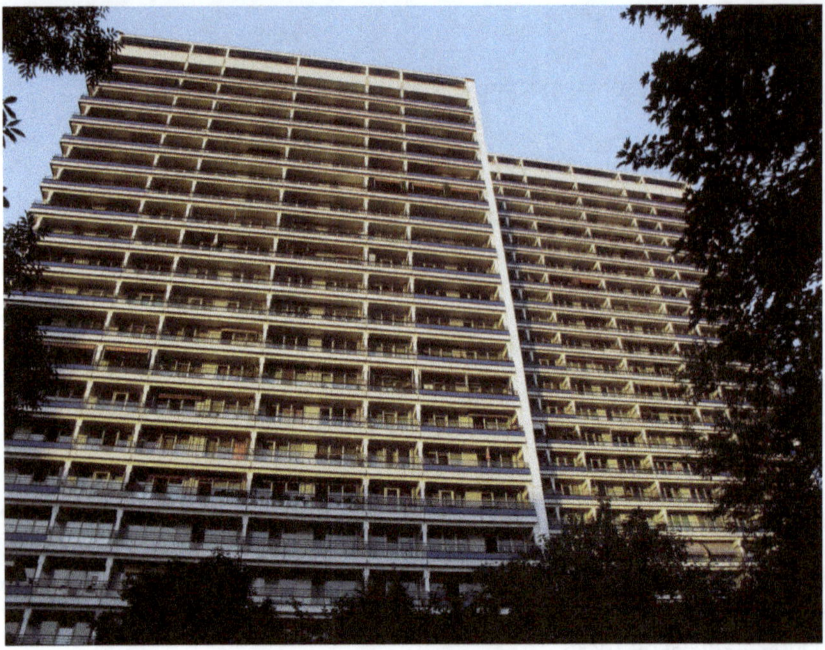

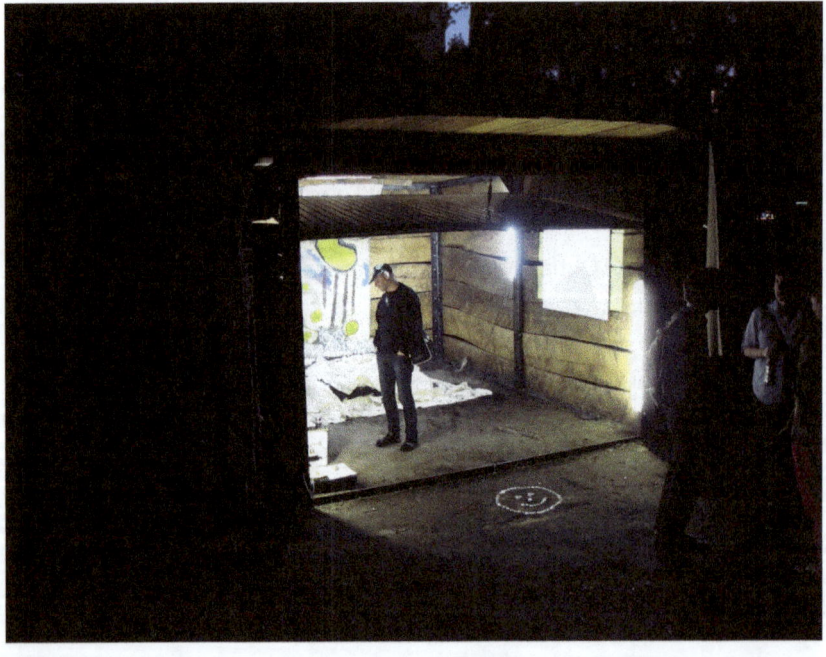

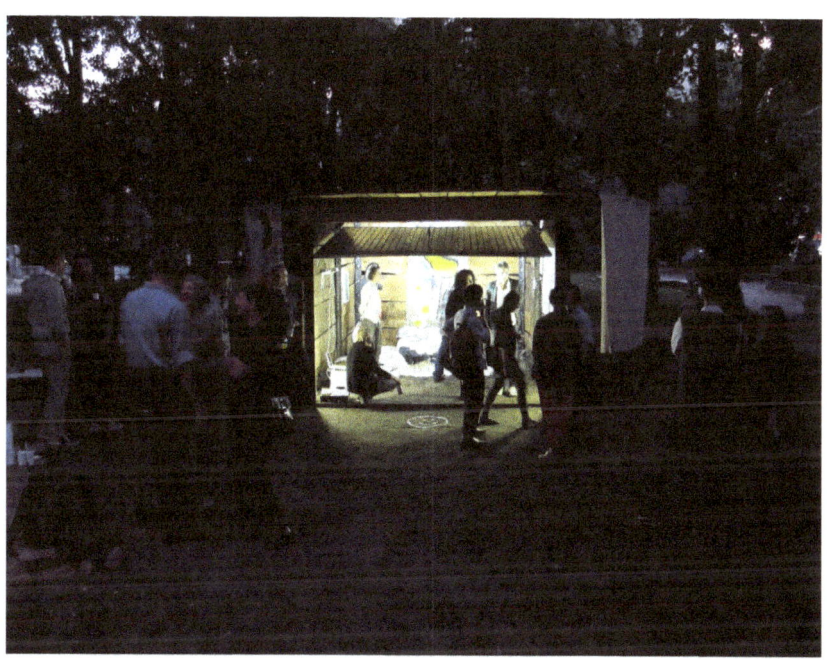

The hut, the Merry Pit, in the afternoon and dark evening, under the linden trees. People gather.

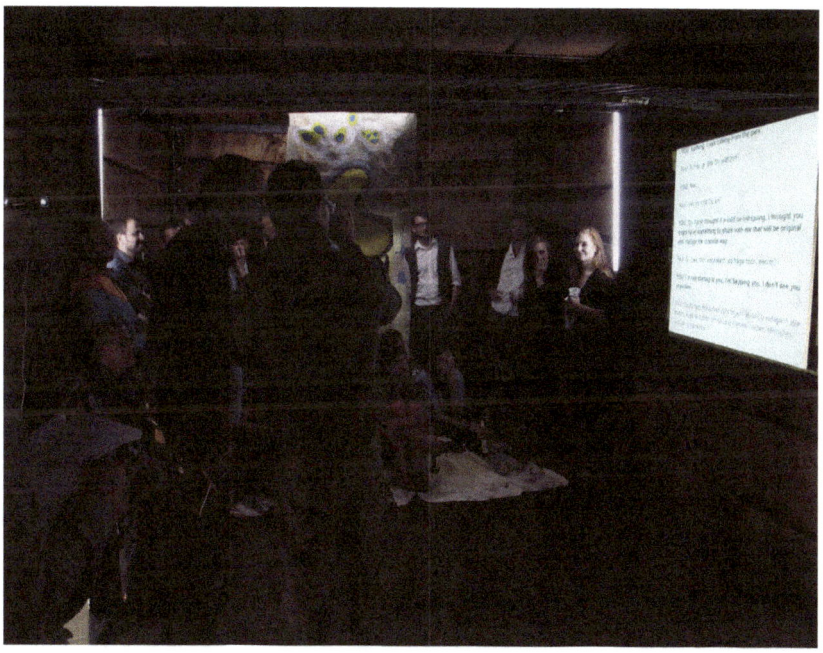

Paul Outlaw Skypes and texts from a nearby apartment as people read Asher's script.

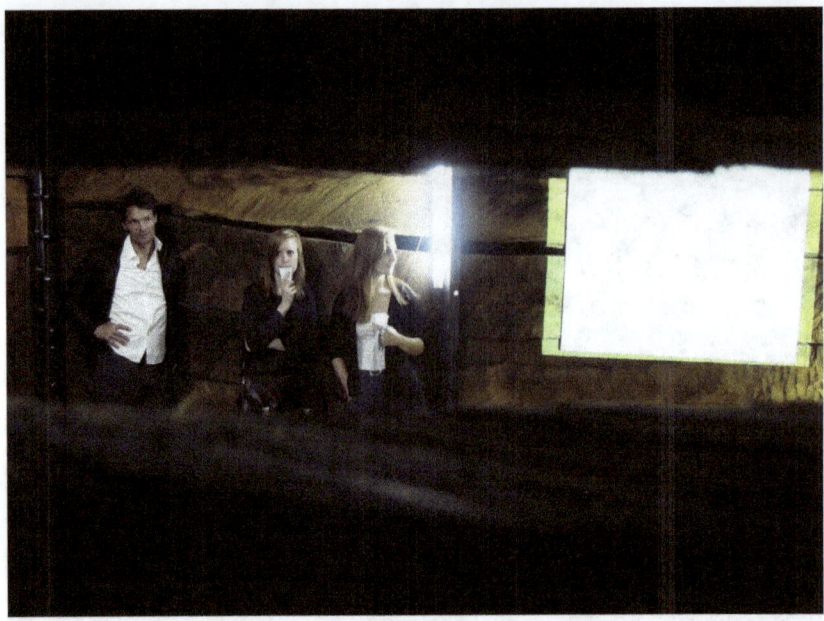

A lucky architectural quirk of the hut are the cracks in its envelope: the oak planks are thick, the structure is sound, yet vision is allowed, even encouraged. The Merry Pit offers its participants an enlightening, revelatory kind of protection from the elements.

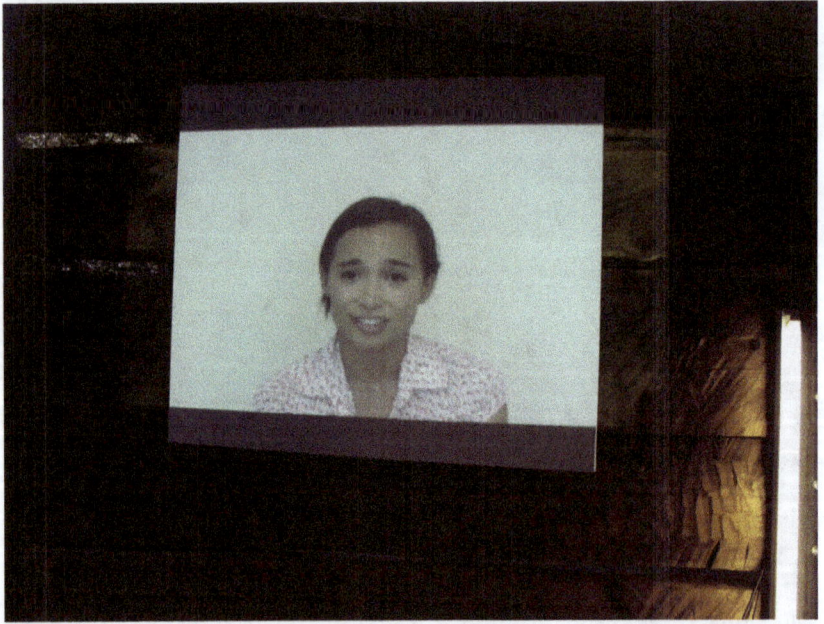

Brianne Latthitham and Anthony Bodlović, *Work Ethic*.

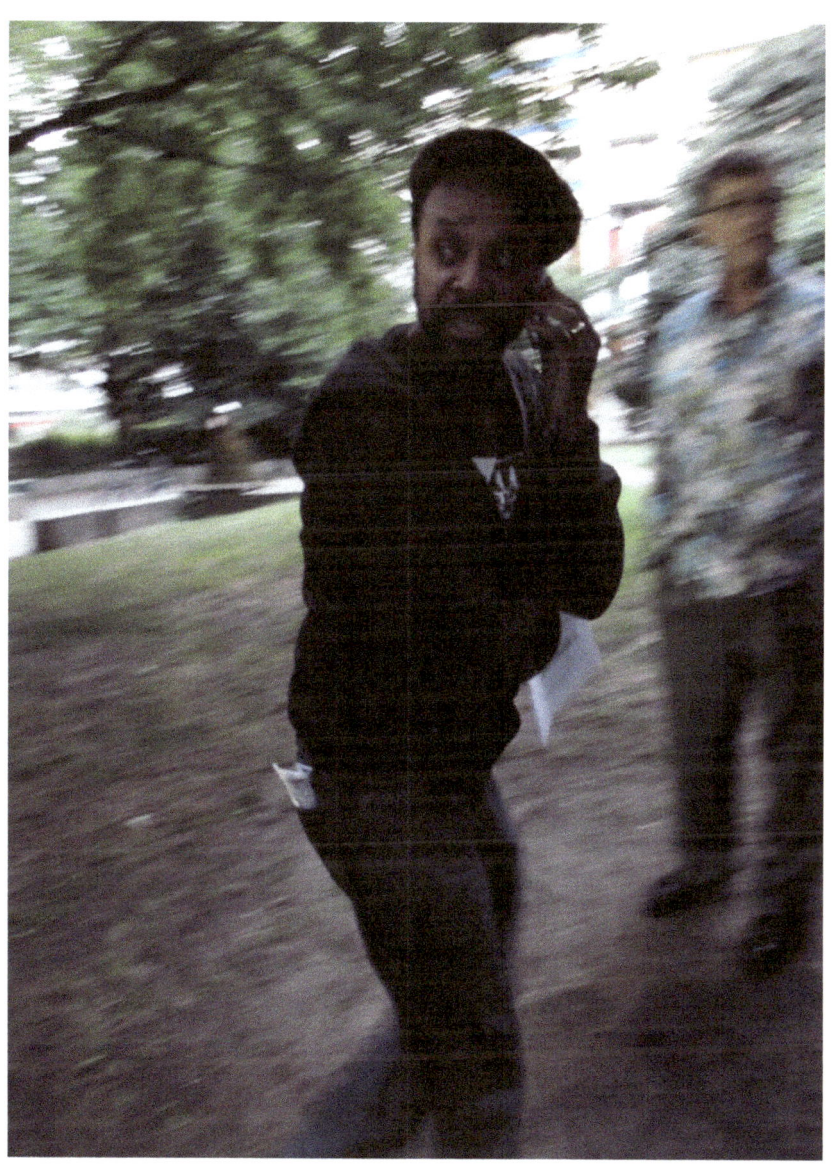

On Saturday, Paul performed again.

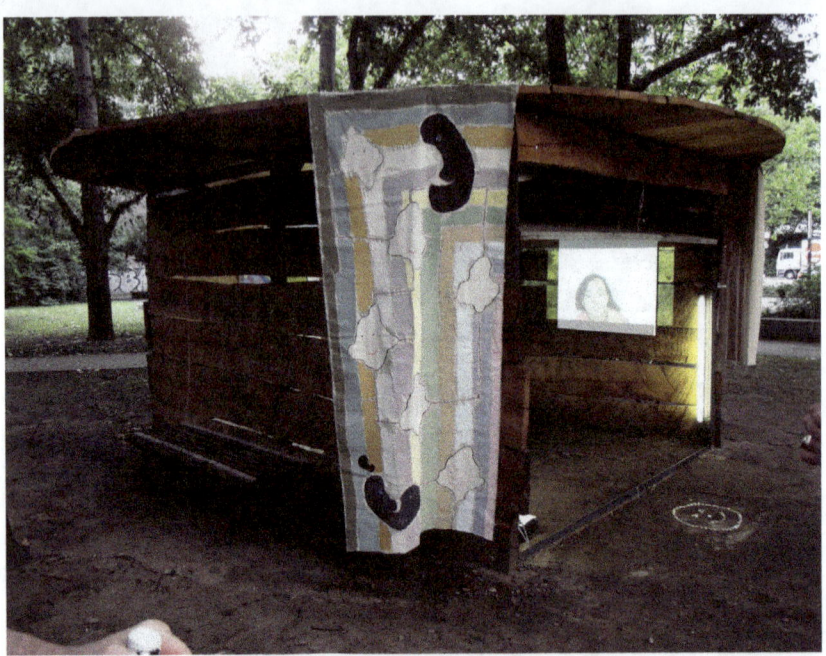

Beer cap, Brianne, happy face, Bingo Bongo Bed Banner, truck, ring, back of David Bell, and the Merry Pit, A vaguely alliterative statement describing a wonderful midday scene

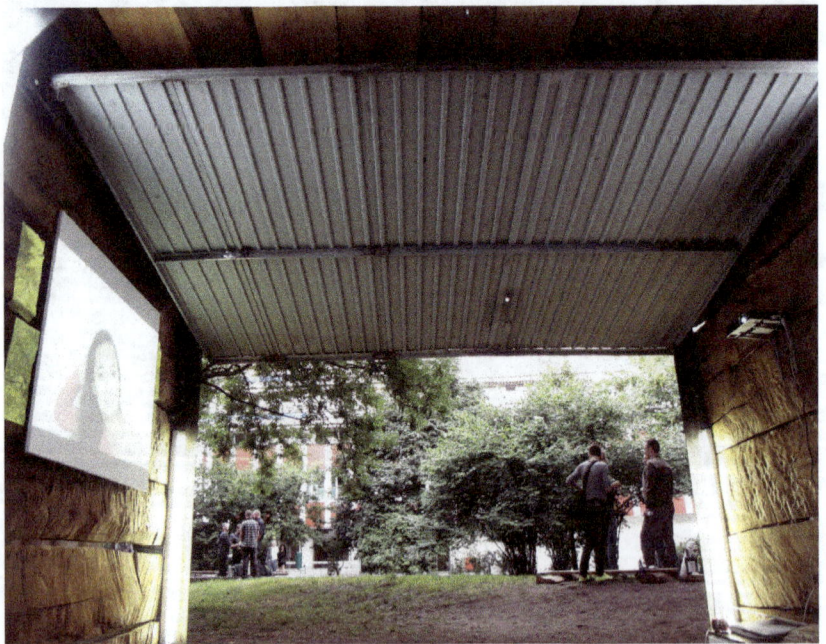

A view from the Bed. Brianne looking glamorous. Standers and talkers. Berlin.

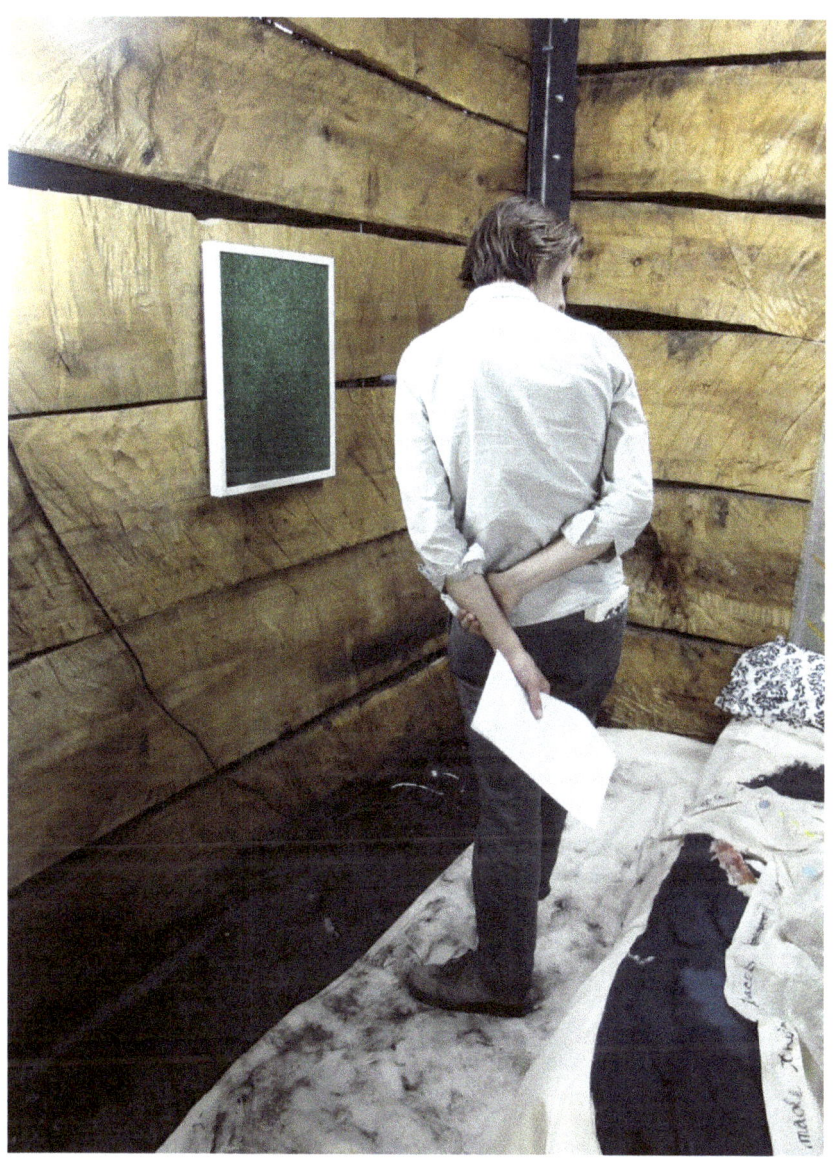

Adam (Feldmeth) trio, number one.

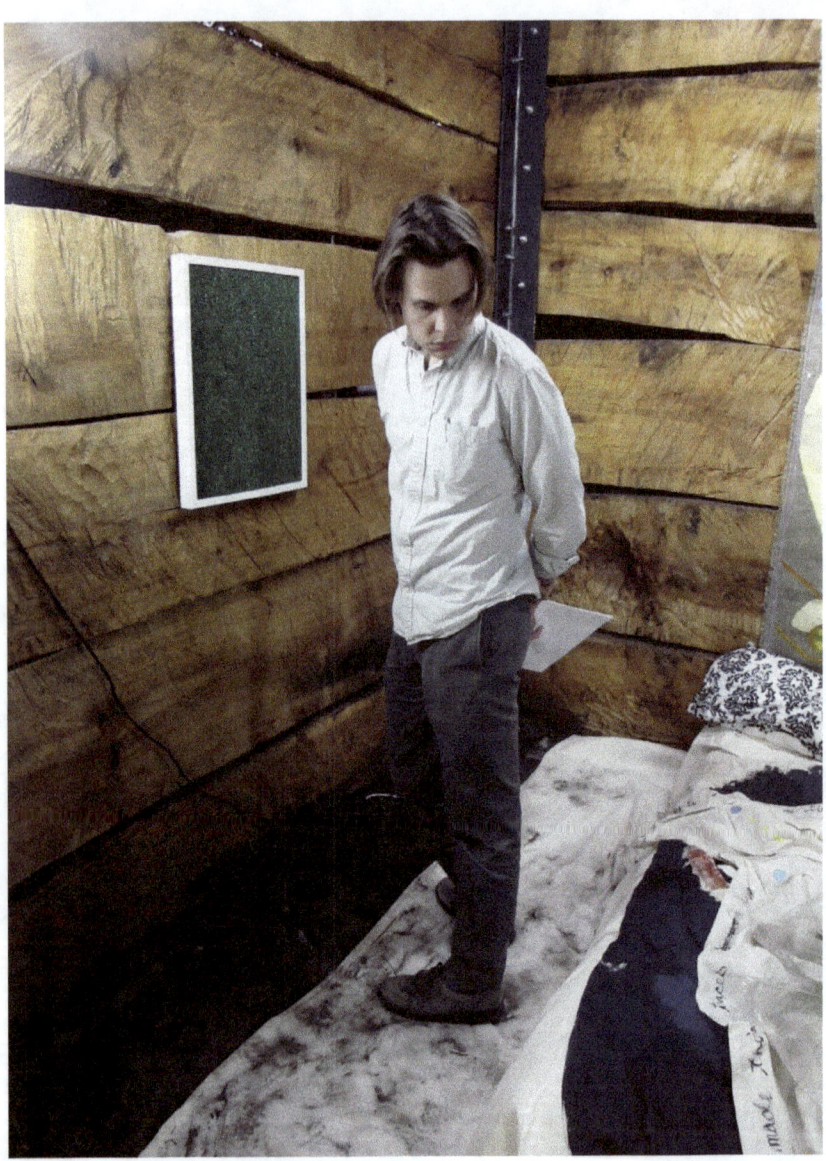

Adam (Feldmeth) trio, number two.

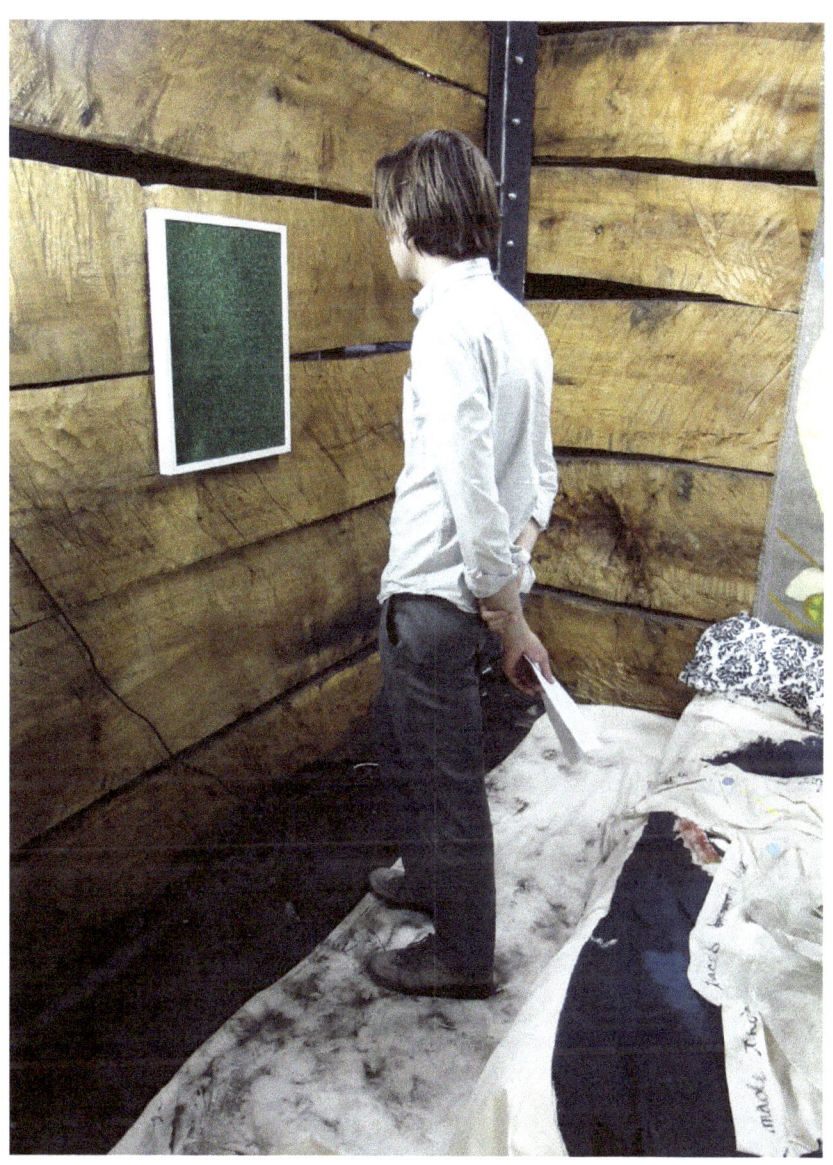

Adam (Feldmeth) trio, number three: Seeing EJ.

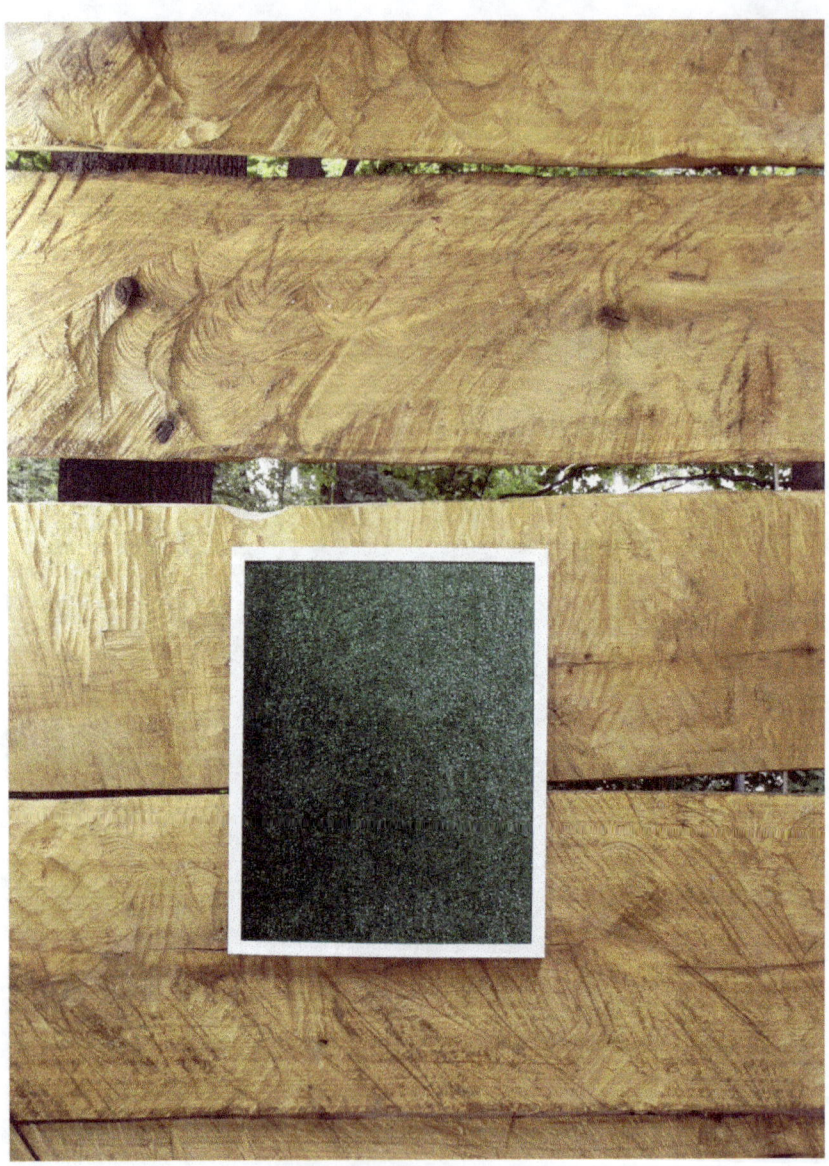

Passing by EJ Hill.

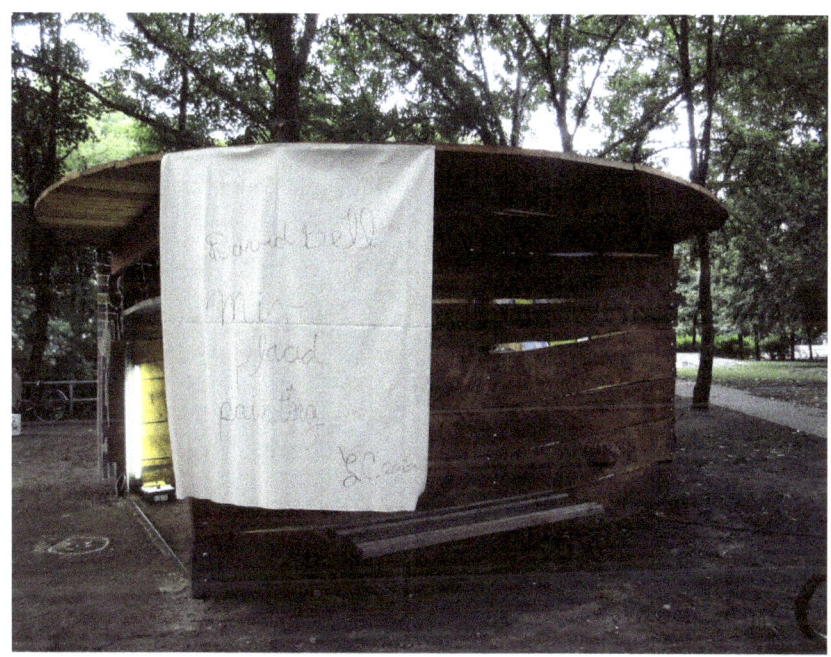

Speaks for itself. I lost the painting. The airport ate it. Or, Lucas Chaddwick, Jr. strikes back. (Isn't "mis-placed" an interesting concept?)

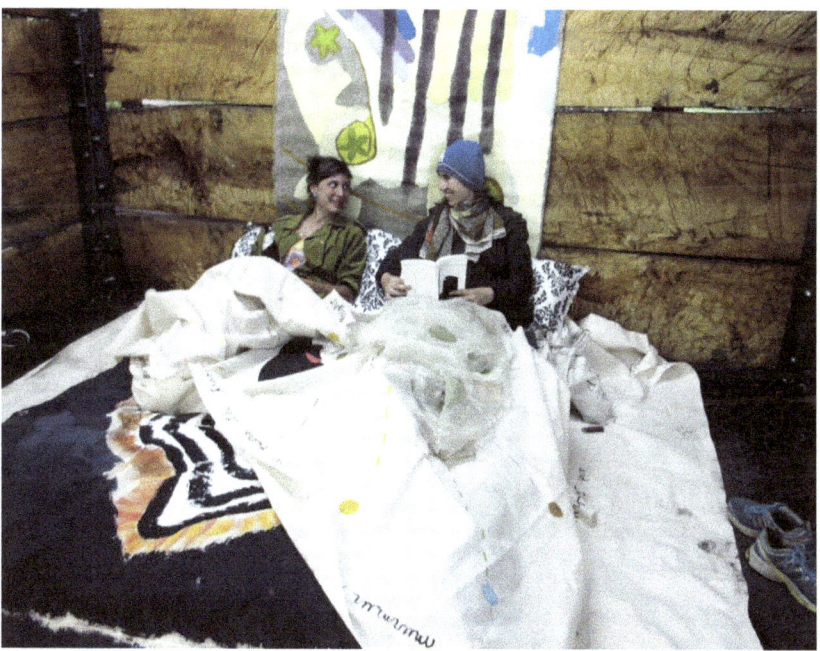

The *Bingo Bongo Bed*, turned down; showing *Jumping Polley* and *Flaming Droolus*.

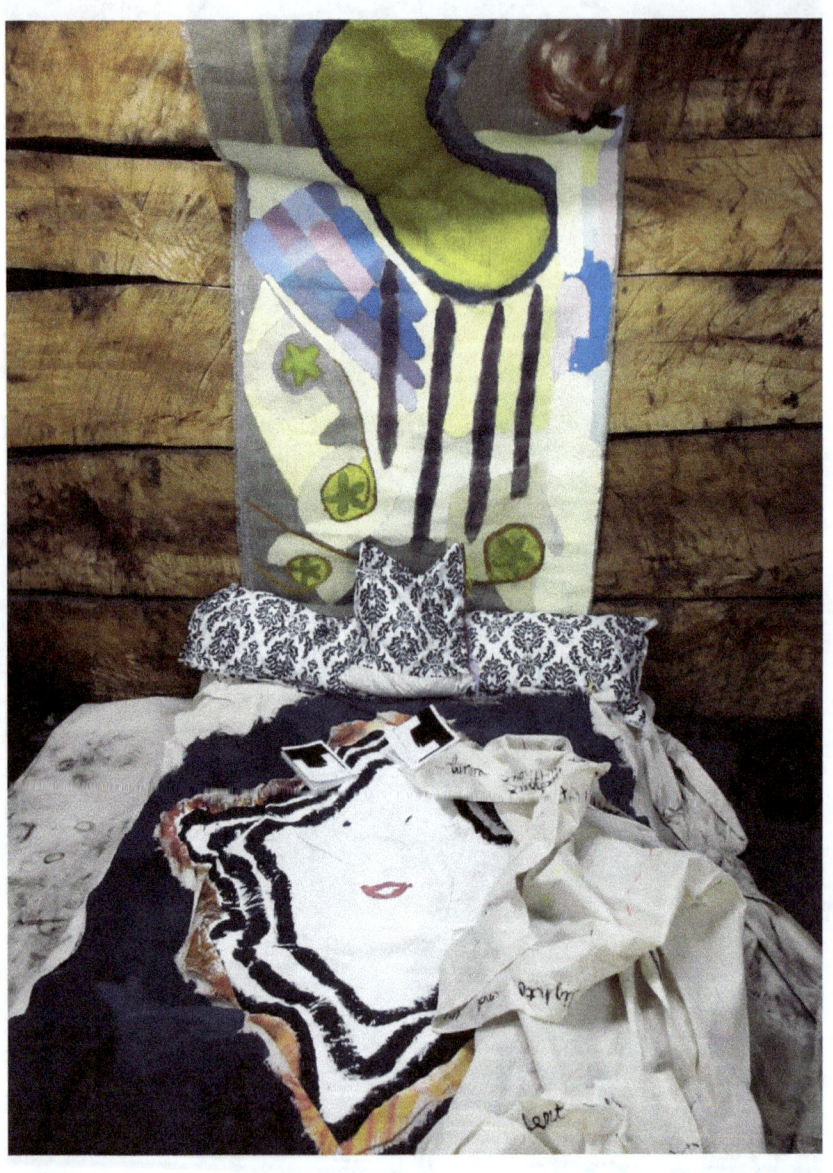

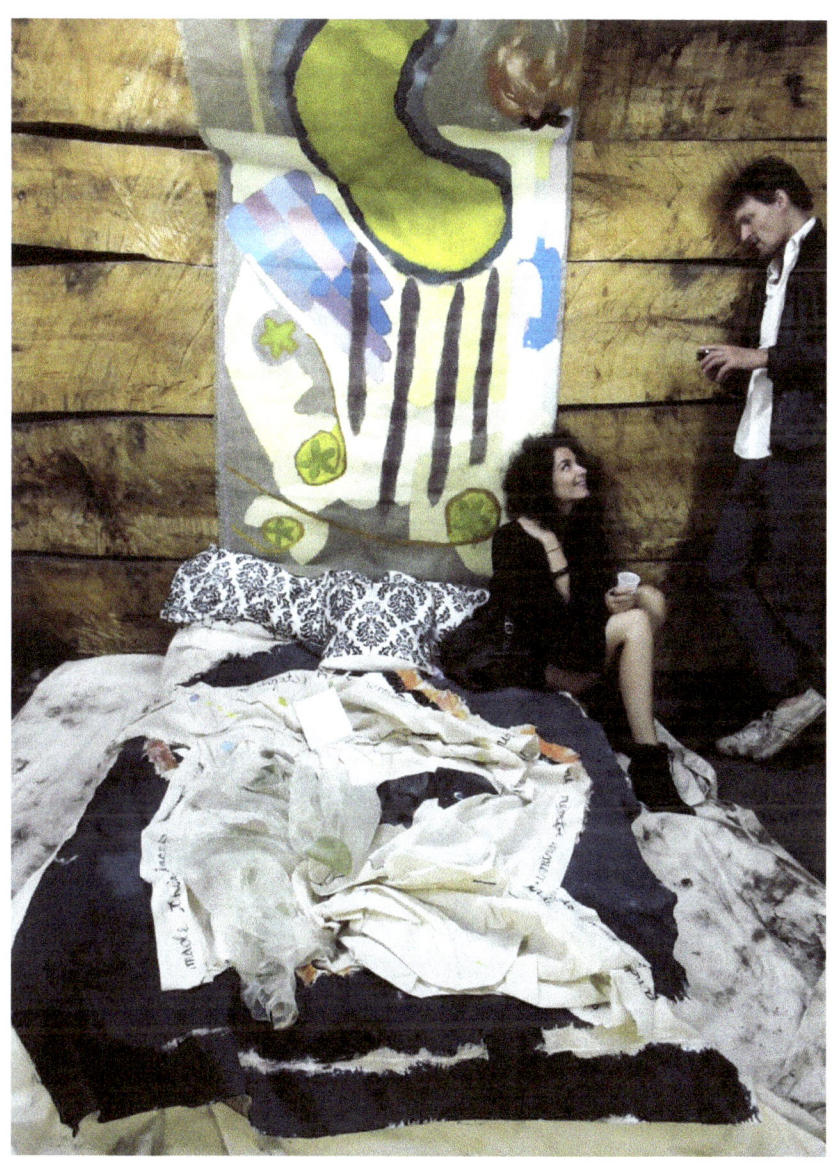

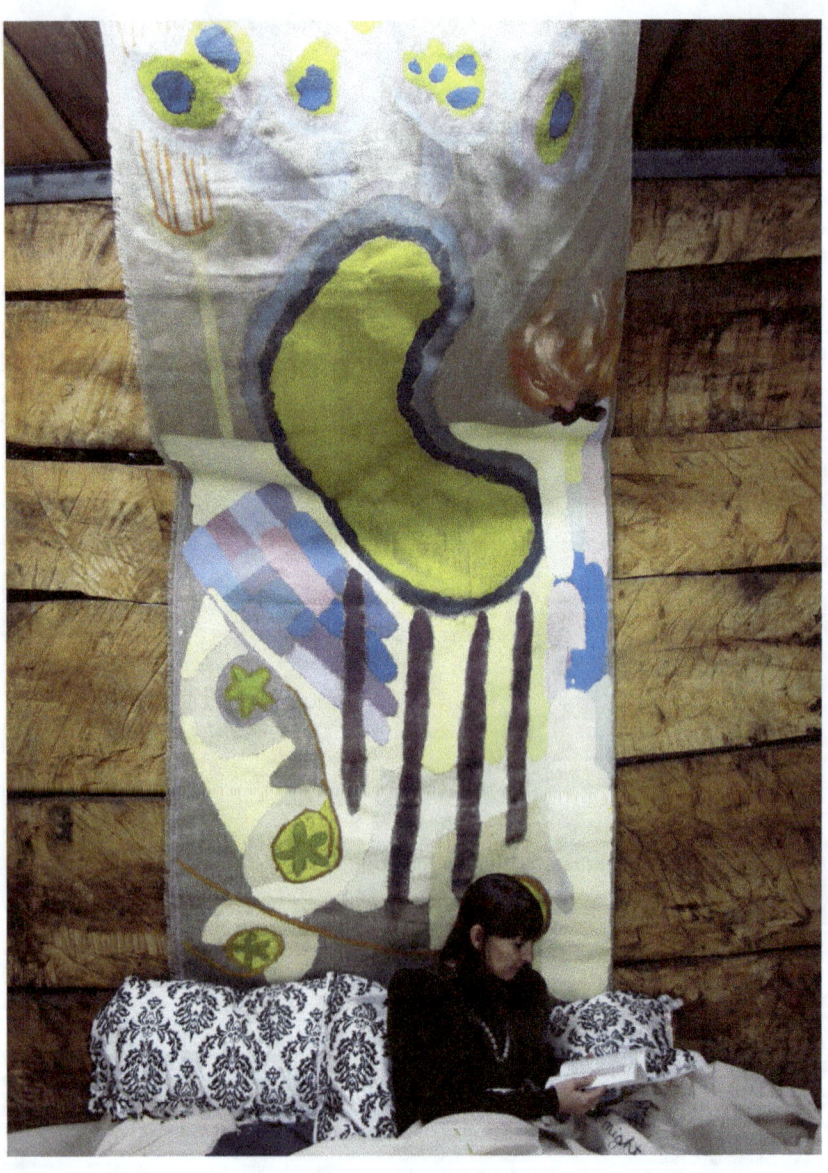

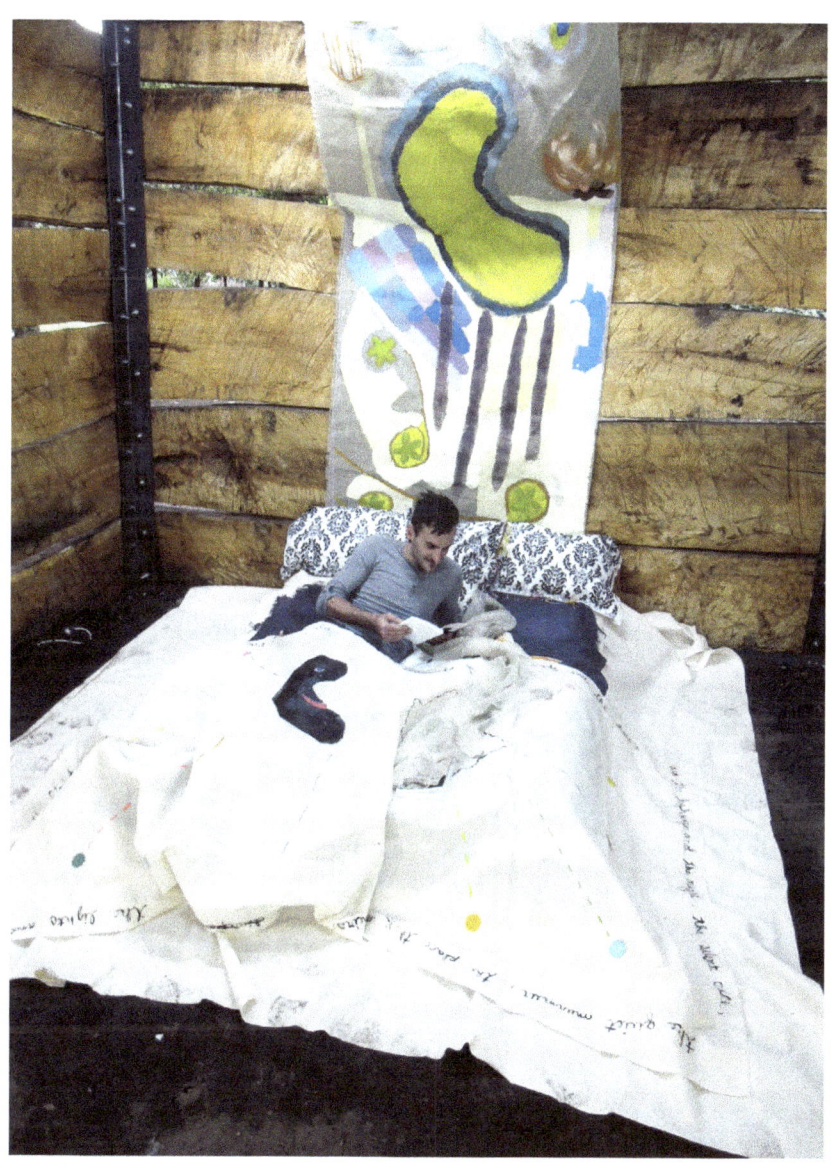

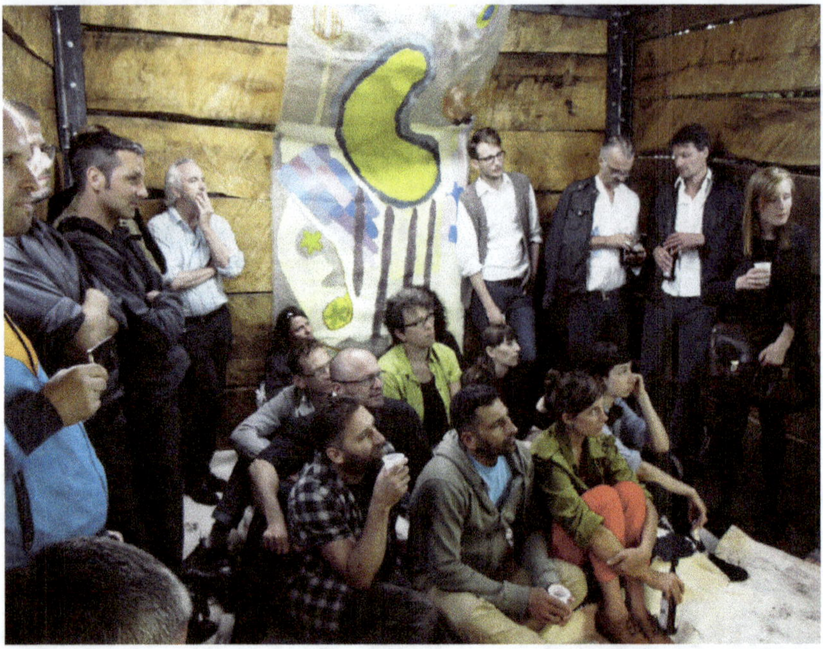

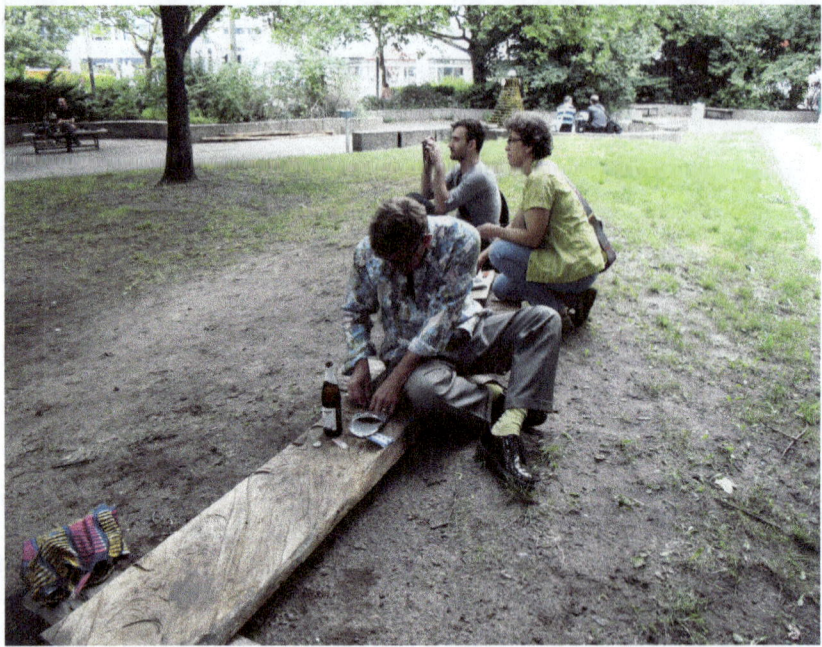

In ones and twos, they come, they gather. Bingo Bongo is an accommodating place.

Some sitting.

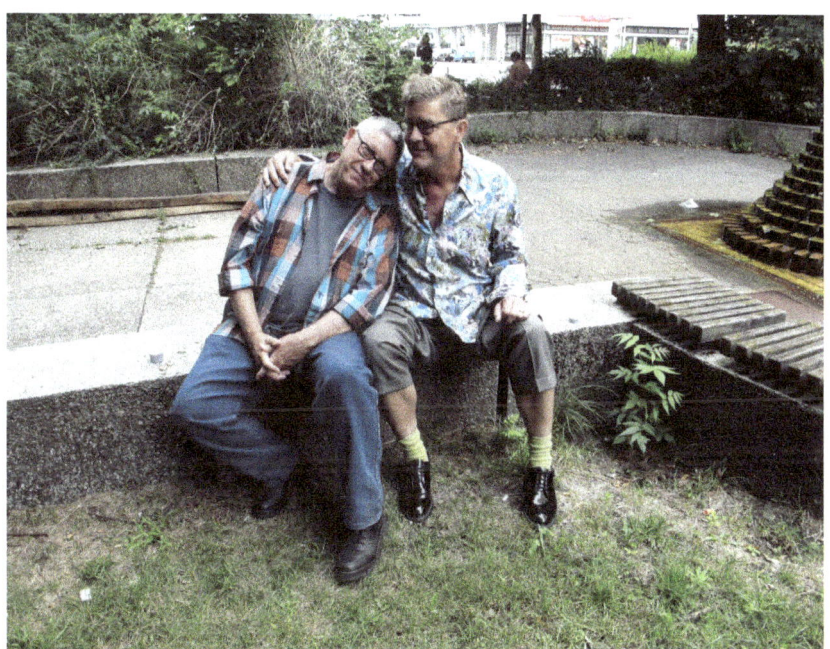

The angel.

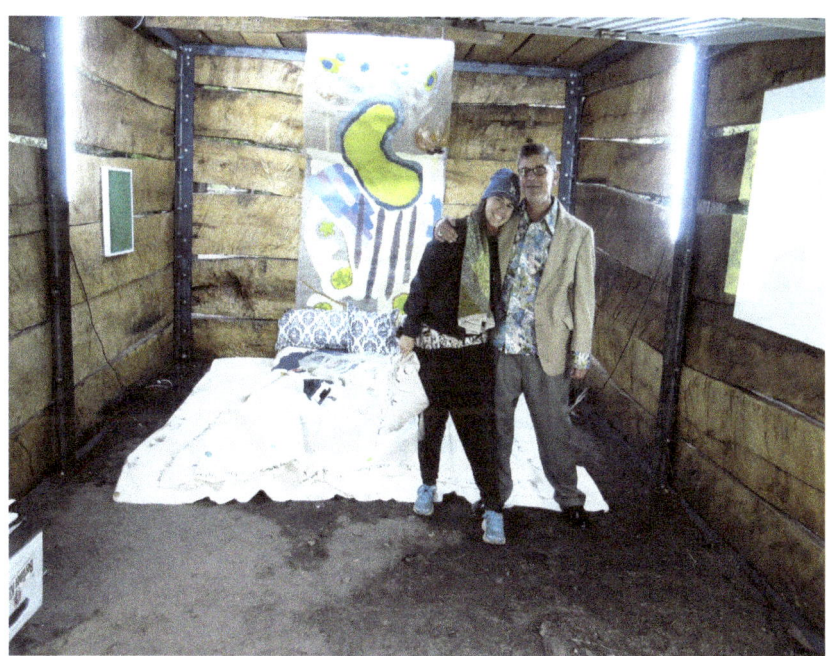

Two. Sonja and Geoff.

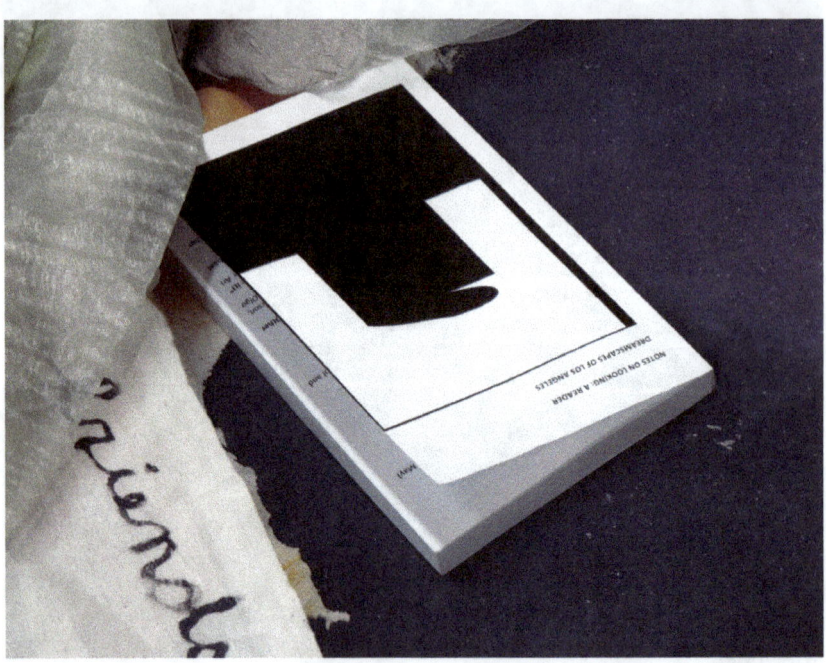

The book. Friends.

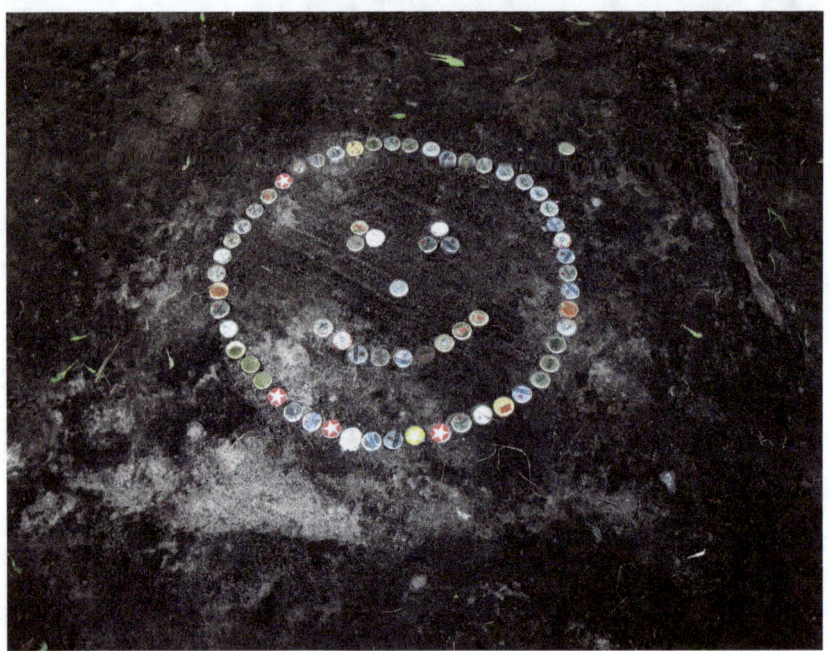

Nowhere to Run, Nowhere to Hide

Works in the Exhibition:

Opportunity for Diversion: A Script for Two Players, 2013
Script and performance
Asher Hartman, Paul Outlaw

Noah Smoking, 2013,
Oil on canvas
David Bell
(*Noah Smoking* was mis-placed at Berlin Tegel Airport. *Mis-placed Painting* represented Mr. Bell in the exhibition.)

Work Ethics, 2013,
looped video, 6:31 minutes
Brianne Latthitham, Anthony Bodlović

Passing, 2013,
AstroTurf, mounted and framed
EJ Hill

Bingo Bongo Bed, 2013
Various weights of muslin, acrylic paint, dirt from Parkfield, fancy window-curtain fabrics, crewel embroidery thread, mattress, book, people.
Geoff Tuck

A bed. Sheets painted with cheerful, yet pathos-evoking characters. A book with references to a real, and yet almost legendary city. As a whole, perhaps this bed is a landscape: a landscape for fantasies and for histories and for nightmares. A place to be born, a place to make love, a place to be alone, a place to die. A place to be violated, a place to sleep. A dreamscape where we meet the consequences of our actions, and where our familiars are the actions of the parents, who made us.

If it is true, as Bertolt Brecht quoted in his song *Denn wie man sich bettet*, from *Aufstieg und fall der Stadt Mahagonny*, that "Denn wie man such bettet, so liegt man / Es deckt einen da keener zu / Und wenn einer tritt, dan bin ich es / Und wird einer getreten, dann bist's du" (For as you make your bed, so you must lie on it / No one will tuck you in / If anyone does the kicking it will be me / if anyone gets kicked, it will be you), then I would propose that within the bed that we all make, and that is made for us, there lies the possibility of transcendence, indeed of liberation.

I invite you to lie in my bed and read from my book of dreams.

The Bingo Bongo Bed is dedicated to the memories of two men: to my father, whose choices in life have caused me so much sorrow and confusion; and to Bryan Thomas White, a young friend who called himself Life's a Dream (L.A.D.), and who struggled bravely to find transcendence and freedom. These two men spent their lives on opposite sides of the fact of childhood sexual abuse, my father as a perpetrator, my perpetrator, as we say in the CSA community, and L.A.D. as a survivor. They both died trying to escape.

I offer my appreciation to Karl Haendel, whose film, *Questions for My Father*, encouraged me on this journey.

Nowhere to Run photographs are by Sonja Gerdes. *The Funny Pit* photographs are courtesy of Alex Gross and *Infernoesque*.